INTERNATIONALIZING DOCTORAL EDUCATION IN BUSINESS

INTERNATIONALIZING DOCTORAL EDUCATION IN BUSINESS

EDITED BY

S. TAMER CAVUSGIL
NANCY E. HORN

Michigan State University Press
East Lansing

All Michigan State University Press books are produced on paper which meets
the requirements of American National Standard of Information Sciences—
Permanence of paper for printed materials ANSI Z23.48-1984.

Michigan State University Press
East Lansing, MI 48823-5202

Printed in the United States of America

02 01 00 99 98 97 1 2 3 4 5 6 7 8 9 10

Library of Congress Cataloging-in-Publication Data

Internationalizing doctoral education in business : viewpoints and proposals for
change / edited by S. Tamer Cavusgil and Nancy E. Horn.
        p. cm.
    Includes bibliographical references and index.
    ISBN 0-87013-424-8
1. Business education—United States—Curricula. 2. Doctor of philosophy
degree. 3. Curriculum changes—United States. 4. International education. I.
Cavusgil, S. Tamer. II. Horn, Nancy E.
HF1131.I585 1996
650'.071'173—dc20   95-51703
                                                                     CIP

To Doris L. Scarlett....
With Love and Appreciation

Contents

Acknowledgments xi
Foreword by Kerry Cooper xiii
Foreword by Al Madansky xvii
Foreword by James B. Henry xxi

Part I: Introduction

Purpose and Overview
  S. Tamer Cavusgil 1
Internationalizing Business Ph.D. Programs:
  How Much Progress Have We Made?
  Peter S. Rose 7
The Internationalization of Doctoral Programs:
  A Survey of Program Directors
  Matthew B. Myers and Glenn S. Omura 25

Part II: Rationale and Conceptual Underpinnings for Internationalizing Doctoral Programs in Business

Introduction
  S. Tamer Cavusgil 43
International Business as a Context, Not a Discipline
  John M. Stopford 45
Internationalizing Business Scholarship: The Essentials
  Brian Toyne 61
Will Globalization Preempt the Need for Internationalizing
  Doctoral Programs: If Not, What Then?
  Robert G. May 97
Internationalizing Doctoral Education in Business:
  Cost-Benefit Considerations
  Lyman W. Porter 105

PART III: INSTITUTIONAL ARRANGEMENTS TO ENHANCE FACULTY COMPETENCE AND INVOLVEMENT

Introduction
  S. Tamer Cavusgil 113

Helpful Institutional Arrangements for Internationalizing
  Doctoral Education in Business Administration
  Edwin L. Miller 115

A Pyramidical Approach to the Internationalization of
  Doctoral Business Education
  Ben L. Kedia 135

Internationalizing Doctoral Programs in Business:
  The Indiana University Experience
  John D. Daniels 149

PART IV: APPROACHES TO INTERNATIONALIZING DOCTORAL PROGRAMS

Introduction
  S. Tamer Cavusgil 163

The Internationalization of Doctoral Education in American Colleges
  of Business Administration: Preserving Our Professional Legacy
  Dale F. Duhan 165

A Dual Approach to Internationalizing Business Ph.D. Programs
  Peter S. Rose 175

Adapting the Ph.D. Program to Ecological Imperatives:
  How to Herd Cats
  Richard J. Lutz 191

Internationalizing the Teaching/Curriculum Dimension of Doctoral
Education: The Ivey Business School Experience
  Paul W. Beamish 201

Internationalization of the Doctoral Program Curriculum:
  A Review of Some Approaches at Toronto
  Daniel Ondrack 213

Dimensions of Internationalizing Doctoral Education in Business in
   Europe: A Discussion of the Concept, Dynamics, and Policy
   Reijo Luostarinen *225*

PART V SPECIFIC INTERNATIONALIZATION STRATEGIES

Introduction
   S. Tamer Cavusgil *245*
Developing and Teaching a Doctoral International
   Marketing Research Seminar: Issues, Experiences and Rewards
   David K. Tse *247*
Multicultural Research: A Lesson in Cultural Diversity
   Barbara Pierce *257*
Foreign Language and Foreign Experience Requirements:
   Are They a Valuable Component of a Doctoral Program?
   William R. Folks, Jr., Sharon O'Donnell and Jeffrey S. Arpan *271*

PART VI: CONCLUSIONS—A GLOBAL CHALLENGE

Introduction
   S. Tamer Cavusgil *287*
Lessons for Doctoral Education from Successful
   International Companies
   James W. Schmotter *289*
Imperatives for the Future
   Charles W. Hickman *299*
The Global Challenge
   S. Tamer Cavusgil *305*

About the Contributors *311*

Index *315*

ACKNOWLEDGEMENTS

This book is the second in the Internationalizing Business Education series sponsored by the Michigan State University Center for International Business Education and Research (CIBER). The first volume, *Internationalizing Business Education: Meeting the Challenge*, was published by MSU Press in 1993. The essays featured in the present volume originated from the Second MSU Roundtable on Internationalizing Doctoral Education held 11-13 September 1994 in East Lansing, Michigan. Accompanying this volume is a companion publication, *Internationalizing Doctoral Education in Business: Issues and Recommendations by Leading Educators*, summarizing key issues and recommendations offered by the experts who contributed to the Roundtable discussions.

As usual, this work is the result of tireless efforts by many talented individuals. First, I must acknowledge all participants of the Roundtable for sharing their wisdom and insights with others. The discussions were highly stimulating, lively, and constructive. They took time to draft their papers prior to the Roundtable, and they revised them subsequently in light of the joint deliberations.

Second, I am grateful to co-sponsors of the Roundtable for their encouragement and support. John Daniels of the Indiana CIBER, Randy Folks Jr. of the University of South Carolina CIBER, Kerry Cooper of the Texas A & M University CIBER, and Chuck Hickman of the AACSB provided valuable guidance and assistance at each step of the project.

Third, I would like to acknowledge the professional editorial assistance of Dr. Nancy Horn. Nancy edited each manuscript, provided feedback to authors for revisions, and prepared the manuscript for publication. Her editorial skills are largely responsible for a manuscript that is well integrated, insightful, and readable.

Next, I must express appreciation for the work of the Michigan State "team." Ms. Tamie Phetteplace's skillful and cheerful secretarial and typing assistance ensured a smooth process. Ms. Kay Fitzgerald, also of MSU-CIBER, provided valuable administrative assistance. Ms. Julie Loehr of MSU Press provided competent, timely, and enthusiastic support in the production process. Thanks!

This book is dedicated to Ms. Doris Scarlett, Associate Director of MSU-CIBER. Doris was primarily responsible for the planning, design, and implementation of this Roundtable. Her extraordinary organizational skills, outstanding interpersonal characteristics, and a most professional attitude ensured a very successful Roundtable. Anyone who had the opportunity to work with Doris offered nothing but admiration. Unfortunately, shortly after the September 1994 Roundtable Doris was diagnosed with a malignant brain tumor, and she passed away December 1995. Thanks, Doris, for touching the lives of so many people and being an inspiration to many more! We miss you a lot!

S. Tamer Cavusgil
The John W. Byington Endowed Chair in Global Marketing
and Executive Director, MSU-CIBER
Michigan State University

FOREWORD

Imagine the following situation. In three or more years of doctoral study in business, students learn little or nothing about the international dimensions of their discipline or the international context in which business is conducted. In preparing these future business school teachers and researchers, most faculty members responsible for prescribing their educational program make no particular effort to address international business issues. Traditional courses are viewed as sufficient for coverage of the international "institutional details." Advanced theoretical treatises and sophisticated statistical methods are regarded as essential. The implicitly operative assumption is that there is no time for international business course work, study abroad or other international experience, or foreign language or area studies. The students read innumerable scholarly articles, pass their examinations, and write dissertations—all with minimal treatment of the international aspects of their discipline or globalized business issues. These freshly-minted Ph.D.s then set forth to educate and to create new knowledge unburdened by any significant knowledge of the nature of multinational enterprise, cross-cultural awareness and skills, or how the international financial system or the international marketplace affect their discipline.

Could such an inherently absurd business doctoral program actually exist in a real university in the U.S.? The painful truth is that, only a few years ago, the above scenario characterized the education of a typical doctoral student in most U.S. business schools. Even after more than a decade of internationalization consciousness-raising efforts by the AACSB and six years of aggressive proselytizing by numerous CIBERs, this description is entirely too close to reality in many doctoral business programs in this country. Why does this perverse omission of such a critical dimension of business—so evidently absurd in today's global economy—persist?

Neglect of international aspects of business in U.S. higher education has many causes. The deepest resistance to their inclusion and emphasis is found in doctoral business education. Internationalization is not the only dimension of business education that has been neglected to a degree that appears inexplicable to an informed observer. The culture of academe—its values, morals, and habits of behavior and thought—often clashes with what needs to be done to prepare undergraduate and MBA students for careers in business, and doctoral students for careers in teaching and research about business. As "professional schools," business schools differ from other units of the educational institutions of which they are a part, but they necessarily operate in much the same manner as the larger entity. As products of the academic culture, business educators inevitably embrace much the same values as other academics and thus see the world in much the same fashion. Performance measurement and reward systems in business schools tend to mirror the rest of academe. All these phenomena are major barriers to change in modes and content of business education and, even more critically, to recognition of the need for change.

Traditional academic values tend to dictate an allocation of time and other resources between teaching and research that is often not in the best interest of business students. But the greatest dialectical tension is perhaps between the traditional academic culture and business student needs for the development of relevant *skills* and *attitudes*, which is perhaps more difficult than the simple imparting of knowledge. Communications and team-melding abilities and attributes are salient and familiar examples; cross-cultural language skills are also very important, but are largely ignored and their importance to business students is not recognized or understood.

What can be done about the fact that the culture of academe, as it shapes the ends and means of business education, acts as a barrier to the internationalization of doctoral education for business students? In developing strategies to cope with the problem it is important to recall two fundamental reasons that all cultures are change-resistant.

First, adherents to a culture often hold unexamined assumptions and unquestioned beliefs that no longer possess validity (if, indeed, they ever did), but still shape behavior. This source of resistance to change can crumble when the flawed paradigm is scrutinized and its adherents gain knowledge and experience that expose the paradigm's baselessness. (Witness the change in behavior and attitudes of "internationalized" faculty members as they gain international experience that reshapes their understanding of business.)

Second, in any organization or institutional arrangement, the existing order often provides benefits to individual members that may be lost if institutional arrangements are altered. The prospect of change poses costs and creates uncertainty for organization members. This source of resistance to change is both powerful and difficult to manage. But, just as in the more benign case of discrediting mythical beliefs, this obstacle must be recognized, confronted, and overcome if change is to be accomplished—and change is imperative!

This book is about recognizing, confronting, and overcoming the obstacles to internationalizing doctoral education that exist, in varying degrees, in most business schools. Unfortunately, there are no standard prescriptions or packaged solutions that can be readily adapted for any given case. In overcoming the challenge that any particular culture of any given business school poses, we can take comfort in the fact that the need for internationalization of business education stems from the way the modern world is—not as some assume it to be OR wish that it were. This is a powerful change-inducing force, indeed, and is the fundamental reason why we will succeed. In due time, reality prevails over myth.

Kerry Cooper
Director, CIBER
College of Business Administration
Texas A&M University

FOREWORD

One should view the issues addressed at this MSU Roundtable within a broader context—that of the general criticism expressed of late about doctoral programs in business. These programs have been under fire for lots of general reasons: production of poor teachers; irrelevance of dissertation research to business practice; dedicated too much to the production of specialists; . . . This Roundtable addressed a much more specific charge: business practice is globalizing, yet our Ph.D. programs have not "internationalized." Having written[1] about the validity of the general charges made about business Ph.D. Programs and whether and how we should react to them, I'd like to recast some of my thoughts so that they address this specific charge.

In my paper, I said of doctoral programs in business that "(t)he mission of such programs is to produce scholars who, given their mastery of a corpus of knowledge and their ability to create new knowledge, will continue to create new knowledge and disseminate it." And that, Ph.D. programs do, and do quite well. Consequently, if there were a specific body of knowledge that can be labeled "international," then it would already be represented in business Ph.D. programs, and it would not be necessary to hold a conference such as this to create such a program. If, on the other hand, "international" is merely a "slant," one might take on existing bodies of knowledge (or, as Stopford might term it, a "context"), then only individual researchers' tastes and/or the influence of the market for scholars with this orientation will "internationalize" doctoral programs in business.

The surveys of Rose and of Myers and Omura, as well as the contextual-definition given by Toyne, shed light on which of these two alternatives is the reality of the day. It appears that it is the latter. And so, most of this volume (sections III, IV, and V) describes mechanisms (e.g., incentives, reorganizations) designed to tilt the market so that the production of "international" scholars increases to meet the demand. But perhaps all this is unnecessary, if, to paraphrase May, in the long run, as business globalizes, the study of business will perforce be the study of international business.

In particular, Hickman's paper addresses the underlying issue well. There are lots of "flavors of the month," each with advocates seeking to have it incorporated in some way into the business Ph.D. program. (One of the more notable of late is Quality Management.) If a "flavor" develops a specific body of knowledge, it becomes a field in the doctoral program.[2] If a "flavor" does not qualify as such a field, it becomes a judgement call of the business school faculty and administration as to whether and how to integrate this "flavor" into the fabric of the Ph.D. program. Perhaps our problem is that Ph.D. programs are "field-oriented," and it will take some visionary academic leadership to pronounce, "It's not vanilla with some chocolate mixed in; it's a new staple called chocolate-ripple."

When I spoke to the general charge leveled at business schools about doctoral research, and, by implication, faculty research in general, I said:

> Change can only be brought about if business school faculties, the trainers of the future business researchers, buy into the proposition that current business research is irrelevant to business practice; modify their research behavior to make their research more relevant; and subsequently reflect that modified research agenda in the training programs for future business researchers—that is, Ph.D. programs.
>
> Recognizing that one cannot change the academic business community as a whole, the critics of academic business research want to modify the system by changing the output of the pipeline. They want the business school faculty to provide Ph.D. students with a broad enough training so that they can both do research that is not only judged to be good (by traditional standards), but that is also more closely attuned to business practice.

My recommendations for dealing with this general issue were a set of mechanisms to be added to the Ph.D. Program for sensitizing the doctoral student to the general set of research needs and evaluative criteria of the business community. Some of those suggested mechanisms could be particularized to address the more specific problem of sensitizing the doctoral student to the research needs of the business community with respect to the globalization of business practice. But there's no longer a need to do that—look instead into this Roundtable volume for the wealth of more concrete suggestions it contains for pursuing this sensitization.

Albert Madansky
Director, CIBER
Graduate School of Business
University of Chicago

NOTES

1. "Fine-Tuning Business Doctoral Education: Who Should Do It?" *Selections* (Autumn 1994), 4-7.
2. As models of this transition, one need merely look back at the history of Marketing and of Management Science as fields in business schools.

FOREWORD

Current doctoral programs in business are under attack from various quarters. Equally important, the forces of change in global business warrant a re-examination of Ph.D. programs. How should we prepare doctoral candidates who will be responsible for training of young people assuming management positions in international companies? How can we develop positive attitudes among doctoral candidates toward a lifelong inclusion of international dimensions? What are some alternative visions for structuring doctoral education programs in business?

These and similar challenges were the focus of the second Roundtable on Internationalizing Business Education organized by the Michigan State University Center for International Business Education and Research. They were explicitly defined and then discussed by a select group of leading educators. The essays contained in this volume represent the richness of perspectives, experiences, and ideas for change. It is gratifying to see that these scholars have given extensive thought and consideration to such critical issues, and are now sharing their proposals through this publication. The ideas presented here will undoubtedly be of interest to many change-minded faculty, doctoral program directors, and administrators elsewhere.

Of special interest is the discussion of alternative models for internationalizing the doctoral student, the faculty, and the program. Here, we have a lot to learn from each other, including those programs outside of North America. It is also important to encourage and support experimentation. Based on their clientele and core competence, graduate schools should be allowed to develop unique and innovative programs. Those that seem to respond well to the ongoing challenge of internationalization can then become candidates for adoption by other schools.

We are proud to have had the Michigan State University CIBER organize the conference that led to this important publication. Congratulations are due to all co-sponsoring CIBERs and the AACSB for focusing on such a critical issue in business education. Our gratitude goes to Ms. Susanna B. Easton, Senior Program Administrator at the U.S. Department of Education, for her encouragement and support of this project.

James B. Henry, Dean
The Eli Broad Graduate School of Management
Michigan State University

I. INTRODUCTION

PURPOSE AND OVERVIEW

S. Tamer Cavusgil

The successes of the development of business education are to be found in corporate board rooms, government departments, colleges and universities, hospitals and businesses around the globe. The ideas and values instilled in students by their professors have created a cadre of individuals who have the ability to accept the challenges of the changing landscape of market forces. The decisions made in leading and subsidiary industries today are a reflection of the training young people received in the past. The question facing business education today is: Are current faculty prepared to teach future business cadres to assume leadership in a vastly different climate, one inextricably linking countries in a global web of capital transfers, trade, comparative advantage and employee mobility? Can the professorate prepare future students to assume their positions in a global corporate world?

As the context of business changes from a domestic to a global focus, universities—responsible for providing cutting-edge insight into the business world of tomorrow—are searching for the most appropriate means to meet the research demands of business and to instruct the future professorate in issues relevant to our changing economic times. It is in this spirit of searching to improve the way we educate future professors—and indeed how the current professorate educates undergraduate and graduate students—that the Center for International Business Education and Research (CIBER) in the Eli Broad Graduate School of Management at Michigan State University (MSU) (East Lansing, Michigan, USA) hosted a Roundtable conference to explore how doctoral education in business can be made more relevant internationally.

Representatives of some of the leading Ph.D.-granting institutions in the U.S., Canada (Toronto and Western Ontario), Europe (London Business School and Helsinki School of Economics and Business Administration), and East Asia (City Polytechnic of Hong Kong) were invited to present position

1

papers on a number of subjects, all of which appear in this volume. The Roundtable, the second to be held at MSU, on Internationalizing Doctoral Education in Business, held 11-13 September 1994, was co-sponsored by the CIBERs at Indiana University, University of South Carolina and Texas A & M University, and by the American Assembly of the Collegiate Schools of Business (AACSB). Twenty-six business faculty and administrators gathered in East Lansing to share their perspectives and experiences and to brainstorm about approaches to internationalizing doctoral education in business. These educators are eminently qualified to serve as resource people: each brought a unique perspective on internationalization from their leadership positions at a diverse set of business schools, the Academy of International Business (AIB), the American Assembly of Collegiate Schools of Business (AACSB), and the U.S. national resource centers in international business education (CIBERs).

The 1994 Roundtable was convened to identify strategies in which business schools could carve out a future for their doctoral education programs that would be more in tune with the current and future trends in the globalization of business. The Roundtable was essentially a forum of leading business educators (doctoral program directors, deans, graduate faculty, and representatives of educator groups) allowing for exchange of experiences and ideas regarding internationalization of doctoral programs in business.

The specific objectives of the Roundtable were to:

- articulate issues and viewpoints related to internationalization of doctoral education (through position papers written by Roundtable experts);
- share experiences and brainstorm about strategies for implementing initiatives that would lead to change in doctoral education; and
- formulate recommendations for possible adoption by graduate schools of management, and disseminate them.

The Roundtable experts met in small discussion groups organized into six thematic topics that represent the internationalization challenges facing business school doctoral programs. Although they overlap to some extent, these categories were helpful in crystallizing key issues.

1. Rationale for and Objectives of Internationalization (Facilitator: Kerry Cooper)
2. Models for Internationalizing the Doctoral Student (Facilitators: Paul W. Beamish, William R. Folkes, Jr., and Reijo Luostarinen)

3. Approaches to Enhancing Faculty Competence and Involvement (Facilitators: Richard J. Lutz, Robert G. May, and Charles W. Hickman)
4. Institutional and Administrative Arrangements (Facilitators: Edwin L. Miller, Dan Ondrack, and Lyman W. Porter)
5. Reinventing the Ph.D. Program: Articulation of Alternative Visions (Facilitators: William Broesamle, Jeffrey S. Arpan, and John M. Stopford)
6. Generating Recommendations and Setting Future Agendas (Facilitators: James W. Schmotter, Brian Toyne, and Ben Kedia).

Each group grappled with its respective challenges to address specific problems and solutions in the internationalization process. A facilitator moderated each group, and a rapporteur recorded the highlights of the discussion. A summary of each discussion session was then prepared and shared with all Roundtable participants. A Delphi process was used to arrive at the final set of recommendations emerging from the discussion sessions. All participants responded to a version of the document and offered amendments before it was finalized into the companion report to this volume, *Internationalizing Doctoral Education in Business: Issues and Recommendations by International Educators*.

IN SEARCH OF RELEVANCE

The changing parameters of business call into question the relevance of the business education our current bachelor's, master's and doctoral students are receiving. Of particular concern is the content and process of education provided to future professors who will be educating generations to lead the global business community in directions that will mean better lives for ourselves and our world neighbors. As each of the Roundtable sessions evolved, several overarching questions dominated our discussions: Why is the demand for Ph.D.s in business declining? How can the education of future professors be improved to take into account the internationalization of business? What does internationalization mean? How can this be accomplished by the range of business schools operating not only in the U.S. but also in Europe, Asia, Latin America and Canada? With declining educational budgets, how can doctoral programs provide both the depth and breadth of understanding needed to conduct research and teach in the business schools of tomorrow?

Because the future of MBAs and BAs—and of the professorate itself—is in the hands of today's doctoral students, several questions must be posed:

- Are the doctoral students prepared to train their students for the 21st century?
- Will they be able to acquire skills required for them? For example:
- managing in an intensely competitive global economy;
- ability to develop successful business partnerships across cultures; and
- cross-cultural effectiveness.

Core to the ability of a business school to internationalize its doctoral programs are the professional attitudes and values held by faculty members and administrators. Themselves a product of doctoral programs, faculty and administrators have been trained largely in a "silo enhancer" Germanic model of doctoral education in which the emphasis is on functional specializations such as accounting, marketing, management and the like. Since international business is both the context in which doctoral education takes place and a subject currently studied, the question arises as to whether the paradigm for educating Ph.D. students in business should not be more integrated and reflective of the Renaissance model of training. Should each one of the functional areas be internationalized, or should internationalization occur at the seminar level for all doctoral students? If such a paradigmatic shift in doctoral education is to occur, what will be lost? Will universities be doomed to churn out "mushy generalists," or can the integrated model still produce specialists able to conduct cutting-edge research relevant to the changing needs of business?

The answers provided to these and other questions appearing in a survey of doctoral program directors conducted by Matthew Myers and Glenn Omura and in several surveys of the dimensions of internationalization in U.S. business schools reported by Peter Rose point out the complexities of changing the culture of doctoral education in business. A key dilemma is how to reorient a business school and its faculty to meet the changing global realities of business when the faculty themselves have achieved their own status on the basis of a different model. Doctoral programs, as so many authors assert, are the locus in which faculty reproduce themselves in their students. The values and attitudes faculty accepted while they were students are passed along to their students in the classes they teach and the research topics they design. While there appears to be general acknowledgement that internationalization should be undertaken, little agreement has been reached on how this should occur and who should be responsible. An abundance of "sacred cows" exist in the teaching profession, and professors who earned their reputations on the basis of the understandings they had reached in their particular discipline are unwilling to alter or adapt their practices for fear that they will not be competent in accepting this new challenge. What internationalization means to faculty is ceding autonomy and professional identity in favor of an unknown quantity that itself is shifting. Aspects of business touted as "universals," these faculty argue, will not benefit from internationalization because, after all, isn't international business just an adaptation of what is commonly accepted as the norm? Internationalization, they argue merely means looking at how the universal model is applied in a multinational or cross-cultural context. As a result of these attitudes and values, accepting the challenge of internationalization is extremely difficult for faculty and administrators.

THE QUEST FOR A NEW PARADIGM

The prevailing issue in internationalizing doctoral programs in business, then, is how to convince faculty and administrators that in order for them to adequately train future business professionals, they must adapt their teaching and research to the new international imperatives. **Section II** of this volume— Rationale and Conceptual Underpinnings for Internationalizing Doctoral Programs in Business—addresses the rationale for internationalization and presents compelling arguments addressed to faculty and administrators concerning the nature of business, the purpose of Ph.D. programs, the levels of internationalization that might be sought at different institutions, and how culture varies the definition of business. Also addressed in this section are the more philosophical issues in doctoral education, i.e., if the Germanic, "silo enhancer" model should continue to guide the development of doctoral programs, or whether the Renaissance, "integrated" model should become the new norm.

The articles appearing in **Section III**—Institutional Arrangements to Enhance Faculty Competence and Involvement—discuss the institutional context in which internationalization takes place and the roles of key administrators in creating an environment in which risk taking and experimentation are acceptable. Also addressed, on an institutional level, are the incentives that must be provided to faculty to entice them into changing their own professional, discipline-specific culture in order to incorporate international perspectives. The authors appearing in this section each identify a range of strategies for internationalization of the faculty, from identifying the level of literacy each faculty member should achieve to learning models to enhance international pedagogical and research excellence.

Section IV—Approaches to Internationalizing Doctoral Programs—begins with articles that set forth different conceptual models to guide internationalization. These include changing the values and culture of the institution and the faculty, issues to address on both micro and macro levels, and faculty incentives to enhance the employability of students. The second part of this section presents the internationalization experiences of several business schools: Western Business School, Ontario, Canada; the Faculty of Management at the University of Toronto; and the Helsinki School of Economics and Business Administration in Finland. Each program was developed within the particular culture, enhancements and constraints of the school represented, and authors caution that what has worked for them may not work in the same way for others.

In **Section V**—Specific Internationalization Strategies—several authors describe a particular internationalization activity they experienced or developed at each of their institutions. A course in international marketing research is described, a research process involving international students is analyzed, and the results of a small survey on the usefulness of foreign language and foreign experiences in internationalizing a doctoral program in the U.S. are presented. These authors illustrate how to translate a vision of internationalization into praxis in specific areas.

Section VI—Conclusions—The Global Challenge—sums up many of the conclusions drawn during the process of the Roundtable and revisits the imperatives for internationalizing—which parallel the imperatives driving business to accept the global challenge. The volume concludes on the specifics of that challenge and how doctoral programs in business can respond.

Internationalizing Business Ph.D. Programs: How Much Progress Have We Made?

Peter S. Rose

Introduction

The call for internationalizing the graduate and undergraduate programs of business schools is not new. Nearly ten years ago the American Assembly of Collegiate Schools of Business (AACSB) stipulated that business curricula must have significant international content or the schools offering those curricula might face a challenge to their accreditation. Today many business schools proclaim that "internationalization" is a key component of their research, teaching, and service missions. Indeed, a recent extensive survey of U.S. and foreign business schools sponsored by the Academy of International Business (AIB), AACSB, and the Center for International Business Education and Research of the University of South Carolina (USC) and authored by Professors Arpan, Folks, and Kwok (1993), found that 57% of responding business schools had included specific references to international business in their written mission statements. This same survey found that 75% of U.S. business schools and more than 80% of European business schools reported having strategic plans that included specific international business objectives.

Unfortunately, the gap between words and reality is often very wide. There is a nearly universal *intent* to internationalize graduate and undergraduate business curricula, but carrying out that intention frequently requires more in resources and in change of focus than many schools are able or willing to undertake. This certainly seems to be true of business Ph.D. programs today where the internationalization process seems to be proceeding slowly, if at all. The result *may* be that the majority of new business Ph.D. graduates are ill-equipped to teach and conduct research in the international dimensions of their principal disciplines.

7

In this chapter I seek to provide an empirical basis for today's call for internationalizing business Ph.D. programs. This study looks first at previous survey evidence on the internationalization of U. S. business Ph.D. programs and extends that evidence through a very recent updated survey of leading American business schools. As you will soon see, the results are mixed at best with some evidence of progress and other evidence of retreat. Clearly much remains to be done by those who value highly the goal of internationalizing future generations of business Ph.D's.

SURVEYS OF THE DIMENSIONS OF INTERNATIONALIZATION IN U.S. BUSINESS SCHOOLS

AN EARLIER SURVEY OF THE INTERNATIONAL DIMENSION OF BUSINESS PH.D. PROGRAMS

The number of U. S. colleges and universities that have internationalized their doctoral programs in a formal way—that is, offering a major, minor, or at least a course concentration in international business—does not appear to be very high. For example, Dr. Robert Kuhne's (1990) survey of U. S. business doctoral programs at the close of 1987 reported that only twenty-eight universities offered a Ph.D. major or minor or both in international business. Many business schools apparently regarded the market for Ph.D's in international business at that time to be too limited in scope, or demanding of more college resources than were likely to be available, or, perhaps, believed that international business is an inherent component of each traditional business discipline and, therefore, should not be regarded as a separate field requiring a separate curriculum.

However, Professor Kuhne's survey found in the late 1980s that at least eight business schools *did* operate International Business Departments, though growth in the number of international business majors was modest (rising only about 9% over the 1984-1987 time period). The majority of participating majors (about 65%) appeared to be non-U. S. citizens, whose numbers were apparently increasing faster than the number of U.S. citizens enrolled as majors.

International Finance led all other international fields as a choice for Ph.D. students majoring in international business at that time; however, International Management appeared to be growing the fastest as a major during the 1980s. Most schools responding to Dr. Kuhne's survey imposed *no* foreign language requirements on their doctoral students and the majority of responding Ph.D. programs did *not* require their students to teach or to travel abroad. Professor Kuhne expressed the fear that

> This large group of future educators does not have the skills to provide a complete educational program and will most likely limit their lectures and research to only the U. S. component of their functional area. Their students, therefore, will not be properly trained to do business in a global market (Kuhne 1990:98).

A MORE RECENT SURVEY OF PROGRESS TOWARD INTERNATIONALIZING BUSINESS SCHOOL PH.D. PROGRAMS

In the Spring of 1994 the present author conducted a follow-up survey of the leading U. S. business Ph.D. programs offering either majors or minors or both majors and minors in international business that were first identified by Professor Kuhne in 1987. These particular schools, along with their major and minor offerings, are listed in Exhibit 1.

Schools Offering Ph.D. Majors and Minors—These leading business schools were asked if they offer a major or minor in international business for their Ph.D. students, following up on a question posed in Dr. Robert Kuhne's survey nearly seven years earlier. There were also questions focusing upon the number of internationally-oriented business Ph.D. students in the current year (1994) compared to a benchmark period five years ago, the number and proportion of doctoral students currently writing dissertations with significant international content, the proportion of women enrolled in international business Ph.D. programs, the global geographic distribution of international business Ph.D. majors and minors, the field specialties chosen by international-business doctoral students, international business course requirements and optional courses offered to these Ph.D. students, any requirements imposed on business doctoral students or faculty for foreign travel or study abroad, the possible existence of separate international business departments within each leading school, the proportion of international faculty in each business school, the foreign language skills of doctoral students and faculty, and whether or not these leading business schools have coordinators or directors responsible for international studies at the doctoral level.

The results suggested that, overall, only *limited* progress toward formalizing and/or expanding international business doctoral programs (at least

Exhibit 1. Leading U. S. Universities Offering Doctoral Programs with a Major or Minor in International Business as Reported in 1987 and 1994.

The 1987 Survey by Dr. Robert Kuhne	Offer a Major	Minor	The 1994 Survey by Peter S. Rose	Offer a Major	Minor	Change in Offerings Observed Between 1987 and 1994
University of Alabama	No	Yes	University of Alabama	No	No	Minor Dropped
Arizona State University	No	Yes	Arizona State University	No	No	Minor Dropped
University of California - Berkeley	Yes	No	University of California-Berkeley	No	No	Major Dropped
University of Chicago	Yes	No	University of Chicago	Yes*	Yes*	Minor Possible*
George Washington University	Yes	Yes	George Washington University	Yes	Yes	No Change
Georgia State University	Yes	No	Georgia State University	No	No	Major Dropped
Harvard University	Yes	No	Harvard University	Yes	NA	No Change
University of Hawaii-Manoa	Yes	No	University of Hawaii-Manoa	No	No	Major Dropped
University of Houston	No	Yes	University of Houston	No	Yes	No Change
University of Illinois-Urbana	Yes	Yes	University of Illinois-Urbana	Yes	Yes	No Change
Indiana University	Yes	Yes	Indiana University	Yes	Yes	No Change
Kent State University	No	Yes	Kent State University	No	Yes	No Change
M.I.T.	Yes	Yes	M.I.T.	Yes	No	Minor Dropped
University of Michigan	Yes	No	University of Michigan	Yes	No	No Change
Michigan State University	No	Yes	Michigan State University	No	Yes	No Change
New York University	Yes	Yes	New York University	Yes	No	Minor Dropped**
Ohio State University	Yes	Yes	Ohio State University	Yes	Yes	No Change
Pace University	Yes	No	Pace University	Yes	Yes	Second Area of Emphasis in International Now Possible. ***

Exhibit 1. (cont.)

The 1987 Survey by Dr. Robert Kuhne	Offer a Major	Offer a Minor	The 1994 Survey by Peter S. Rose	Offer a Major	Offer a Minor	Change in Offerings Observed Between 1987 and 1994
Pennsylvania State University	Yes	Yes	Pennsylvania State University	No	No	Major Not Offered, But There is a Supporting Field.
St. Louis University	Yes	Yes	St. Louis University	Yes	Yes	No Change
University of South Carolina	Yes	Yes	University of South Carolina	Yes	Yes	No Change
Temple University	Yes	Yes	Temple University	Yes	No	Minor Dropped****
Texas A&M University	No	Yes	Texas A&M University	Yes	Yes	Major Possible*****
University of Texas-Austin	Yes	Yes	University of Texas-Austin	Yes	Yes	No Change******
University of Texas-Dallas	Yes	No	University of Texas-Dallas	Yes	No	No Change
Texas Tech University	No	Yes	Texas Tech University	No	Yes	No Change
University of Washington	Yes	Yes	University of Washington	No	Yes	Major Dropped
University of Wisconsin	Yes	Yes	University of Wisconsin	Yes	Yes	No Change

*   Students at the University of Chicago can sit for a preliminary exam in the applied field of international business; the school does not use the terms "major" and "minor." The major field at the University of Chicago is called "International Economics."

**   Doctoral students at NYU must choose a co-major in another business discipline along with the field of international business.

***   Pace University asks students to choose two areas of emphasis, one of which can be in international business.

****   Temple University no longer distinguishes between major and minor in international business. Majors commit to taking 6 courses; other students can take one or more international business courses.

*****   Doctoral students accepted by the Center for International Business can pursue a major or minor in international business through one of the academic departments in the Graduate School of Business at Texas A&M University.

******   The Marketing Department offers a specialty major in International Marketing at the University of Texas, and there is an unofficial minor.

Sources: 1987 survey results extracted from Robert J. Kuhne, "Comparative Analysis of U. S. Doctoral Programs in International Business," *Journal of Teaching in International Business,* Vol. 1 (314), 1990, The Harvard Press; 1994 results are from a written and a follow-up telephone survey by the present author.

among the schools responding to the survey) has been made and, indeed, some retrenchment has occurred between Dr. Kuhne's survey in 1987 and the author's 1994 survey. In fact, some schools (e.g., Kent State University,[1] the University of Alabama, the University of California at Berkeley, the University of Hawaii,[2] Georgia State University,[3] Penn State University, and the University of Washington) appear to have de-emphasized or even dropped their separate international business major or minor Ph.D. degree programs. The general trend today appears to call for *blending* major or minor international specializations into programs offered for more traditional business Ph.D. majors—Accounting, Finance, Management, Computer Systems/ Operations Research, and Marketing. Many business school administrators now seem to regard international business, *not* as a separate discipline, but rather as an integral part of existing business disciplines. At Penn State University, for example, faculty that were formerly in a separate international group now appear to have been spread out across the business school into their respective traditional fields.

On the whole, most business schools found by Dr. Kuhne in 1987 to be offering a Ph.D. major or minor in international business were, in 1994, apparently still offering major or minor areas of specialization in international business. In 1987, twenty-one of these twenty-eight leading schools offered a major in international business, twenty offered an international business minor, and thirteen offered both major and minor programs. By 1994 only seventeen of these schools still offered a formal major in international business, just fifteen offered a formal minor, and eleven offered both a major and a minor international concentration.

As was true in the 1980s, some business schools (e. g., MIT, the University of Michigan, and Temple University) reported operating Ph.D. programs for international *majors*, but did not appear to offer a formal international business minor at the doctoral level. Major schools offering a Ph.D. degree in international business outnumber schools not offering Ph.D. majors in international business by a ratio of about 1.5 to 1. However, these same business programs come closer to being equally divided between offering and not offering *minors* (or a second areas of emphasis) in international business for their Ph.D. students.

Clearly, the current trend definitely appears to be away from formal majors or minors in international business toward more traditional business disciplines, each of whose boundaries are now viewed as *global* in scope. The perceived need for a separate international "label" inside business Ph.D. programs appears to be waning. Moreover, among those schools *not* offering international business majors for their Ph.D. students, the proportion of their students writing dissertations with significant international business content appeared to have declined slightly or, at best, held steady between 1987 and 1994.

Overall, the number of international business Ph.D. *majors* appeared to have risen over the most recent five-year period, rising about 24%, on average, for those schools reporting their current enrollments and estimating their enrollments as of five years ago. But the enrollment experience of these leading business schools seemed to be highly mixed. For example, the Ohio State University, the University of Wisconsin at Madison, the University of Michigan (Ann Arbor), and Georgia State University all reported substantial declines in international Ph.D. majors over the past five years. On the other hand, Temple University, the University of Illinois at Urbana-Champaign, the University of Texas at Dallas, and the University of South Carolina saw substantial gains in numbers of international Ph.D. majors. The remaining schools (including such key programs as Indiana University, the University of Texas at Austin, George Washington University, and MIT) experienced relatively steady enrollment of international business majors in their doctoral programs.

The trend among international business *minors* at the Ph.D. level is also mixed. Some schools (e.g., The Ohio State University and the University of Wisconsin at Madison) reported enrollment decreases in their international business minor programs, a few tallied substantial increases (e.g., Texas Tech University, the University of Houston, and the University of South Carolina), and others (e.g., Indiana University and George Washington University) indicated relatively steady enrollments in programs where an international minor or supporting field in international business was made available to doctoral students. Overall, Ph.D. students enrolled as *minors* in international business increased an average of almost 31% over the past five years ending in 1994 among those schools reporting specific enrollment figures.

Women's Enrollment—The proportion of women students enrolled in international business Ph.D. programs still appears to be relatively low, as Exhibit 2 (which summarizes many of the most recent survey's findings) illustrates. The average across all schools responding to the survey was a women's enrollment of only about 16% of all international business Ph.D. majors. Just over 28% of those doctoral business students minoring in international business were women. Still, these percentages are slightly higher than the 14% figure for women Ph.D. students majoring in international business and the 22% figure for women doctoral candidates minoring in international business found by Professor Kuhne in 1987. While progress is being made, current Ph.D. programs still appear to have a gender bias that is likely to be corrected only through significant recruiting efforts in the future.

Geographic Backgrounds of Students—Most international doctoral students enrolled at leading U.S. business schools are from the United States, as shown in Exhibit 2. Among international *majors*, about half were U.S. residents with Asian students accounting for almost 40%, North and South America (outside the U.S.) 4%, Europe 5%, and the rest of the world about 2%. Thus, the relative paucity of European-origin Ph.D. students enrolled in leading U.S. schools that was observed by Robert Kuhne during the 1980s appears to have continued to the present time. U.S. residents account for a slightly higher percentage of doctoral students *minoring* in international business (about 61%), while Asian students represented most of the remainder (26%) of all international minors. For the most part, these relative proportions of Ph.D. minors in international business across different regions of the globe seem to have changed little since the mid-1980s. However, the relative proportion of U.S. citizens among all international majors appears to be rising.

Principal Fields of Study—For those graduate business schools responding, International Management appears to have become the leading major field in international education at the business Ph.D. level, followed by International Marketing and International Finance. However, some schools apparently define management more broadly than others do so that we need to exercise caution in interpreting these field labels. This finding reflects trends already evident from Professor Kuhne's survey in 1987 which found International Finance to be the leading discipline, but International Management was growing rapidly and International Banking was on the decline.

Most responding schools (about 59%) indicated that they *require* all of their business Ph.D. students (whether or not they are international majors) to take at least one course predominantly focused upon international business. The leading types of seminar offered are in International Management,

Exhibit 2. Selected Statistics from the 1994 Survey of Leading U. S. Collegiate Schools of Business with International Ph.D. Programs

The Mean Proportion of Women Enrolled As International Business Ph.D. Majors and Minors:

International Majors	15.9%
International Minors	28.1%

Geographic Distribution of International Business Ph.D. Majors and Minors:

Area of the World	Proportion of Majors	Proportion of Minors
United States	49.2%	60.7%
North and South America Outside U.S.	4.2	7.7
Asia	39.2	25.6
Europe	5.0	0.9
Other Areas	2.4	5.1

Proportion of Leading Business Schools Surveyed
Requiring Their Ph.D. Students to Take Courses
Focused on International Business 58.8%

Proportion of Leading Business Schools Surveyed
Offering All Their Ph.D. Students *Optional* Courses
Focused on International Business 94.1%

Proportion of Leading Business Schools Surveyed
Requiring Ph.D. Students to Study a Foreign Language 25.0%

Proportion of Leading Business Schools *Requiring*
Ph.D. Students to Travel or Study Abroad 6.3%

Proportion of Leading Business Schools Surveyed
Requiring Ph.D. Students to Have Foreign Travel or
Foreign Business Experience *Before* Gaining Admission
to the Ph.D. Program 0.0%

Proportion of Leading Business Schools Surveyed Having
a Separate International Business Department 35.3%

Exhibit 2. (cont.)

Estimated Proportion of Current Business Faculty at
Surveyed Schools Who Can Speak or Write in a
Foreign Language 28.5%

Proportion of Leading Business Schools Surveyed
With a Specific Person Serving as Coordinator or Director
of International Business Studies at the Ph.D. Level 63.2%

followed closely by International Finance, Marketing, and Trade. Ninety-four percent of the schools responding said they also offer *optional* courses in international business which their non-international Ph.D. students may take and count toward meeting their degree requirements.

Language and Travel Requirements—When asked if they *required* an international business student to study a foreign language while enrolled in the doctoral program, a large majority (75%) of the schools responding said "no"—a finding that again parallels Professor Kuhne's 1987 survey findings. Moreover, as Exhibit 2 shows, an even larger percentage of responding schools (nearly 94%) said they do *not* require an international business Ph.D. student to travel or study abroad before his or her doctoral program is completed, though many schools indicated that they often *recommend* overseas study and make opportunities available for their students to travel abroad. None of the responding schools appeared to impose a formal requirement that international students should have traveled or studied abroad or have possessed foreign business experience *before* they are admitted to the doctoral program. (However, two leading schools mentioned that their admissions committee effectively requires foreign travel, study, or business experience in screening applications, even though there is no formal requirement to possess overseas experience.)

Parallels with an Earlier Global Survey—Overall, these results seem consistent with the findings of a recent AIB-AACSB-USC-sponsored study on "International Business Education in the 1990s: A Global Survey (1993)," which observed that the internationalization goals generally set by U. S. business schools are quite low. For the most part surveyed business schools seemed content to create a general "awareness" of the global business environment among their students rather than to promote real understanding or even international expertise (what some would call "global competence"). Only about one fifth of business schools responding to the AIB-AACSB-USC sponsored study declared that they sought to provide "international expertise" in a single functional discipline. More discouraging perhaps for American business schools, European schools were nearly three times more likely to provide international expertise in at least one functional business field than were U.S. business schools. Moreover, this same study found that, on average, only one U.S. business school in ten reported that developing the international expertise of their doctoral students was a stated goal. The AIB *et. al.* study concluded that "the lack of commitment of doctoral programs to the internationalization of their students continues unabated" (Arpan, Folks, and Kwok 1993:16).

The Trend Away From International Business Departments—Most of the leading business schools responding to my survey did *not* have separate international business departments, though about 35% *did* report having such a specialized department, as Exhibit 2 relates. However, most schools responding (75%), including a few institutions that *do* have international business departments, thought that such departments were unnecessary or unwise (particularly if only Ph.D. students were involved, though most respondents suggested that such specialized departments might well be justified at the MBA or undergraduate levels). The majority of schools with verbal comments on this question expressed a desire to see international business integrated with all other areas of the business school rather than being isolated in a single department separated from the rest of their faculty.

The International Focus of Business Faculty—The survey asked each graduate school to indicate the number of its faculty devoted to international business and inquired as well into the overall size of each school's business faculty. On average, the self-designated "international business faculty" represented just under 9% of all college faculty members. This figure must be regarded with extreme caution, however, because defining exactly what constitutes "international business faculty" is a difficult, highly subjective process and the survey did not supply a specific definition. It was left to each business school to decide which faculty members could be considered a part of its "international faculty." Obviously some faculty members not considered a part of the formal international program might still be classified as "international" if the focus of their research is international business or if the material they present in the classroom is heavily flavored with international content.

In response to a question on what proportion of a business school's faculty can speak or write in a foreign language, many schools either did not know or were unsure. Among those who made an estimate of the foreign-language capability of their faculty, the average was 28.5% (as reported in Exhibit 2), but with considerable variability from school to school. When asked if foreign language capabilities would be more important in their *future* hiring decisions about 86% of the responding schools said "no."

Overwhelmingly these business schools responded in the negative when asked if they *require* their faculty members to travel abroad, though many schools responded that they encourage foreign travel and make the opportunity to travel overseas readily available to their faculty. As one business school administrator noted, "we encourage but would not want to require foreign travel by faculty." Finally, the majority of schools—about 63% of those replying—reported having a specific person serving as coordinator or director of their international business studies at the Ph.D. level (see Exhibit 2). Other responding schools could find *no* particular need for having an international business coordinator.

Lack of Commitment to Internationalization—The foregoing observations seem to be consistent, once again, with the study of U.S. and European business schools by Arpan, Folks, and Kwok (1993) that was cited earlier, which shows that, in 77% of the U.S. and foreign business schools surveyed, the internationalization of business *research* did *not* include someone assigned administrative responsibility to oversee the development of an international business research program and 64% of the responding schools did *not* include internationalization activities as part of the annual performance evaluation of their business faculty. Moreover, 61% of U.S. business schools and 53% of European business schools did *not* appear to have a specific plan for the future internationalization of their faculty. This AIB-AACSB-USC study specifically noted what it called "the continued lack of commitment of U. S. business schools overall to the development of meaningful faculty incentives for internationalization activities" (Arpan, Folks, and Kwok 1993:15).

Other Business Schools With Doctoral Programs—It must be noted that several business schools not on Professor Kuhne's original survey list as having international Ph.D. programs apparently do operate internationally-oriented business doctoral programs today. This was revealed in the 1993 AIB-AACSB-USC survey alluded to above which found at least eleven other business schools with international major or minor programs at the doctoral level. These additional doctoral-granting schools are listed in Exhibit 3.

It is obvious from Exhibit 3 that these eleven additional graduate business schools offering international programs to their doctoral students have gone heavily into minors or "supporting areas" rather than choosing to offer international business majors. Only three of these eleven degree-granting institutions reported offering *majors* in international business and all three of these institutions apparently provide no minor or supporting area in the field.[4]

Following a survey of these eleven schools plus eleven other U. S. business schools that also appear on Professor Kuhne's original list, this 1993 AIB-AACSB-USC study concluded that 70% of business doctoral students received either "no or minimal international business education" (Arpan, Folks, and Kwok 1993:16), double the proportion for European business schools. The AIB *et al.* study concluded that a lack of adequate financial support and a lack of interest on the part of the faculty represented the principal roadblocks to further progress toward internationalization of business doctoral programs. Part of the lack of faculty interest apparently sprang from the limited international education that current business school faculty frequently have received. Nearly 70% of current U. S. business school faculty members surveyed reported minimal prior education or training in the international field. Still, over 90% of the AIB-AACSB-USC surveyed schools believed that their faculty's knowledge of international business had increased over the past five years (especially among AACSB-accredited schools).

CONCLUSIONS AND IMPLICATIONS OF THE SURVEY EVIDENCE

In summary, the latest survey results suggest that, while some business schools are still undecided about where international business "fits" in among the traditional disciplines of accounting, finance, marketing, management, and computer systems/operations research, a substantial segment of the respondents seems to have concluded that international business is part of, rather than separate from, traditional business disciplines and can be successfully grafted onto or infused into existing academic fields. Enrollments in

Exhibit 3. Other Universities Offering International Business Majors, Minors, and/or Degrees.

s School	International Business Major	International Business Minor	Dual International Business Degree	Specialized International Business Degree
University of California Los Angeles	Yes	No	Yes	Yes
Florida International University	Yes	No	No	No
University of Maryland	No	Yes*	No	No
Memphis State University	No	No	Yes	No
University of Miami	Yes	No	No	No
New Mexico State University	No	Yes**	No	No
Oklahoma State University	No	Yes***	No	No
University of Pittsburgh	No	Yes	No	No
University of Rhode Island	Yes****	No	No	No
Virginia Commonwealth University	No	Yes	No	No
Washington State University	No	Yes*****	No	No

* The University of Maryland's minor in international business (established in 1990) requires a minimum of 4 courses devoted to various areas of international business.

** There seems to be a disagreement among sources of information regarding New Mexico State University. The AIB-AACSB-USC study contends that this business school has an international business minor, but a survey by this author was answered "no" for *both* an international business major and minor.

*** Oklahoma State does not offer an official minor; however, a student can choose to create an area of concentration in international business.

**** Rhode Island reports in a follow-up survey by the present author that there is no official international major or minor but that a student can focus through independent study or through a suitable dissertation project on international business.

***** Washington State University lists this program as a "supporting area."

Source: Jeffrey S. Arpan, William R. Folks, Jr., and Chuck C. Y. Kwok, *International Business Education in the 1990's: A Global Survey* (1993), with supplemental survey information obtained by the author.

international business at the Ph.D. level appear to be increasing, though several leading degree-granting schools reported declines or have apparently reached a steady state in their overall enrollment picture. Students of U.S. origin now seem to dominate both international Ph. D. majors and minors enrolled at leading U.S. business schools, while the number of women students remains in the minority but seems to be slowly gaining ground. Moreover, few U.S. programs *require* foreign languages or foreign travel for either their doctoral students or their faculty and, based upon earlier survey results from the 1980s, this has not changed appreciably in several years.

Nevertheless, we must remain cautious and not rush immediately to the conclusion that today's undergraduate and master's students are being poorly prepared for the challenges of international business or that future business faculty graduating from today's doctoral programs will not be adequately equipped in the principles and practices of international business. Surveys such as those cited here do not effectively measure how the *content* of established courses within traditional business fields may have changed to reflect growing awareness of the importance of international developments. The bottom line for business education is that labels probably do not matter, but the real content of educational programs clearly does matter. To the extent that graduate, as well as undergraduate, business courses and curricula today are more heavily infused with international topics and issues and reveal a trend toward increasing international emphasis, then the overall direction of change must be regarded as favorable, even though the level of international exposure still appears to be inadequate for most business schools.

Unfortunately, the surveys discussed cannot measure well these ongoing changes in educational content. A dynamic analysis in the form of an *ongoing* survey and study of business school courses and curricula is definitely needed for the future if we are to gain a deeper understanding of what is really happening to the internationalization process in today's business schools. We need new measures of "internationalization" that capture the often subtle changes underway inside traditional business fields, courses, and degree programs. In the future, it will no longer be adequate merely to count international and non-international degree programs or majors and minors. Increasingly, international business is being viewed "as a context," not as a discipline. The changes going on today in business doctoral programs seem to lie deeper inside at the level of the individual course or seminar and in the mind set of individual business faculty members. If we are to succeed in fully internationalizing business Ph.D. candidates for the future, we must find ways to shift the focus of individual faculty members, the courses they teach, and the research programs they pursue.

NOTES

1. Information received by telephone indicates that Kent State deleted the international business major portion of its Ph.D. program about five years ago. However, their marketing program permits an international concentration for Ph.D. students. Kent State is working with two other area schools to establish a new master's level international business program.
2. Information received via telephone indicated that the University of Hawaii is currently working on a new international business Ph.D. program, though it apparently had not yet received official sanction.
3. Georgia State University's international business Ph.D. program was reported over the telephone to have been inactive over the past five years. The University does have plans underway for a Master of Science program containing an overseas internship, however.
4. The author conducted a follow-up survey of the eleven business schools added through the AIB-AACSB-USC survey and found their replies to the survey form similar to the schools on Professor Kuhne's (1990) original list. Responding programs were about evenly split between offering and not offering majors and minors in international business. There was some evidence here of declining numbers of majors in international business, but a somewhat greater portion of women enrolled as international business majors. International economics and management ranked highest as desirable majors. Once again, however, none of the responding schools required foreign language training, travel, or experience before or during the program. These responding schools generally avoided separate international departments and one school noted specifically that: "the whole emphasis is to integrate international research into *all* our courses rather than separating these issues into specific courses." On average, these schools reported that 11% of their faculty were in the international field and only about 25% of the faculty could speak or write in a foreign language. There were no requirements for faculty to travel abroad, but the schools were about equally split over whether this should be required and whether an international coordinator was in place or might be needed in the future.

REFERENCES

Arkin, Anat. "How International Are Britain's Business Schools?" *Personnel Management.* 23(11) (November 1991): 28-31.

Arpan, Jeffrey S., William R. Folks, Jr., and Chuck C. Y. Kwok. 1993. *International Business Education in the 1990s: A Global Survey,* jointly sponsored by the

Academy of International Business, the American Association of Collegiate Schools of Business, and the University of South Carolina.

Cannon, Steve. 1991. "Current Trends in European Graduate Management Education." *Selections*. (Autumn): 22-28.

Cavusgil, S. Tamer (ed.). 1993. *Internationalizing Business Education: Meeting the Challenge*. East Lansing, MI: Michigan State University Press.

Kuhne, Robert J. 1990. "Comparative Analysis of U. S. Doctoral Programs in International Business." *Journal of Teaching in International Business*. 1(3/4): 85-99.

Lutz, Richard J. 1994. "Adapting the Ph.D. Program to Ecological Imperatives: How to Herd Cats." in this volume.

Madura, Jeff. 1991. "Internationalizing the Ph.D. Program." *Journal of Teaching in International Business*. 3(1): 21-26.

THE INTERNATIONALIZATION OF DOCTORAL PROGRAMS: A SURVEY OF PROGRAM DIRECTORS

Matthew B. Myers and Glenn S. Omura

INTRODUCTION

In an effort to increase interest in the internationalization effort among business faculty, the AACSB began in 1977 a series of seminars targeting deans and faculty. Although the response was encouraging and a significant increase in new international curricula was introduced in business schools by 1987, Nehrt (1993) warned that only a small percentage of business faculty participated in the workshops, and that these individuals cannot be expected to produce a significant change in each of their school's curriculum.

Another approach to internationalizing faculty is to provide international education during doctoral studies. According to a survey conducted by Nehrt in 1976, 25% of doctoral students had studied business within the international context. In 1987, a similar survey was conducted of 53 doctoral programs of business that produced 92% of all doctoral degrees. Of the 1,690 doctoral students who had completed their coursework and were expected to graduate within three years, only 17% had been exposed to one or more international business courses, indicating a decline in international studies at the doctoral level when increased need called for just the opposite.

Nehrt (1993) argues that there are two solutions to the problem of internationalizing doctoral programs. First, the doctoral committee of each school must change the prerequisite coursework requirements for all doctoral students so as to include an international business course. Second, the school could opt for each department that offers a major to require a core international course in its discipline. Nehrt adds that while these solutions appear simple, their actual implementation is not. He suggests that reaching a consensus among faculty and administrators often proves difficult when curriculum change is proposed.

25

In order for today's business schools to produce graduates competent in international matters, business school faculties must become committed to global issues within the curriculum. Long term internationalization goals dictate that the future professors of business—the doctoral students of today and tomorrow—be exposed to international issues and be convinced of the importance of an international perspective. Participation by doctoral students in international studies could provide a trickle-down effect necessary to bring all undergraduate business students and MBAs on line in order to compete in the globally competitive markets.

THE QUESTION OF INTERNATIONALIZATION

VIEWS ON THE INTERNATIONALIZATION PROCESS—IS IT REALLY NEEDED?

The complexity of the internationalization issue is compounded by what some see as the teaching/research dichotomy—is the goal of the doctoral program to produce individuals competent in research methods, pedagogical methods, or both? Studies such as the Gordon and Howell report of 1959 as well as subsequent remarks by Howell (1993) state that there is a tension between the models of doctoral education—that which stresses the accumulation of knowledge (the late-Renaissance model) and that which focuses on the creation of knowledge (the 19th century German model). As Howell states, the debate centers around whether the simple accumulation of knowledge is sufficient for teaching at the college level, or whether methodological competence for creating knowledge should also be required. This is an important point since business education is shaped by the professional attitudes and values of the business school faculty (Kedia 1994). How faculty deem the importance of research (the creation of knowledge) could affect their opinion of more managerially relevant trends such as internationalization. There is little doubt that Ph.D. granting institutions expect strong research competence among their faculty and doctoral students, following the German model. However, the increasing importance of managerial relevance, reflected in such MBA program evaluations as those of *U.S. News and World Report* and *Business Week*, is causing most of the institutions to re-think their self-conceptions. As a result, the late Renaissance model seems to be gaining in popularity. The conflict is that due to the variety of programmatic commitments in our institutions, there continues to be a need for high-quality faculty capable of integrating established analytical models based in the social and behavioral sciences with practice, both in teaching and research (Alutto 1993).

Because of the different missions of individual schools, staffing models among organizations differ. Alutto (1993) categorizes these staffing models into "integrator" and "silo-enhancers." The integrator staffing model helps to operationalize the late-Renaissance doctoral education model, whereas the silo-enhancing staffing model assists the implementation of the German doctoral education model. Integrator schools expect integration to occur within each faculty member, with areas of commonality, such as internationalization. A weakness of this model may be an insufficient level of internationalization as individual faculty focus on their discipline, resulting in minimized competency in internationalizing their teaching or research. Silo-enhancing schools expect a few integrative faculty specialists to perform integration (internationalization) for the whole. A weakness of this model may be insufficient depth of knowledge in a specific discipline in order to competently teach or perform research.

According to Daniels (1993), business schools will never internationalize all of their courses until all doctoral students are required to study and become proficient in the international nuances of their own areas. Only then would we begin to see a larger cadre over time that would include international dimensions in their own courses and texts. Daniels states that before any significant changes can be made in any doctoral curriculum, however, the faculty and administration of the business schools must be convinced of a) the value of the internationalization process, and b) the feasibility of a curriculum change. These opinions may vary according to the perceived importance of such issues as research and teaching, as well as the individual backgrounds of the faculty members. To determine the attitudes of faculty toward the internationalization process and its relevance to teaching and research, several questions need to be posed:

1. Upon graduation, should doctoral students be proficient in teaching international business courses?
2. Upon graduation, should doctoral students be adept in conducting research on international issues?
3. If it were determined that a doctoral program should prepare students to integrate international issues when teaching business courses, what would be the major barriers to changing the doctoral program in order to do so?

To address these questions, 130 questionnaires were sent to doctoral program directors throughout the U.S. and Canada. After two weeks, a second mailing was sent, resulting in ninety-four responses, for a response rate of 72% . The instrument addressed the three major questions listed above and included some classification variables, including the age of the individual programs, the size of the programs measured in the number of students graduated in recent years, as well as the number and types of disciplines offered as majors within the program. With this information, some basic issues may be addressed and conclusions made regarding current attitudes toward internationalization, perceived barriers to the process, modifications of programs, and faculty development.

SENTIMENT ON INTERNATIONALIZING TEACHING

To determine the attitudes of program directors regarding international skills in the classroom, we asked what the international teaching capabilities of the graduated doctoral student should be (see Table 1). There seems to be support for individuals capable of integration in their teaching skills rather than specialization (the silo-enhancer). Most directors (59.6%) believe that newly graduated Ph.D.'s should be able to integrate international issues when teaching managerial courses, as opposed to being able to teach an undergraduate international introductory course in their discipline (6.7%). However 13.5% of respondents felt that new Ph.D.'s need only be competent in their specialty area without the ability to integrate international issues, and one-fifth believed that personal sensitization to international issues was sufficient. Hence, 34% are not receptive to integration in teaching. Directors are not particularly interested in an international specialist or an individual completely insensitive to international issues; rather, faculty members who can integrate international issues and offer their students an international perspective while teaching are more desirable.

SENTIMENTS ON INTERNATIONALIZING RESEARCH

Given the differing attitudes discussed by Howell toward the research issue, it might be expected that a question regarding the importance of international research capability would receive somewhat bi-polar responses. This was not the case (see Table 2). When asked of the importance of international research capabilities of graduated doctoral students, almost 70% of directors

Table 1.

Should your doctoral program require that all graduated students . . .	% Responding Yes
Be able to teach undergraduate introductory international course in their discipline	6.7%
Be able to integrate international issues when teaching managerial courses	59.6%
Be personally sensitized to international issues	20.2%
Be competent in specialty area without ability to integrate international issues	13.5%

Table 2.

Should your doctoral program require that all graduated students . . .	% Responding Yes
Be able to do competent research on international issues and develop a career in the international track of their discipline	2.2%
Be able to do competent empirical research on international issues	13.2%
Be able to search for and integrate the international literature of their discipline in literature reviews	69.2%
No special effort should be made to internationalize the research competency of our students	15.4%

said that Ph.D.'s should be able to search for and integrate the international literature of their discipline in their research. Very few (2.2%) thought that faculty should be able to develop a career in the international track of their discipline through international research, but 15.4% responded that no special effort should be made to internationalize the research competency of doctoral students. A significant percentage of new Ph.D.'s have not been encouraged to internationalize their research competency.

Table 3.
Relationship between School Rankings and Perceived Importance of
International Issues in Teaching

	School Rankings*					
	Top 25	25-50	Unranked	Non-U.S.	Total	n
Teach Int'l Course	8.3	0.0	8.3	8.3	6.7%	6
Integrate Int'l Issues	33.3	70.6	62.5	58.3	59.6%	53
Be Personally Sensitized	16.6	23.5	23.0	8.3	20.2%	18
No Ability to Integrate	41.6	5.9	6.2	25.0	13.5%	12
Total	100%	100%	100%	100%	100%	n=89

Table 4.
Relationship between School Rankings and Perceived Importance of
International Issues in Research

	School Rankings					
	Top 25	25-50	Unranked	Non-U.S.	Total	n
Develop Career In Int'l Track of Their Discipline?	8.3	0	0	8.3	2.2%	2
Competent Empirical Research on Int'l Issuers?	0	5.9	23	0	13.2%	12
Integrate Int'l Literature in Their Research?	75.0	88.2	58.0	83.3	69.2%	63
No Special Effort Be Made to Internationalize	16.7	5.9	20.0	8.3	15.4%	14
Total	100%	100%	100%	100%	100%	n=91

BUSINESS SCHOOL LEADERS

To assess the value of internationalization, the sample of program directors were categorized by their school's ranking in the *U.S. News and World
Report* (March 1994). Breaking the respondents down into four categories
(Top 25, 26-50, unranked, and non-U.S.), we cross-tabulated these divisions
against the responses to our above questions (see Table 3). There is no difference in the response pattern for the ranked versus the unranked in teaching
or research. At least two conclusions are possible. Either internationalization
is unrelated to being a top-ranked school, or top-ranked schools are as obliv-
ious to the need to internationalize as are unranked schools. In either case,

this is not inconsistent with the view that top ranked schools are dominated by research oriented models of doctoral education (Leavitt 1993), and in these schools "faculty members value colleagues that are narrowly trained in core disciplines with little concern to think in a holistic manner about professional application of their basic disciplines" (Kedia, in this volume, p. 155).

BARRIERS TO INTERNATIONALIZATION

In an effort to determine the hurdles associated with internationalizing the doctoral programs, we asked the program directors to assume that it was mandated that their doctoral program must prepare students to integrate international issues when teaching managerial courses. The respondents were then asked to identify the three most significant barriers to implementing change in their program (see Table 5). Nine possible answers were provided, with the option to write in additional responses if necessary. Twenty percent responded that there would be no problem, since their program was already sufficiently integrated. The top-ranked schools stood out in their opinions on the issue (see Table 6). Fifty percent of the responding top twenty-five schools believed they were already sufficiently internationally integrated, compared with only 30% of the twenty-six to fifty schools, and 9.6% of unranked schools. Top ranked schools apparently believe they are more internationalized than schools not ranked. Still, a large proportion of ranked schools believe they would have problems if forced to internationalize. While it may be said that these top schools are generally seen as intensive research schools, as Alutto (1993) points out, virtually all doctoral degree granting institutions are designed to be silo-enhancing, research oriented units, regardless of the type of overall school orientation.

It is apparent that top ranked schools view internationalization differently than the others. Many feel that international issues are not a necessary component to the teaching exercise, and half feel that they are sufficiently integrated internationally in their doctoral programs. Our survey does not allow us to infer why these highly ranked schools seem averse to change.

FACULTY

When perceived barriers to implementing change were identified, however, one point became clear—that the barriers are overwhelmingly associated with the faculty. Fifty-five percent of the respondents stated that "faculty who teach doctoral classes lack the international expertise to prepare students" was one of three major obstacles, 43.9% state that there is "insufficient faculty commitment to integrate international issues into their courses," while 29.8% chose "insufficient faculty commitment to change their doctoral program" as one of the three significant barriers. If the faculty are indeed the barrier to the internationalization process, who will train the future educators? As Kuhne (1990) states, the result will be a population of educators without the skills to provide a complete education to their students, limiting their lectures to domestic topics and failing to provide their students with the tools necessary to succeed in a global business environment. All of this tends to support Kedia's (1993) statement that the most urgent need is to internationalize faculty in order to internationalize schools of business.

FUNDING

Given contemporary factors, such as the downturn in enrollment levels in business schools, it might be expected that funding problems would be seen as significant barriers to internationalization. Surprisingly, only 28.7% of the respondents identified "insufficient funding" as a major hurdle to implementing change, suggesting that funding is not an insurmountable barrier. This is perhaps due to a wide variety of funding sources or the belief that simple "integration" isn't a costly process.

LACK OF CHANGE AGENT

According to Cavusgil (1993), it is essential that one or more "change agents" emerge in each institution, providing support and encouragement to the internationalization effort. Yet, only 25.5% of the respondents believed that a lack of an individual champion supporting change would be a significant barrier to the internationalization of their doctoral programs. This may be due to the failure to realize the need for a champion, or the outright rejection of the need for one. In either case, Nehrt warned the small percentage of faculty participants in the AACSB seminars might not provide the necessary leverage to make changes in the programs.

Table 5.
Hurdles in Internationalizing Programs

	% Responding Yes
No problem. Our program is sufficiently integrated	20.2%
Insufficient funding	28.7%
Not sure we would know how to integrate	18.1%
Faculty who teach doctoral students lack the international expertise to prepare students	55.3%
No individual champion to support change	25.5%
Insufficient faculty commitment to integrate into their courses	43.9%
No flexibility in the program to properly integrate international issues	7.4%
Insufficient faculty commitment to change their doctoral program	29.8%
Interdepartment politics would stymie change	6.4%

Table 6.
Relationship between School Rankings and Perception of International Hurdles

	School Rankings*				
	Top 25	25-50	Unranked	Non-U.S.	Total
No Problem	50.0	30.0	9.7	38.5	20.2%
There is a Problem	50.0	70.0	90.3	61.5	79.8%
Total	12.8%	18.1%	55.3%	13.8%	n=94

POLITICS

To a lesser extent, lack of flexibility in the doctoral programs and interdepartmental politics were seen as barriers, with few respondents believing these to be hurdles. These last issues are surprising for several reasons. First, due to the extensive core requirements of most doctoral programs, flexibility in adding international courses or adjusting the program to include international issues would seem to be limited. Second, it seems natural that each department would wish to control its own curriculum; any attempt to force requirements across departmental boundaries would be cause for conflict. Still, these two issues were not identified as significant hurdles. It must be remembered, however, that this is the point of view of the program directors, and not the independent faculty members or department heads.

No Core International Faculty

Given the different viewpoints regarding the faculty staffing models mentioned above, the role of international specialists in the college of business might be subject to debate. Can a few core internationally specialized faculty infuse the college with internationalization? Those schools offering majors in international business at the doctoral level were cross-tabulated with those respondents answering "no problem, our program is already sufficiently (internationally) integrated," and only 23% responded that their program was indeed sufficiently integrated. It seems that either the presence of a core faculty of international specialists may not be infusing the doctoral programs with the internationalization needed, or champions have not evolved from this group. This supports the criticism of the silo-enhancing staffing model provided earlier.

STRUCTURAL FACTORS

It is obvious that with 130 institutions offering doctoral programs in business there will be a wide variety of program types, sizes, majors and minors, and qualities. In order to determine what structural factors influence an institution's commitment to the internationalization process, we attempted to answer the following questions:

1. What effect does the size of a doctoral program, measured in the number of students graduated in the past five years, have on a program's commitment to internationalization?
2. Are newer doctoral programs (those developed within the last ten years) more likely to be receptive to the internationalization theme than more established programs?

Program Size and Age

To determine the relationship between these variables and a program's commitment to international issues, the doctoral program directors were asked about the size of their programs, whether the program was started in the past ten years, and what disciplines are currently being offered as majors. These factors were cross-tabbed with the responses regarding barriers to internationalization, international teaching capabilities, and international research capabilities.

Table 7.
Relationship Between Program Size and Perceived Importance of
International Issues in <u>Teaching</u>

	Program Size (Number of students graduated in last ten years)						
	<10	10-19	20-29	30-39	>40	Total	n
Teach Int'l Course?	0.0	13.3	0.0	0.0	0.0	6.8%	6
Integrate Int'l Issues?	70.6	40.0	71.4	66.7	57.6	60.2%	3
Be Personally Sensitized	23.5	13.3	21.4	22.2	18.2	19.3%	17
No Ability to Integrate	5.9	33.3	7.1	11.1	12.1	13.6%	12
Total	100%	100%	100%	100%	100%	100%	n=88

Table 8.
Relationship Between Program Size and Perceived Importance of
International Issues in Research

	Program Size (Number of students graduated in last ten years)						
	<10	10-19	20-29	30-39	>40	Total	n
Develop a Career in Int'l Track of Their Discipline?	0.0	6.7	0.0	0.0	3.0	2.2%	2
Competent Empirical Research on Int'l Issues?	22.2	6.7	13.3	0.0	15.1	13.3%	12
Integrate Int'l Literature in Their Research?	72.2	4.7	73.3	77.8	72.3	68.9%	62
No Special Effort Made to Internationalize	5.5	40.0	13.3	22.2	9.1	15.6%	12
Total	100%	100%	100%	100%	100%	100%	n=90

Table 9.
Relationship Between Program Size and Perception of
Internationalization Hurdles

	Program Size (Number of students graduated in last ten years)						
	<10	10-19	20-29	30-39	>40	Total	n
No Problem	21.0	18.7	18.7	0	24.2	19.4%	18
There is a Problem	79.0	81.3	81.3	100	75.8	80.6%	75
Total	100%	100%	100%	100%	100%	100%	n=93

Table 10.
Relationship Between Program Age and Perceived Importance of International Issues in __Teaching__

	Program Age (Was your program developed in the past ten years?)			
	Yes	No	Total	n
Teach Int'l Course	0%	8.4%	7.1%	6
Integrate Int'l Issues	78.6%	56.3%	60.0%	51
Personally Sensitized	21.4%	18.3%	18.8%	16
No Ability to Integrate	0%	17.0%	14.1%	12
Total	100%	100%	100%	n=85

Table 11.
Relationship Between Program Age and Perceived Importance of International Issues in __Research__

	Program Age (Was your program developed in the past ten years?)			
	Yes	No	Total	n
Develop Career in Int'l Track of Their Discipline	0%	2.9%	2.3%	2
Competent Empirical Research on Int'l Issues	14.3%	14.1%	13.8%	12
Integrate Int'l Literature in Their Discipline	85.7%	69.0%	70.1%	61
No Special Effort to Internationalize	0%	17.0%	13.8%	12
Total	100%	100%	100%	n=87

Table 12
Relationship Between Program Age and Perceived Fully Integrated
Program

	Program Age (Was your program developed in the past ten years?)			
	Yes	No	Total	n
No Problem	7.1%	23.7%	21.1%	19
There is a Problem	92.9%	76.3%	78.9%	71
Total	100%	100%	100%	n=90

From an education standpoint, larger doctoral programs may be slower and/or more resistant to changes in curriculum modification. Bound by tradition, the same could be said of the older programs and their outlook on the internationalization process. Smaller, newer programs, however, would be expected to be receptive to "newer" ideas and innovations, and therefore more receptive to the internationalization issues. Surprisingly, the general responses of the program directors did not agree with our expectations. While the very smallest seemed more receptive, the small sample mitigates any definitive conclusion.

In evaluating program size, the respondents were asked approximately how many students graduated from their Ph.D. program in the last five years (see Tables 8 and 9). We found little general relationship between the size of the doctoral program measured in students graduated and the views on international research and teaching capabilities of graduated doctoral students. Similarly, program size had little relation with those respondents who felt their programs were already sufficiently integrated internationally.

To determine the effect of age, we cross-tabbed age of the program with the director's views on teaching, research, and the internationalization process (see Tables 10, 11,and 12). Like program size, there was very little relation between the age of the doctoral program and the views on the importance internationalization.

CONCLUSION

The issue of internationalization of doctoral programs is still a controversial one despite the obviously increased importance of understanding the global economy. Even those who agree that internationalization is necessary differ in their beliefs on how it should occur, whether through faculty development, integration of international issues in doctoral program curriculum, or even at the undergraduate and MBA levels of study. Opinions on just how Ph.D. programs should be modified, if at all, vary according to the type of program and the backgrounds of faculty and administration. Surprisingly, however, the perceived need for internationalization, especially from an integration standpoint, does not follow the traditional boundaries or schools of thought, such as research or teaching concentrations, or program sizes and age.

The problems with faculty may be due in part to the fact that international issues have not been a traditional measuring stick in their own careers—according to the study by Arpan, Folks, and Kwok (1993) the majority of schools in their survey do not include international activities in the annual performance evaluations of their business faculty (64%). Given the results of past studies showing the small percentage of business faculty that have been exposed to international topics, however, some effort must be made to better provide the future professors of business with the tools necessary to prepare business students for the hyper-competitive global economy.

REFERENCES

Alutto, Joseph A. 1993. "Whither Doctoral Education? An Exploration of Program Models." *Selections*. (Spring): 37-43.

Arpan, J. S., Folks, W. R., and Kwok, C. Y. 1993. *International Business Education in the 1990's: A Global Survey*. University of South Carolina.

Cavusgil, S. Tamer. 1993. "Internationalization of Business Education." in *Internationalizing Business Education: Meeting the Challenge*. East Lansing, MI: Michigan State University Press.

Daniels, John C. 1993. "Perspectives on Curriculum: Indiana University." in *Internationalizing Business Education: Meeting the Challenge*. East Lansing, MI: Michigan State University Press.

GMAC. 1992. Current Issues in Business Doctoral Education: A Report on the Dallas Invitational Conference. *Selections*. (Autumn): 9-26.

Gordon, R. A. and Howell, J. G. 1959. *Higher Education for Business*. New York, NY: Columbia University Press.

Howell, J. G. 1993. "The Business School and the Doctorate." *Selections*. (Winter): 12-21.

Kedia, Ben L. 1993. "The CIBER Agenda." in *Internationalizing Business Education: Meeting the Challenge*. East Lansing, MI: Michigan State University Press.

Kedia, Ben L. "A Pyramidical Approach to the Internationalization of Doctoral Business Education." in this volume.

Kuhne, Robert J. 1990. "Comparative Analysis of U.S. Doctoral Programs in International Business." *Journal of Teaching in International Business.* 1(3/4): 85-99.

Leavitt, Harold J. 1993. "The Business School and the Doctorate." *Selections.* (Winter): 12-21.

Nehrt, Lee. 1993. "Business School Curriculum and Faculty." in *Internationalizing Business Education: Meeting the Challenge.* East Lansing, MI: Michigan State University Press.

Nehrt, Lee. 1987. "The Internationalization of the Curriculum." in *Journal of International Business Studies.* Volume 18, 83-90.

"The Best Graduate Schools." *U.S. News and World Report.* 21 March 1994, 66-98.

II. RATIONALE AND CONCEPTUAL UNDERPINNINGS FOR INTERNATIONALIZING DOCTORAL PROGRAMS IN BUSINESS

Introduction

S. Tamer Cavusgil

The articles in this section capture the conceptual and practical reasons for internationalizing doctoral programs in business. **John Stopford** argues that all business is international and that this is the context that doctoral programs must address, not by "bolting on" an international business seminar to a parochial program, but by expanding methodology courses, increasing the diversity of faculty and the student body, and by redefining research topics, all to emphasize facets of the international context of business.

Brian Toyne provides a framework in which individual programs can tailor and focus their internationalization efforts. He reminds us of the purposes of Ph.D. programs in business, analyzing the problems of shifting priorities, internal and external pressures, and the types of scholarship conducted in the internationalization process. Having presented his framework, he then explores the levels of internationalization that each institution might seek to achieve. He establishes a base level that all institutions should achieve and then discusses how an institution might accomplish awareness, understanding and competency levels of international business literacy.

Robert May adds to the rationale and our conceptual understanding of internationalization by asserting that business might be the same everywhere, but that culture varies that definition. Reconceptualizing doctoral programs, he asserts, requires that faculty overcome their own culture in order to be able to prepare students to meet the international business challenges of the 21st Century.

Lyman Porter rounds out this discussion by identifying what can be gained and what can be lost in the internationalization process. Instead of conceptualizing changes as all encompassing, he advocates a targeted, incremental approach in which selected schools, departments, faculty and students

43

are first exposed to the ideas of internationalization, i.e., consciousness-raising, and then proceed to deeper levels of understanding and competence.

The reader of this section will gain an appreciation for the changes business has undergone over the past decade and why it is necessary to address these issues in doctoral education. In addition, the reader will—as did the authors—struggle with some of the conceptual issues of moving from the historical, Germanic roots of "silo-enhancer" doctoral programs to the more integrated, Renaissance model that seeks to create more broadly prepared specialists in each of the fields of business.

International Business as a Context, Not a Discipline

John M. Stopford

Introduction

The debates about the nature of international business (IB) as a subject for study have raged for as long as the field has existed. Some argue that business is essentially the same the world over, and that national and cultural diversity merely add complexity to familiar domestic issues. Others point out that IB has some specific issues that are absent in domestic studies (for example, Robock and Simmonds [1989] emphasize political risk and currency issues) and therefore IB is differentiated from other business subjects. Yet others are concerned to draw a distinction between *comparative* management and cross-border *international* management. Whereas for some, IB is a quasi-discipline in its own right; others consider the whole field to be a *melange* of underlying subjects and disciplines, each with its own non-domestic component.

In this paper I do not wish to address all the issues implied in these debates, for they have occupied many pages in journals such as the *Journal of International Business Studies*. Instead I wish to pick up just a few of the arguments as a way to make the case for considering "international" more as a context for research than as a separate field of study. Promoting greater internationalism in doctoral research can yield far-reaching consequences, some of which are illustrated by the development of the doctoral program at the London Business School (LBS).

London is just one example of the European experience, about which I am wary of generalizations. This is itself an example of the difficulties in the international field—how to capture some regularity of behavior when there are so many different structural variables involved. Even so, there is a strong commonality in the approach of considering "international" as the context

45

for teaching and research. Perhaps because of history, custom and the pressures of smaller national markets, most European schools start from a much more intuitively international view of the world than seems to be the case in the U.S. The vast internal market makes many in American education and business ask what benefits there are to gained from an international perspectives—even in these days of global competition. Besides, many of the basic management models started in the U.S. and their domination of so much of European thinking adds to European openness to ideas from abroad.

WHY ADD THE INTERNATIONAL DIMENSION?

Conducting research in an international rather than a national setting adds complexity to the phenomenon under study and to the data required for adequate analysis. Because complexity adds cost, we must ask whether the needed incremental returns, in terms of greater insight or even new theory, are likely to be reaped. At least four answers are possible, depending on the particular subject and the particular issue. Sometimes the answer seems to be that universalism prevails; an international setting adds little or nothing. A second answer is that internationalism adds to the range of particular outcomes, because of local influences rather than any change in the underlying theory. A third is that by looking across borders, one can conjure with many alternative explanations and avoid the trap of simplistic, single-cause answers. Finally, internationalism can be seen to be changing the nature of the phenomenon itself, thus requiring research to start from international assumptions and then "work backwards," so to speak, to implications for national environments.

Universal paradigms dominate many of the discipline-based business subjects and also subjects like accounting. The fundamental notions of score-keeping remain the same, regardless of the regulatory provisions and the particular procedures that are permissible for recording taxable profits. If one is interested in debits and credits, the setting is a matter of indifference. If, however, one is interested in, say, the effect of regulatory and tax codes on investment behavior, the setting becomes of crucial importance. But even here, the issues are those of *comparative* management—does behaviour in these matters in China differ from behaviour in France?—not *international*.

Even so trivial an example as this shows how easy it is to redefine the subject to fit it into the second category of answer: where the application of the theory needs adjustment at the margin to cope with a wide variety of special cases. One could, for example, develop an international theory of cultural and regulatory influences on the application of accounting disciplines on investment behaviour. Whether that would change the understanding of accounting as a whole remains a moot point.

Take a more difficult example from economics. The theory of industrial economics has been developed principally from U.S. data. The underlying (tacit) assumption has been that the U.S. market provides representative data (or was it just that many of the crucial developments were made in the U.S.?) and various tests in other markets have generally supported the American propositions. This can be taken as *prima facie* evidence that there is a universal theory of industrial economics that applies with only minor modification to all markets. But if one changes the focus slightly and adds the issue of cross-border competition and market interdependencies, the sense of certainty evaporates. The strong correlations seen at the national level between, say, market share and profitability disappear when the market is defined to include (as in the European Community) many nations. Economists might object to this argument on the grounds that the market is defined in Marshalian terms by the law of one price and that broadening the scope of the market across borders breaks that definition and changes the question. Yet, close inspection of industry-by-industry price data can show both variations within the U.S. that are greater than transport cost differences and also similarities across Europe. The point is not that industrial economics should be revised fundamentally, but that the extra discipline that comes from studying the complexities of international markets should help to focus attention on the underlying assumptions by making them explicit and open to enquiry. Such a focus can yield greater insights into the importance of the boundary conditions of both the model being used and the data set employed for the empirical test.[1]

The third answer applies to a wide range of the "softer" issues of management: an understanding of the international context enriches the stock of metaphors can be used to explain otherwise confusing differences in the observed regularities in behavior. A purely domestic approach to a problem can blind the research to alternative possibilities and provide temptation to draw false conclusions. The issue applies to some of the "harder" disciplines as well. For example, the rapidly increasing stock of Foreign Direct Investment in most industrialized economies serves to challenge some assumptions of industrial economics. What may look on the surface to be a purely domestic contest can be an international one. If oligopolists are playing exchange-ofhostage games in several countries, price behavior in each national market will not readily be explained by national-only variables. Yet, many national studies ignore the issues of nationality of ownership and of corporate fights across borders and produce analytical interpretations that may be no more than elegant rationalizations of imperfectly understood data. The concern is that an illusion of rationality can be created, simply because the researcher did not start from a sufficiently broad conception of the possible causes of behavior.

The fourth possible answer is that, for some subjects, the nature of the phenomenon itself is changing. For example, in the field of strategic management, the complexities of organizing the giant multi-industry multinationals are provoking researchers to ask new questions. Big business is no longer a national matter, with some overseas offshoots; it has become global, at least in some of its managerial dimensions. Prahalad and Doz (1987), Hedlund (1986), Bartlett and Ghoshal (1989), among many others, are finding that previous administrative and structural concepts need serious modification if they are to address the central questions of the contemporary organization.

Similarly, the theory of comparative advantage is being challenged by the development of global competition. Originally, the Ricardian assumptions of the immobility of resources made the theory applicable as an exercise of *comparative* analysis, as its name implies. Today, however, many of those assumptions are being challenged by the growth of the multinationals and the increasing mobility of some resources that can be channelled within their managerial systems. Perhaps curiously, Porter (1990) did not consider to any serious extent these cross-border developments in his exploration of national competitiveness, preferring to concentrate on the issues of immobile resources. Yet, it now seems abundantly clear that the sources of competitiveness for the multinationals are mobile and immobile. Combining them into novel combinations provides a new challenge for both the understanding of global strategy and public policy (Stopford, 1994). The underlying theory itself seems due for an overhaul to reflect the *international* dimensions that increasingly drive the contest among nations. Without modification, the theory can lead to dangerous illusions and inappropriate policy prescriptions (Tyson 1992).

A simple conclusion from all these examples is that researchers need to be aware of the power of the context or setting for their research. It is not that the international context necessarily changes the theory or the problem under investigation; it is that an unthinking framing of the problem in purely domestic terms runs the risk that false generalizations will be drawn from the results. A greater degree of internationalization of doctoral work would seem, therefore, to be highly desirable. Early in their careers, scholars can learn the richness of the international metaphors and be aware of the pitfalls of unduly parochial thinking. There are, however, many obstacles to be overcome, for the desirable outcome has its price.

EDUCATIONAL TENSIONS

One way to think of the obstacles against internationalizing doctoral education is to conjure with a series of competing tensions. Rather than try to decide whether A is better than B, the designer of an international program is forced to search for ways to balance the seemingly opposite forces; there are no absolutes in these arguments. Consider first the classic tension for all doctoral programs between those that stress the accumulation of knowledge (the late-Renaissance model) and those that focus on the creation of new knowledge (the 19th-Century German model).[2] Professor Howell of Stanford considers that the German model has triumphed on most American campuses and that has caused a great problem for the 75 to 90% of people who earn doctorates and do no further published research. "Except where there is research, the training of most professors is completely orthogonal to the job at which they spend most of their time—teaching students who themselves are not going to be scholars."[3] The addition of the complexities of the international context worsens this tension. What precisely is "new" knowledge that comes from the study of a familiar problem, but in a foreign setting?

Is it reasonable to expect that young scholars under instruction will be able to master the complexities of the foreign environment, the extant literature on the subject simultaneously devise novel methodologies and lines of interpretation? The Renaissance model would make it easier to legitimize reportage from abroad using known methodologies to add understanding of the extent of the range of sites of application. The German model, however, raises the stakes by making it difficult if not impossible to choose between making a contribution in terms of methodology and doing so in terms of new knowledge.

There are high costs to be paid if this tension or dilemma is not resolved. Consider a hypothetical thesis on political risk. This is a caricature, but I have seen theses from leading schools with all of the elements described below. Great effort is spent on devising a new methodology to fill in the lacunae (well known to scholars of this branch of IB) of previous theoretical models.

The schema produced calls for data on variables alpha (1-n) in ten countries. Unfortunately, an exhaustive search reveals that reliable and comparable data are available only on variables beta (1-n). Great effort is then devoted to constructing an argument as to why beta is an acceptable surrogate for alpha. The data on beta are collected and the original schema of analysis used. The results are then interpreted as though alpha had been used all along. The creative theorizing that led to a novel and promising conceptualization of the issue has been drowned out by the noise from an inappropriate empirical test. For many candidates, it would seem easier to choose a topic with fewer dimensions of required novelty. Most often something has to give way in the name of practicality, and that can mean sticking to a domestic setting and missing much of the dynamic that is changing so many contemporary markets and managerial activities.

A second tension is introduced by the fact that "international" almost always requires elements of multi-disciplinary work. To be responsive to the foreign environment requires the researcher to broaden the range of analytical variables, as my earlier examples indicated. The difficulty is that the dominance of the German model has been allied with a tendency for research to be located within a single discipline. That tendency is reinforced by the difficulty of getting multi-disciplinary work published in the scholarly journals. Doctoral candidates are routinely advised to stick to one discipline. How then to encourage more candidates to go against this kind of well-meaning advice?

A third tension is the length of time needed to complete all the required demonstrations of research skill. International complexity adds to the time needed for most theses in the field. When there are severe financial pressures on candidates, there are equal pressures for speed and simplicity in the research design. Surely the complexities can be added later in post-doctoral work? Evidence from casual observation suggests, sadly, that few people break the mold set by the style of their original training and thesis. Thus, if the complexities are not adequately addressed during the doctoral period, the researcher is likely never to broaden her or his research "scope" later on. The demands of time to learn how to survive in the classroom add to the pressures to remain narrow during the early post-doctoral years, thus worsening the problem.

Quite clearly, there are no simple ways to resolve these tensions in any field. Individuals have to make up their own minds as to the risks they want to take and the pressures they want to endure. To work in the international field requires extra effort, for candidates must master the underlying theory or set of concepts as well as master the external complexities.

I, personally, believe it wise to conceive of internationalization of the doctoral training as implying an additive process. There is a need to preserve the worth of the existing curriculum. If internationalisation is treated as then there is a real danger of a diminution of standards. The moment colleagues begin to regard those in the international department as "soft," the cause is lost. Managing an additive process requires a re-consideration of the available resources and a search for solutions that yield an acceptable way to resolve, or at least reduce, the dilemmas to manageable proportion.

There is a steep learning curve for each institution seeking to internationalize its doctoral offering. Each institution has its own administrative and philosophical context (another dimension of the contextual nature of the issue), so the applicability of experience across institute boundaries is imperfect. Nevertheless, some experience from Europe can be used to illustrate how the inherent dilemmas are being resolved.

EUROPEAN SCHOOLS

One might think that European schools' more immediate exposure to international forces would make them all well placed to promote the cause of greater internationalization. The evidence, however, suggests that though they may share intuitive assumptions about the internationality of their environment, they are struggling up the learning curve at different speeds. Considering the development of teaching of IB as a measure of institutional investment in the capability to resolve the dilemmas, a recent report showed that there had been a steady growth of IB as a subject throughout the 1980s—part of the basis of the demand for more internationalized doctorates.[4] By 1990, of the 197 schools surveyed, 16% had limited their efforts to international as an extension of existing subjects; 39% had developed separate IB courses, often in the form of electives within the degree course; and 44% had developed separate IB programs. Only 2% were judged to have reached the "mature" stage of "thoroughly internationalized education."[5] Of these, INSEAD in France and IMD in Switzerland were the exemplars. One should note, however, that INSEAD has only recently decided to create a doctoral program, the first degrees having been awarded in 1994.

Similar variation marks the progress in the developing doctoral programmes in business. Many schools seem uncertain why they have Ph.D.

programmes, what they expect as inputs (e.g., type of student; mature, experienced executives or novices with newly minted masters degrees) and what
they expect as outputs (e.g., placement of graduates and the return earned on
the resources used). Access to doctoral programs varies from procedures
familiar in the U.S. to much looser arrangements, as in Scandinavia where
students have the right to register for a higher degree once they have completed their first degree. The issue of language is a complicating factor; some
schools have introduced a parallel English track in order to recruit people
from outside their own linguistic boundaries. Though the main market is the
traditional Ph.D. (as defined in each country), there have been recent exper-
iments in the UK where two schools have set up DBA courses. The initial
response has not been good, mainly it seems because the market is unclear
about the comparative advantage of this degree with its greater emphasis on
practitioner issues.

Generalization about the internationalization of these programs is impossible for lack of comparable data.[6] There is, however, one aspect of the
European experience that deserves attention. This is the use of consortia for
the teaching and exchange of doctoral students. These have been funded by
the European Commission as part of the investment in education as a means
of promoting greater continent-wide integration. The strengths of these consortia are that they often bring together Anglo-Saxon and Mediterranean-
type cultures in a working environment. Assumptions that might go
unchallenged in a mono-cultural setting are explicitly discussed, to the benefit of staff and students alike.

THE LONDON BUSINESS SCHOOL AS AN EXAMPLE

The London Business School is another European school that has reached
this "mature" phase of attempting to work on the basis that the environment is essentially international and that "international" is not something
to be bolted on to a parochial system.[7] The school as a whole has been promoting the values of internationalism for students and faculty alike as a
central driver for progress. The doctoral program has been evolving within
this context.

The LBS doctoral program has existed for many years, but it is only within
the last five years or so that it has been expanded and a strong structure of
methodology course requirements and a formal thesis proposal examination
added. At present, there are about eighty candidates registered. Admissions

are running at eighteen to twenty a year and degree awards are in the range of ten to fifteen a year. The completion rate is less than admissions, partly because the recent expansion of admissions has yet to pass through the entire system. In part, also the program is not in steady state, because we have yet to resolve the tension of time, for many candidates are taking longer to complete than before. The lengthening period of study reflects two basic problems. One is to do with the relative paucity of funds, so that many candidates without scholarships are forced to seek part-time employment. The other is more central to the issues of this paper: most candidates are addressing international issues and having to deal with the resultant complexities and difficulties of obtaining accurate and appropriate data.

The international profile of the program can be measured on at least six dimensions. The first is the student body itself. At present, about 40% are local nationals; 40% are from the rest of Europe; and about 20% are from the rest of the world, randomly scattered across all continents. This mix provides a rich multicultural setting that is further enriched by the fact that about one-third of the candidates are female (LBS actively recruits and offers scholarships for women).

In such a setting the question naturally arises as to how the particular needs of different cultures are managed. The LBS approach is to create a strong program culture that is driven by the values of scholarship, of empiricism and of the drive to publish in the top international (English language) journals. There are, to be sure, heavy cultural overtones in that set of values. Nonetheless, the program culture seems to create considerable freedom for individual behavior. National cultural differences can be respected without culture becoming an issue for explicit management.[8]

One benefit of the sense of freedom is that the plurality of nationalities and languages (all instruction and thesis examination is in English, but much informal conversation is a tower of Babel) acts to broaden many people's perceptions of possibilities elsewhere. For example, most of the UK candidates seem to get "bitten by the international bug," as one put it, and do not wish to get left behind by studying only parochial problems.

A second measure of internationality is provided by the content of the theses undertaken. The sense of "infection" for the excitement of international settings is indeed pervasive and seems to have been growing in recent years. During the 1970s, the proportion of completed doctorates that had some form of international, border-crossing or comparative dimension was 17%. During the 1980s, that proportion rose to 36%, and so far during the

1990s it has been well over 60%. More complex data bases, more travel time for field work, and slower, more tortuous data interpretation are all causes for the lengthening time taken to complete. It is, of course, very hard if not impossible to sort out reality from excuses, but our impression is that the reasons for delay are real. Where once we hoped that improving information technologies would alleviate the first of these problems, we are now of the view that only a small portion of the data needs of most internationally oriented theses can be met by harnessing the power of IT.

The fact of being in London may have something to do with why LBS students choose to work at a level of internationalism far greater than is common in U.S. schools. London is an international hub and the domestic market is small in world terms. This has long been the case, but the candidates' moves away from purely domestic study may have been encouraged in part by the growth of the foreign student population. In part also, candidates may increasingly be taking the view that the UK does not represent a fertile ground for study of best practice and that cutting-edge issues demand a larger setting. Especially if they view their career futures on the international market, they will quite rationally choose, where appropriate, subjects that give them mobility.

It is now rare for a thesis to be exclusively on domestic matters, though there remain good reasons why a purely domestic setting may be appropriate. One example of a current thesis in corporate strategy underscores the point made earlier about the difficulties of combining novelty in setting or of methodology. This work is on the impact of regulatory change in one national industry, a subject of repetitive study in many countries. Instead of using conventional research approaches, this thesis has been constructed on novel methodologies that simulate dynamic interactions. Though the main contribution of the work will probably, in the first instance, be methodological, the results are so promising that they hold out hope for a major challenge to received wisdom in industrial economics. The challenge of devising novel and testable methodology in a contentious area is so great that a relatively simple setting was needed to keep the work within reasonable proportions. Later on, to realize the full potential of the work, the candidate in question will have to accept the challenge, alluded to earlier, of breaking the mold and internationalizing the empirical settings. In this case, one-step-at-a-time seems the sensible advice to give and the encouragement of the peer group should go a long way to making the psychological shift possible.

A third measure of internationality is the curriculum. At LBS, the principal taught portion of the Ph.D. is on methodology. Consonant with the values of the program as a whole, methodology is approached on a universalistic basis. The aim is to expose candidates to state-of-the-art concepts and to train them to be able to publish in top journals. Because of the topics chosen for study, the advanced methodology courses dealing with current work are naturally international in setting. Rather than attempt to regulate the extent of internationality, effort is directed to ensuring that all candidates are exposed to both quantitative and qualitative approaches. In the more specialised, subject based courses, the extent of explicit international training varies enormously according to the needs of the subject and the preferences of the instructor.

A fourth measure is the extent of exchange with schools in other countries. LBS tends to discourage individual exchanges unless they are required for the purposes of data collection or as part of one of the European consortia mentioned above. Recently, however, LBS and INSEAD have begun to use an institute-level exchange whereby the candidates in both schools meet for a few days collectively. The purpose here is to allow research in progress to be debated in the friendly atmosphere of peer review—faculty have so far been excluded. The results have been extremely encouraging. One tentative conclusion is that the multicultural aspects of the event contribute positively to the learning and do not create distracting "noise," precisely because both schools share the same values of scholarship and the same standards of achievement.

A fifth measure is the nationality of the faculty. The LBS faculty is predominantly Anglo-Saxon—British, American, Australian and Canadian—with relatively few from other cultures. Though this mix is changing slowly to broaden the nationality mix, the main emphasis has been and will continue to be on excellence of the individual. Provided the experience of the individual is sufficiently broad—and enhanced by all the normal possible mechanisms of faculty exchange, etc.—LBS does not consider the faculty measure to be a strong influence on the internationalising process.

Sixth and finally, in this listing of measures is the placement record. Before the recent expansion of the program, many of the graduates went into consultancy rather than teaching. More recently, however, more stringent admission standards have tilted the balance towards those whose career intentions are academic. Recent graduates have found jobs in many countries, but few have done so at leading U.S. schools. Whether this is a matter of standards or of relative neglect by the supervisors to mastermind the campaign needed in the tightly contested contemporary job market is hard to say. Whatever the cause, this feature of the LBS placement record needs improvement, for a record of success in the top schools is a critical indicator of world-standard excellence. Graduates become "academic ambassadors" and their professional success helps promote the interests of their *alma mater*.

The Ph.D. program does not have a committee structure as is the norm in the U.S. Instead, reliance is placed on individual supervisors and a thesis examination system conducted by outsiders. When needed, candidates have to beg for the marginal time of other busy faculty. As a personal observation, I regard this as a weakness in the LBS system for the international subjects that are necessarily multi-faceted, with some facets beyond the expertise of a single supervisor. Ease of access to faculty is important if candidates are to be afforded the best possible chance of stimulus for knowledge creation and the avoidance of methodological mistakes.

CONCLUSIONS

My first conclusion is that LBS still has a long way to go before all the tensions are managed adequately. Progress in managing them has been at different speeds. Our students' enthusiasm has made them tackle increasingly complex issues, though some of the faculty are of the view that the risk of reducing intellectual standards has been managed wholly satisfactorily. We have not made as much progress as many would like in encouraging a multidisciplinary approach. The Germanic School remains in the ascendancy here, as in the U.S. We are experimenting with an increase in the number of postdoctoral fellowships to help make the one-step-at-a-time approach work for some individuals who are willing to make another investment in their research careers before going far on the teaching front. The results are mixed, suggesting that the problems of early type-casting in the style of research have not been resolved. We have not therefore resolved the tension of time.

One manifestation of this differential progress is shown in the equally disparate trends in the six measures of internationalization. Our student body is more international and equipped with better language capabilities than the faculty, though imbalance is slowly being eroded. Their choices of international topics are acting to extend the faculty's capabilities; a reversal of the usual supervisor-student role. We are considering ways to harness our students' experience and capability more fully, not just for the benefit of faculty but also for the whole student body. We have deliberately kept the methodology part of the taught course on a universalistic basis and feel no pressure to change this. Indeed, our belief is that the contextual nature of "international" demands some unifying "glue" to hold it all together.

Nonetheless, we believe that LBS is already far down the track of demonstrating that the costs of encouraging international work are well worth paying. Considering "international" as a context, not a discipline, has allowed a wide variety of initiatives to be pursued simultaneously. Rather than try to choose between the relative merits of the Germanic and the Renaissance Schools, we are attempting to combine the best features of both. We aim to add to knowledge by freeing our students to enrich the scope of the questions asked. The contextual dimension of the scholarship makes it legitimate for the faculty to demand much tougher analysis and to expect that candidates will have been exposed to thinking and evidence from many countries. We deliberately avoid the issue of whether or not to make some international course mandatory—a lively debate in many North American schools—because of the experience and perspective our students bring when they arrive.

The LBS conception of "context" has deliberately been kept broad. We have not felt it necessary to create departments of regional specialization to foster that dimension of the context. Even where we have a regional unit, the CIS-Middle Europe Centre, this recent initiative was set up to foster cross-disciplinary work and to place local work clearly within an international, cross-border context. We have much to learn about how to make the best of the combinations and to limit the costs of the complexities of subject matter within the Centre, but the early achievements seem encouraging by their indication of, not work.

Whether the LBS experience has any message for other schools is an empirical question. London has evolved in a particular and idiosyncratic way, given the accident of geography and the balance of faculty skills and philosophy. Few North American schools enjoy such a broadly experienced student body. Equally few appear to question the constraining blinkers that an implicit reliance on the scale and importance of their domestic market imposes on the curriculum. If exposure to the international marketplace is to improve scholarship and the grooming of first-class faculty connected with the discipline of IB, then there is a need for a radical re-examination of basic principles. Until the additive and conceptually challenging nature of IB is fully understood, the filed will remain of marginal importance in North American Schools.

NOTES

I am grateful to Dr. Raymond Madden for a thoughtful reflection on the LBS experience, and to the participants at the Roundtable for lively commentary aimed at sharpening the arguments.

1. For one industry study using international price data to reveal many paradoxical relationships, see Baden-Fuller and Stopford 1991.
2. The dialogue at the 1992 Dallas Conference of the AACSB on this tension is illuminating. For a summary, see Blood 1992.
3. Howell, cited in Blood 1992:6.
4. For a useful review of the state of development of International Business as a subject, see Luostarinen and Pulkkinen 1991.
5. Defined by Luostarinen and Pulkkinen as schools where the "whole business education is international by nature and perspective. All the courses and programmes have mainly or fully internationalized contents, the contents of teaching may have a regional or global focus" (41).
6. A profile of all the leading European doctoral business programs has recently been prepared by the network of program directors. The EDAMBA survey provides some data on the international content, but the version I have seen does not give wholly comparable information. In part, the problem is linguistic; terms have different meanings, leading to different definitions being used.
7. LBS was excluded from the original survey, so the rating of the school's position is a purely personal one.
8. Foreign students have particular needs that do not apply to most home nationals. In the main, however, these are to do with logistics, pastoral care, networks, and contacts. The School's support system is established to meet these needs, either on campus or by using the much more broadly distributed resources of the University of London as a whole.

REFERENCES

Baden-Fuller, Charles, and John M. Stopford. 1991. "Globalisation Frustrated: The Case of White Goods." *Strategic Management Journal.* 12(7), October, 493-507.

Bartlett, Christopher A., and Sumantra Ghoshal. 1989. *Managing Across Borders.* Boston, MA: Harvard Business School Press.

Blood, Milton. 1992. "Report from AACSB/GMAC Doctoral Education Project." July, mimeo.

Hedlund, Gunnar. 1986. "The Hypermodern MNC: A Heterarchy?" *Human Resource Management.* (Spring): 9-35.

Luostarinen, Reijo, and Tuija Pulkkinen. 1991. *International Business Education in European Universities in 1990*. Helsinki School of Economics and Business Administration, a report prepared for the European International Business Association.

Porter, Michael. 1990. *The Competitive Advantage of Nations*. New York: Macmillan.

Prahalad, C. K., and Yves Doz. 1987. *The Multinational Mission*. New York: The Free Press.

Robock, Stefan H., and Kenneth Simmonds. 1989. *International Business and Multinational Enterprise* (4th ed.). Homewood, IL: Irwin.

Stopford, John M. 1994. "The Growing Interdependence between Transnational Corporations and Governments." *Transnational Corporations*. 3(1), February, 53-76.

Tyson, Laura. 1992. *Who's Bashing Whom? Trade Conflict in High-Technology Industries*. Washington, D.C.: Institute for International Economics.

INTERNATIONALIZING BUSINESS SCHOLARSHIP: THE ESSENTIALS

Brian Toyne

INTRODUCTION

The purpose of this, the second Michigan State University Roundtable, is to make recommendations for the internationalization of U.S. doctoral programs of business. However, as we all know, doctoral programs are very expensive for students, faculties, and schools both in time and resources. They are also built on strong, not easily changed convictions, and designed to satisfy an assortment of needs that are currently in flux. As Ernest L. Boyer, President of the Carnegie Foundation, recently noted (1990:xi) ". . . the work of the academy has changed throughout the years—moving from teaching, to service, and then research, reflecting shifting priorities both within the academy and beyond." Thus, lacking a clear understanding of the reasons for doctoral programs, the forces that effect their orientation and content, and the markets they serve could raise serious questions concerning the viability and appropriateness of any particular recommendation, and could result in solutions that are at best of short duration.

To be of value, the recommended internationalization approaches need to be tailored to meet the specific goals and objectives of a school's program. Thus, it is first necessary to examine the goals and objectives served by doctoral programs, and the external and internal forces shaping these goals and objectives. On the basis of this examination, a classification framework can then be developed to assist in selecting those internationalization approaches most appropriate for a particular situation.

I believe it is also necessary when making such recommendations to show how U.S.-bound business education and inquiry are enriched by being internationalized. The doctoral program's faculty must be convinced of the merits of internationalization from their respective viewpoints, since it may be

61

impossible for a school's administration to mandate such a requirement (see, for example, O'Reilly 1994).

Since most of the papers presented at this Roundtable will probably make concrete recommendations concerning the internationalization of the content of doctoral programs, I decided it would be useful to develop a framework that can help in focusing and tailoring these recommendations to individual programs. I also examine in paradigmic terms the relationships that exist between U.S.-bound business research and education, on the one hand, and international business (IB) research and education, on the other hand. Unless these relationships are made clear, the internationalization recommendations cannot be tailored to specific doctoral programs, nor can those responsible for doctoral programs be persuaded to adopt them. Finally, I present what are, in my estimation, the core internationalization essentials. They are based on the changing demands challenging business schools today, and are presented as general recommendations and as IB literacy levels of awareness, understanding, and competency.

WHAT PURPOSES ARE SERVED BY U.S. DOCTORAL PROGRAMS IN BUSINESS?

Why do doctoral programs exist? Who do they serve? Although seemingly unnecessary questions, the current debate on the content and process of business education suggests that there is no consensus, even within the business academy. From the student's perspective, for example, a doctorate satisfies a combination of possibilities including the acquisition of necessary credentials for a life of teaching, research, or consulting. Institutions, on the other hand, view their doctoral programs as sources for undergraduate teachers, and as adding prestige and recognition to their institutions, and thus their ability to attract leading scholars and obtain research grants. From the faculty's perspective, particularly those involved in doctoral education, these programs provide interested, motivated research assistants and collaborators who can also be socialized to a particular point of view and set of values.

While it is important to recognize the several constituencies that have an interest in doctoral programs and the different pressures that they may exert on the content of these programs and the resources devoted to these programs, perhaps a more useful approach here is to examine the needs ultimately satisfied by such programs. That is, what is ultimately required (possibly demanded) of the graduates of these programs in the way of knowledge, skills, and professional commitment? The answer, of course, is scholarship. But, as we shall see, the meaning of scholarship can and does vary from one institutional setting to another, and how it varies is important when making internationalization recommendations.

Boyer's Schema of Scholarship

Boyer (1990:16) classifies scholarship in the United States as having "four separate, yet overlapping functions." These are (1) the scholarship of *discovery*, (2) the scholarship of *integration*, (3) the scholarship of *application*, and (4) the scholarship of *teaching*. Elements of these four scholarship functions are found in all business schools and doctoral programs, but not necessarily given equal attention or weight.

The Scholarship of Discovery

The scholarship of discovery is closest to what is often called "research" by today's business academics. It is a commitment to the production of knowledge (for its own sake). The parenthetical statement is deliberate and necessary for this is what distinguishes those who seek to understand for the sake of understanding and those who seek to understand for the sake of application or because of application. Even within academic circles, even within individual researchers, the two views often stand against one another. Thus, we often speak of basic and applied research as if they are distinct, even mutually exclusive, and attach greater "value" to one or the other depending on our philosophical inclinations. Importantly, "cultures" differ on the relative importance placed on basic and applied research. For example, Boyer (1990:22) points out that the British and Germans tend to regard scholarship as "an end in itself," and Americans tend to view it as "equipment for service."

It is also important to recognize that the scholarship of discovery can be *unidisciplinary, multidisciplinary,* or *interdisciplinary*. For our purposes, unidisciplinary research is the study of business phenomena from a single functional perspective (i.e., accounting, finance, information systems, management, marketing, and so on). Multidisciplinary research is the study of a specific business phenomenon from two or more functional perspectives simultaneously. Interdisciplinary research is the study of business phenomena from a functionally integrated perspective[1] (e.g., the co-joining of strategic management and marketing at a higher level of abstraction).

THE SCHOLARSHIP OF INTEGRATION

The scholarship of integration is the "bringing together" of knowledge across the social sciences and the business disciplines, the placing of specialties in a larger context. In contrast to the "renaissance man" of yesteryear, the scholarship of integration for today's scholar means the ". . . serious, disciplined work that seeks to interpret, draw together, and bring new insights to bear on original research" (Boyer 1990:19).

Such scholarship is important because of the call for relevance by the business community and by such representatives of the business education community as Porter and McKibbin (1988), the American Association of Collegiate Schools of Business (AACSB), and the Graduate Management Admission Council (GMAC) (1990). In addition, if current trends continue and the various business disciplines become even more specialized (see, for example, Toyne 1993), it becomes increasingly necessary for unidisciplinary scholarship of discovery to be interpreted within the greater, more generalized body of business knowledge.

THE SCHOLARSHIP OF APPLICATION

In contrast to the investigative and synthesizing traditions of discovery and integration, respectively, the scholarship of application shows how knowledge can be applied to important problems and how important problems can define an agenda for scholarly investigation. Like the scholarship of discovery, the scholarship of application can be categorized as unidisciplinary, multidisciplinary, or interdisciplinary.

The implications of the scholarship of application for the content of doctoral programs go beyond the issue of research. For example, the GMAC report (1990:17) specifically calls for ". . . a new synthesis between rigorously developed knowledge and managerial practice." This call, of course, is at the heart of Boyer's fourth function of scholarship, teaching.

THE SCHOLARSHIP OF TEACHING

Boyer (1990:23) also observed that teaching becomes scholarship when it educates and entices future scholars to further discovery, integration, and application. Thus, the last of the four functions of scholarship, teaching, is simultaneously the means by which the results of the other three functions are disseminated,[2] and the inducement to further discovery, integration, and application. Again, for our internationalization purposes, it is important to note that *what we learn depends on what we have learned, why we have learned it, and how we have learned it.* That is, learning is influenced by cultural, historical, situational, and philosophical factors that vary from one locale to another, or one "culture" to another. Moreover, the doctoral student is socialized to a set of values, norms of behavior, etc. (Leavitt 1993). Collectively, learning and socialization ultimately have a pronounced effect on how the student sees (conceptualizes) and questions reality, and what body of knowledge he or she will use when "educating" others.

ALUTTO'S SCHEMA OF SCHOOLS AND DISCIPLINES

While Boyer's schema recognizes that scholarship involves four functions, it is silent on those institutional specifics that have an important bearing on which functions are emphasized. In addition, he appears to view the scholarship of teaching as monolithic. But teaching, like research, can be classified in several ways; ways that are dependent on the institutional setting in which it occurs. For example, Alutto (1993:38) suggests that business schools can be subdivided into *integrators* and *silo enhancers*:

> Integrators are those institutions that truly reflect the integration of discipline-based functional frameworks in *all that they do*. Silo enhancers are institutions that pursue minimal integration while maximizing the focus on individual functional specialties (emphasis added).

Besides distinguishing between the scholarships of unidisciplinary discovery and integration, this schema makes two points that are of value to our discussion. First, Alutto's schema recognizes that institutions tend to support single forms of research. Second, he breaks down Boyer's monolithic concept of teaching by suggesting that there are at least two forms of teaching that are determined by the type of research undertaken at an institution (or vice-versa).[3] That is, there is silo enhancing teaching (unidisciplinary teaching) and integration teaching (multidisciplinary or interdisciplinary teaching). A point not made by Alutto, but one worth noting is that silo and integration teaching can be conceptual (e.g., generalized abstractions), applied (e.g., case analysis) or some combination of these two.

Alutto also classifies business schools as *teaching-dominant schools*, *research-dominant schools*, and *mixed-focused schools*. The faculty requirements for these are as follows:

TEACHING-DOMINANT SCHOOLS

The primary mission of these schools is teaching, and the most important faculty skill set is the ability to teach. Possibly because of this classroom emphasis, other skills often sought include an ability to work with the business community and as a member of a multidisciplinary teaching team.

RESEARCH-DOMINANT SCHOOLS

Knowledge production is viewed as the primary mission of these schools, and the most important faculty skill set is the ability to conduct significant research. Other skills include an ability to raise research funds and to remain focused (e.g., not distracted by teaching, executive education, or consulting activities). It is worthwhile noting that research and teaching are primarily the result of individual effort at many of these schools.

MIXED-FOCUSED SCHOOLS

The mission of these schools is to provide a balance between research and teaching. Thus, important faculty skills include an ability to simultaneously undertake significant research while excelling at teaching, and, in integrator schools, to remain broadly aware of multidisciplinary developments, and to interact effectively with the business community. As Alutto notes, the mixed-focused, integrator type of school has the most complex educational task, requiring from their faculties the greatest breadth of personal development.

A SYNTHESIS OF THE TWO SCHEMATA

Although there are other classification schemata, a synthesis of the Boyer and Alutto schemata provides a sufficiently elaborate framework for identifying (1) the factors that influence the content and structuring of doctoral programs, and (2) the faculty needs of institutions hiring the graduates of these programs. Factors such as these need to be considered when making specific recommendations for the internationalization of a particular doctoral program.

Thus, it is strongly recommended that a discriminating model similar to the three-dimensional matrix shown in Figure 1 be used when developing recommendations for the internationalization of specific doctoral programs. This particular classification framework can be used to classify both doctoral programs and the types of faculty sought by institutions of higher learning.[4] The three dimensions highlighted by this framework are (1) the relative emphasis placed on teaching and research, (2) the type of research emphasized; and (3) the type of teaching emphasized.[5]

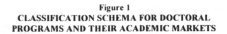

Figure 1
CLASSIFICATION SCHEMA FOR DOCTORAL
PROGRAMS AND THEIR ACADEMIC MARKETS

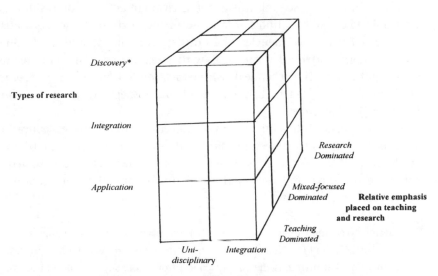

Types of teaching**

*   Discovery can be either unidisciplinary, multidisciplinary, or interdisciplinary
**   Teaching can be either abstract, applied, or some combination of these two

WHAT TRENDS AND PRESSURES ARE INFLUENCING THE CONTENT OF DOCTORAL BUSINESS EDUCATION?

To offer convincing recommendations for the internationalization of doctoral program, a classification schema that simultaneously classifies doctoral programs, and links them with potential "market opportunities" is necessary, but not sufficient. The recommendations must also be responsive to those trends and pressures that will probably have some impact on the types of scholarship demanded of future faculty in the United States.[6]

Within the university setting, particularly within professional schools such as business, engineering, law, and medicine, the argument often heard is that "market forces" must decide what is emphasized, even taught. Even in Britain, such bastions of higher liberal education[7] as Cambridge and Oxford are examples of these forces at work. Recently, both universities introduced business education programs.[8]

Unfortunately, a problem with using "market forces" to shape educational programs is in identifying which "forces" are germane when two markets are involved. In business schools this is not as clear cut an issue, or as simple, as we would like. Unlike schools of law and medicine, business schools satisfy not one but two constituencies: the business community and the business academy (Leavitt 1993). The first deals with educating or training future business practitioners. The other deals with educating or training business scholars who are interested in research, academic respectability, and teaching (probably in that order).

It would appear at this juncture in the development of business education, schools of business have been primarily interested in satisfying the business academy (GMAC 1990). Thus, while "market forces" can be observed to influence the programmatic offerings of institutions of higher education, Leavitt can correctly state:

It seems exceedingly clear that an alarm bell has been sounding for a good while now. The MBA and the Ph.D., as we know them, are not necessarily here to stay. Neither, for that matter, is the current concept of a graduate school of business. We've had a decade of ever-growing complaints about irrelevance. Our MBAs have been stereotyped as arrogant, overly ambitious, number-crunching snobs. Our research has frequently been characterized as trivial and incomprehensible. These are not signals to be ignored.

We exist by courtesy of a society much larger than academia, and we ignore these signals at our own peril. If we insist on keeping today's Ph.D. students—the next generation of faculty—huddled together at the academic end of the academic/professional seesaw, the other children may all run off to play elsewhere (1993:21).

So what trends are germane when recommending changes to the content of doctoral programs and, just as importantly, the socialization of doctoral students? Put differently, what types of recommendations will those in charge of doctoral programs be most receptive to? Discussions within the business education community suggest that there are at least two groups of trends and pressures that need to be examined when thinking about the future content of doctoral programs: changes in the phenomena and relationships under investigation (research), and changes in the structure and content of business programs (teaching). To these I would add a third group—changes within the worldwide professorate.

CHANGES IN THE PHENOMENA STUDIED

Increasingly, business is recognized as a dynamic social process. That is, the business process, and the phenomena created and subsequently influenced by this process, change as the social fabric in which it is embedded changes (Granovetter 1985; Pfeffer 1987; Porter 1990; Toyne 1989, 1995; Zysman and Tyson 1983). Also, a point that needs to be repeated often is that the "social embeddedness" of business is most apparent when studying either business phenomena in other countries, or the influence that foreign business practice may have on domestic business practice.

When compared with today's business environment, the business environment of the 1950s, 1960s, and even the 1970s, was highly stable and relatively simple. That is, the relationship between the firm and its intrinsic parts (generally the focus of attention), and higher levels of the business process (industry, government, society) could be assumed structurally stable (unchanging) for research and educational purposes. This was true because the rate at which boundary conditions were changing within these higher levels that directly or indirectly affect firm-level practice and choice could be ignored or assumed static.[9] Thus, the complicating assumption that the firm is a consequence of a particular socially embedded business process could be safely ignored. As I noted elsewhere (Toyne 1997), "The difference between 'The firm is part of society' and 'Society includes the firm' is a real one, and could be an important one: the first puts the firm as the focus of attention and the second society."

However, between the 1970s and 1990s major changes occurred in both the environment and the form and practice of business that now demand a more explicit understanding of the interactive, recursive nature of national business processes,[10] and the emerging international business (IB) process that these dynamic internal and external interactions have caused. For example, students of business can no longer ignore the historical roots and long-run cumulative effects that have irreversibly affected governments, industries, firms, and individuals, on the one hand, and the relationships that link these various levels of a society within and across countries, on the other hand. Nor can they ignore the impact that technological and communication changes are having on national business processes, the linkages between the levels of these processes, and the indeterminacy of their outputs (e.g., the internal relations of geographically dispersed operations of firms, such as the multinational, and the ability of decision-makers to be in "two places simultaneously" because of advances in communications).

Globalization, cultural diversity of the workforce, rapid and significant changes in technology (especially in the areas of communication, computers, and information), changing societal demands, and political/economic regionalization (e.g., the North American Free Trade Agreement [NAFTA], the European Union) are manifestations of a business environment undergoing fundamental structural change, not just cyclical change.

Moreover, international "interaction" is no longer concentrated and discrete, involving just a few public and private organizations within any particular society. Because of technology (e.g., transportation and communications), education, and the growing interconnectedness and interdependence of nation-states, this interaction is increasingly diffused, spanning all levels of society and an increasing portion of the phenomena within these levels (e.g., from government agencies to the individuals who make up business enterprises). Consequently, firms are experimenting with new organizational structures, new control techniques, new manufacturing techniques, and new human resource practices (see, for example, Anon 1994b).

Changes such as these, and there are many more, are having a cumulative and profound effect on both the business processes of nation-states and the phenomena they create, maintain, and destroy. Therefore, the questions asked of business in the United States and elsewhere are changing just as the paradigms that conceptualize business are also of necessity changing. That is, the business disciplines are in a period of introspection that make them receptive to new conceptualizations, new paradigms, and new methodologies, but not necessarily radical ones.

CHANGES IN BUSINESS EDUCATION

The structural changes impacting and influencing the way business is done within and across countries are also placing considerable pressure on the U.S. business education system for change. As I noted at the last MSU Roundtable:

> Bedeian (1989), Daft and Lewin (1990), Porter and McKibbin (1988), and the Graduate Management Admission Council (GMAC) (1990) have raised serious questions concerning the efficacy of the Ford-Carnegie paradigm upon which much of modern U.S. business education and research is based. Collectively, these critics question the ability of the present education-research system to deliver on the kind of education required in the years ahead. In particular, Porter and McKibbin and the GMAC report argue that the massive and interconnected changes transforming the global environment of business, such as globalization, rapid technological change, and increasing demographic and cultural diversity of the workforce, require different approaches.
>
> . . . the academic leaders of individual schools need to face the important challenge of developing more appropriate approaches for the recruitment and development of faculty members, *including new models of doctoral education* in order to meet the knowledge, skills, attitudes, and values required of faculty members in the future (Toyne 1993:45-46; emphasis added).

Many of the accreditation changes implemented by the AACSB since 1991 reflect the recommendations of the Porter and McKibbin (1988) and GMAC (1990) reports, and the increasingly vocal concerns of the business community and the U.S. government. For example, while acknowledging the importance and significance of research, the AACSB now places greater emphasis on a *combination* of academic rigor, managerial relevance (discussed more fully later), and the humanities.[11] Also, some educators see a need for business, government and the academic community to develop new partnerships to respond to and shape developments in higher education (Anon 1994a).

Ultimately, the changes sought by the accreditation organizations, the business community, and some educators require a reorganization of, and major revisions to, the business curriculum. They also require changes in the way business schools are structured and governed, since both are manifestations of an antiquated firm-level paradigm of business (i.e., functional departmentalization that echoes the structures of companies in the 1950s, not the 1990s). For example, interactive team teaching and cross-disciplinary teaching may yet become norms rather than exceptions, since most faculties are reluctant to reduce the material that is representative of their functional areas and relinquish the high degree of autonomy achieved because of specialization.

Additionally, because of the growing demand for relevance, an increased emphasis on application that accentuates the analytical reasoning skills of students may also replace abstract (conceptual) teaching. As O'Reilly (1994) points out:

> B-schools are under enormous pressure to produce fundamentally different kinds of graduates than those of six or seven years ago. Employers claim too many MBAs in the 1980s were great at narrowly focused skills like accounting and finance but dreadful at motivating colleagues or diagnosing complex business problems. Now, they say, MBAs must be inspiring leaders capable also of applying knowhow to unravel and solve the most convoluted problem.

In addition, the profound effect that NAFTA will have on the U.S. business process cannot, must not be ignored by U.S. business schools. In the relatively near future, most, if not all, graduates of business programs will need to have at least a nodding acquaintance with foreign currency exchange and the business approaches and competitive practices of their Canadian and Mexican counterparts. For example, at a recent symposium on the effects of NAFTA on higher education, representatives of Canada, Mexico, and the United States acknowledged that reform is necessary, and trilateral collaboration required (Anon 1994a).

While not suggesting that doctoral students become embroiled in the administrative mechanics of the current changes in business education, I am suggesting that they need to be made aware of, and understand, the philosophical and praxis implications that such changes may have on their chosen profession and career. If doctoral programs just followed through on this recommendation, the internationalization of business education would be assured. For example, if current trends persist, sometime in the not too distant future, esoteric, highly specialized, U.S.-bound research may not be sufficient to qualify them as faculty members at most business schools. Pendulums do change their directions periodically.

CHANGES IN THE PROFESSORATE

Beyond the well-documented trends in business and business education, there are at least two major trends within the business academy itself that need to be considered when making internationalization recommendations. The first, already alluded to above, is functional specialization and socialization. The second is the mushrooming growth in non-U.S.-based business research and education.[12]

Functional Specialization and Socialization—According to Leavitt (1993:12), business schools have attempted to manage their scholastic and educational responsibilities in a variety of ways. For example, "[o]ne way has been to utilize MBA and executive education as major connections to the business side, while treating the Ph.D. program as a major anchor to the academy." This, the most prevalent approach, has enabled faculties at schools with doctoral programs to become increasingly specialized, since it essentially isolates Ph.D. students from MBA students, and leaves "the education of our next generation of faculty—almost entirely in the hands of the research-oriented subset of any faculty" (Leavitt 1993:12). Moreover, these younger, more research-driven faculties tend to treat their doctoral programs as the most central programs in their schools, and as opportunities to inculcate future faculty with their particular beliefs, attitudes, and ways of thinking. Leavitt amusingly describes the socialization process put in place by this cadre of research-driven faculty as follows:

> Our relationship with doctoral candidates has traditionally been almost parental. We use a lot of one-on-one coaching. We put students through arduous rites of passage. We teach them much more out of the classroom than in it. We marinate them up to their eyebrows in our academic culture, day after day, for endless years. We brainwash them, much as an army or religious sect might. We force them to take terrifying oral exams and to present colloquia before bloodthirsty peers (1993:18).

Functional specialization and socialization have their rewards. The business literature of the last thirty years is an explicit testimony to the tremendous strides made in understanding U.S.-bound business situations and practices, primarily because of unidisciplinary research.

However, there are also very real dangers. Specialization is predicated on reductionistic assumptions that assert that the whole can be understood as a consequence of studying its parts. Since we deal in abstractions (concepts), not reality, this can and does result in gaps in our more general and comprehensive (holistic) understanding of human behavior as it relates to business affairs. Also, when taken to an extreme, it can result in disciplinary isolation because of communication barriers (i.e., disciplinary jargon), and a refusal to seek knowledge and understanding (enlightenment) from alternate, but disparate sources.[13] More dangerous, perhaps, is the very real possibility that specialization, when coupled with socialization, can result in "blind" adherence to beliefs, values and attitudes that become obsolete as a consequence of the progress made elsewhere (see, for example, Gould 1981).

Because of specialization and unidisciplinary socialization, doctoral programs are increasingly at variance with current AACSB and GMAC thinking and business practice. Most programs are designed to produce highly specialized graduates who have academic rigor but *lack* business experience, managerial relevance, and breadth of learning, particularly in the core social sciences (e.g., anthropology, sociology, business history).[14] For example, at some business schools, applicants who have business experience are explicitly excluded from doctoral programs. The argument supporting this policy of business ignorance is the misunderstood need for "scientific objectivity."

Because of external pressures from the business community, the AACSB, the GMAC, and the "buyers" of their output, some changes to the content of doctoral programs can be anticipated in the future. However, to insure internationalization happens requires that those who administer doctoral programs be persuaded of the merits of adding an "international dimension" to the content of their programs. Thus, any internationalization recommendation must take into account the negative aspects of specialization (e.g., limited sensitivity to what is happening outside the area of specialization) and socialization (e.g., entrenchment arising from a fear of change and loss of power).

Growth in Non-U.S. Business Education and Research—Although most of us would agree that the United States was the birthplace of business administration education and business research, these scholarly activities are no longer exclusively U.S. phenomena. Besides the many business schools that have sprung up in other parts of the world, there are increasing numbers of Asian, European, and Middle Eastern business scholars who are interested in the study of business, *but from their respective paradigms, and for their respective needs.*

The fact that many of these schools were established with the assistance of U.S. business schools, and many of their scholars were trained in the United States, does not mean that these schools and scholars "blindly" accept the Anglo-American version of business reality. The schools are busy developing their own programs of instruction, and the scholars are busy developing their own paradigms, and formulating and testing their own theories.[15]

Just as "national culture" influences how we think about reality,[16] and thus what is taught and how it is taught (Locke 1989, 1997), it also influences the questions asked of this reality, and thus the theories and concepts developed to explain it. Consequently, the involvement of Asians, Europeans, and Middle Easterners in business education and research reverberates with the "world views" that are inimitably parts of their indigenous business processes (e.g., Locke 1989).

Disparate points of view are not, of course, unknown to business scholars. However, specialization, socialization, and language limitations introduce the well-known problems of "not invented here," ethnocentricity, parochialism, and ignorance of what is happening elsewhere (e.g., Boyacigiller and Adler 1991). These problems must be consciously guarded against, if for no other reason than intellectual integrity.

THE CONSEQUENCES OF CHANGE FOR DOCTORAL EDUCATION

The commentary so far suggests that because of trends such as those described above, future business faculty will be required to have at least the following: (1) either new ways of seeing the world of business (paradigms, conceptualizations), or at least a sensitivity to, and an understanding of, the educational and research implications of the world views of others; (2) new pedagogical skills, such as multi-disciplinary team teaching; (3) new research skills, such as is required for multi-functional and cross-national research; (4) managerial relevance that comes from either actual experience or direct involvement (consulting) in business activities; and (5) language capabilities.

These recommendations, of course, are based on the assumptions that (1) international colloquy among business scholars is not just desirable, but increasingly necessary, and (2) both business education and business research are global, not parochial, activities. Thus, instead of "blind" adherence to ever narrower fields of human understanding, doctoral programs need to seek to instill in their students a passion for knowledge from all possible sources (e.g., foreign as well as Anglo-American, anthropology as well as economics), combined with an essential open-mindedness that fosters and furthers global scientific discourse. These are attributes that many believe are critical for success in the late twentieth-century world economy (Thurow 1985; Kotkin 1992; Toyne 1993). These attributes, in turn, require an ability to understand, but not necessarily accept, the orientations, paradigms, metaphors, and methodologies of others. Competing orientations, paradigms and theories should not automatically be excluded, or trivialized, particularly out of ignorance. This, of course, means that doctoral students need to be introduced to the philosophy of science debates of today, not just the scientific ones; not an easy task when most scientists prefer to ignore philosophers altogether (Casti 1989).[17]

The new skills of pedagogy, research, and languages are not mutually exclusive. In the same way that firms are responding to environmental challenges by "eliminating" or "consciously reshaping" internal and external organizational barriers, and requiring employees and managers to work as multi-functional, cross-national teams, business scholars of the future will also have to work as multidisciplinary, cross-national teams both as educators and researchers. Just as the paradigms of business in the past "informed" the governance and activities (research and education) of business schools, they will continue to "inform" the governance and activities of these schools in the future. As educators and researchers we live and breathe at the whim of a paradigm. Only philosophers of science have the privilege of sitting above the fray.

WHAT IS THE RELATIONSHIP BETWEEN BUSINESS AND INTERNATIONAL BUSINESS EDUCATION AND RESEARCH?

What do we hope to accomplish as a consequence of internationalizing doctoral programs? The immediate, vocalized goal is the inclusion of our work in the core research and educational agendas of the business disciplines. We no longer believe that IB should be treated as some fringe element; it deserves to be a central element, if not *the* central element, of any business school's activities. It is the emerging world of business, not our needs, that necessitates this change.

Apparently, in the eyes of those whom we seek to convince of the merits of IB scholarship, we suffer from two insurmountable inadequacies. In the eyes of our university brethren we are simply vocational instructors—we train, we do not educate. In the eyes of our immediate colleagues, the business faculty, we provide at best scientific replication, and at worst, interesting, anecdotal, but non-essential, spurious examples of business aberrations. As Feldman (1997) succinctly summarizes, we are being challenged to answer the question, "where's the beef" in what we do. According to functional pundits, our research lacks theoretical and methodological rigor and most students will never operate in the international arena in any event (NAFTA, of course, has changed this, but its message has not yet gotten through).

In other words, what can IB scholars add to the already well defined but splintered body of business knowledge and the well entrenched, somewhat impervious business educational process? Our response, of course, must be to convincingly show that the generalized, certified body of business knowledge being produced by IB scholars has both theoretical and educational value, and that tomorrow's managers need exposure to international business issues, and experience in managing international complexities (e.g., foreign exchange, tax law differences, ad infinitum). And this, I believe, requires showing (1) how the paradigms that underpin IB research and education mesh with those of the business disciplines, and (2) how our "scientific" contributions either confirm what is already known, add distinctively to the body of discipline-splintered business knowledge, or add uniquely to this body of knowledge (see, for example, Toyne 1997).

THE PARADIGMIC ROOTS OF IB INQUIRY

IB inquiry in the United States sprang from a desire to educate future U.S. international business practitioners (see, for example, Fayerweather 1986). Shortly after World War II, when U.S. business aggressively expanded internationally, a handful of U.S. educators, sensitive to and knowledgeable about the socio-cultural and politico-legal differences existing among nation-states, saw a need to address the issues and problems encountered when crossing national boundaries.

To guide them in this educational crusade two paradigms (Vernon 1964) were adopted that still permeate the arguments and thinking of many U.S.-bound business and IB scholars.[18] The first paradigm, *the extension paradigm*, emphasizes the management of functional activities in "foreign economies." The second paradigm, *the cross-border management paradigm*, focuses attention on the integration and management of operations "within the international environment and across foreign economies." A third, more recent paradigm, *the emerging interaction paradigm*, attempts to present a more holistic, multi-level view of international business (Toyne 1989; Toyne and Nigh 1997) that reflects more recent thinking (see, for example, Boddewyn 1997).

The Extension Paradigm—When seen from this viewpoint, IB practice is modified domestic practice. Thus, both IB education and IB research can be, and often are, viewed as mere extensions of domestic business education and research. In fact, judged by U.S.-bound business research standards, much of IB inquiry can be termed "normal science" (Kuhn 1970). It involves using U.S.-bound business knowledge and methodologies, and classifying the output as "international" marketing, "international" management, and so on.

At the core of this paradigm are four assumptions: 1) business is business wherever practiced, only the situations or external circumstances change; 2) business environments converge; (3) as a consequence, there is a propensity for business practices to converge and (4) since, to many, the U.S. is the most economically advanced country in the world, U.S. business practice leads the world in new styles and new techniques.[19] Thus, the questions raised by this paradigm are essentially concerned with identifying factors that have a statistically significant influence on modifying a firm's home-country strategies, operations, and managerial practices when venturing overseas. The questions concerned with these "foreign situations" are limited to those that can be legitimately articulated within the various paradigms accepted by the (U.S.) business disciplines. Thus, according to Vernon, the teaching of IB as extension is better left to functional experts:

> . . . our existing functional groups—to our production people, our marketing people, our control people, our finance people, and so on. I say this because, as all of you know, we have developed a body of hard conceptions and ideas within the fields of production, marketing, control, and finance. These ideas I assume, can appropriately be extended by observant men who are specialists in their fields. It would seem prudent to me to take the discipline as it exists and to see in what sense these ideas have to be adapted to the peculiar conditions of foreign environments. I think we will learn that, with suitable, sensitive adaptation, many principles we now use can be applied to the circumstances of foreign economies and will continue to be valid (1964: 8).

So what can extension-based IB scholarship add to what is already being done as a result of functional inquiry? The answer, of course, is a great deal. First, the scholarships of discovery, integration, and application are enriched by the opportunities that IB provides for replication, and for defining the boundaries of the mid-range theories developed as a consequence of studying U.S. business practice in the United States. Second, the scholarship of teaching is enhanced because parochialism is acknowledged, if not eliminated. At the practitioner level, the student gains a much greater appreciation of the complexities and challenges of operating successful enterprises; particularly when foreign competitors are involved, and the domestic market becomes "regionalized" (e.g., the North American Free Trade Agreement). At the doctoral level, the student gains a broader yet deeper appreciation of the diversity, richness, intricacy and subtlety of human expression (albeit as it relates to business).

The Cross-Border Management Paradigm—The second concept that has had a strong and continuing influence on IB inquiry for at least the last 30 years deals with the problems associated with the movement of goods and capital across national boundaries and the simultaneous monitoring, control and integration from headquarters of operations existing in two or more countries. Vernon (1964:9-10) went so far as to suggest that this paradigm supports the argument that international business is distinct from U.S. business for the following four reasons:

1. IB involves both risks and opportunities of a kind not normally encountered within the domestic economy (e.g., balance of payment risks and opportunities, import restriction risks and opportunities).
2. IB requires an understanding of the vagaries and intricacies of such things as international taxation, foreign exchange, the international patent system, and the special problems of international oligopoly pricing.
3. IB requires dealing with governments, particularly at the point of entry.
4. IB requires the development of an effective operating discipline for understanding the complexities of moving across boundaries and operating in many countries.

In Vernon's view, these peculiarities raise questions not addressed by the "functional groups" in their research or teaching. At its core, however, this paradigm adds nothing in the way of uniqueness, and suffers from the same conceptual constraints as does the extension paradigm. It is a firm-level paradigm that does not challenge the core assumptions of the extension paradigm (i.e., universality of business practice, business practice convergence, and U.S. leadership in new business styles and techniques). Thus, as most U.S.-bound business scholars are quick to point out, IB's distinctiveness is not the result of a different worldview, but simply a distinctive opportunity to practice "normal science." The question asked is "how does a U.S. firm handle these peculiarities?"

So, again, what can IB scholarship based on a cross-border management paradigm add to what is already being done by the business disciplines? And again, the answer is a great deal. In addition to the contributions provided by the extension paradigm, this paradigm draws attention to, and provides opportunities for, the study of and teaching about the *consequences* of cross-coupling national and regional differences for strategic and operational purposes by enterprises. Indeed, how international firms handle the issues of environmental and operational diversity are harbingers of what will probably occur in most "open" societies as a consequence of increasing economic, political, and social interdependence.

An "Emerging" Paradigm of International Business—As I and others have explicitly and implicitly noted (see, for example, Casson 1997; Granovetter 1985; Toyne and Nigh 1997, Chapter 1), the social sciences and the business disciplines are in a period of introspection and are seeking to reformulate the central questions guiding their respective inquiries. Because of this introspection, new paradigms, or new ways of conceptualizing the world, are being sought. In the IB literature, for example, this is most evident in the calls for multidisciplinary research (Dunning 1989), interdisciplinary research (Toyne 1989), the development of more comprehensive theories that requires the"coming together" of two or more branches of the social sciences (Casson 1997), the development of a more comprehensive, multi-level, and perhaps holistic, view of IB's domain (Toyne 1997; Boddewyn 1997), and the suggestion that culture will assume a "center stage" role in the economic explanation of firm behavior (Dunning 1997).

In seeking a comprehensive and holistic definition of IB, I proposed elsewhere a paradigm that views IB as an emerging multi-level, hierarchical (biological) system of interactions between two or more socially-embedded business processes (Toyne and Nigh 1997, Chapter 1). Additionally, this hierarchical system evolves intermittently because of informed hunch, intuition, and vision (learning coupled with inductive thinking) that can originate at *any* level in the process (e.g. supragovernmental, governmental, industry, firm, individual). Thus, the "trigger" for all business-related decisions is a combination of three *culturally* influenced elements or factors: (1) self-interest; (2) the available pool of information, knowledge and experience; and (3) learning (which includes awareness, discernment, interpretation and judgment). A business process and the various phenomena that are the output of this process change because of the self-interested, bounded[20] learning that occurs as a consequence of interaction with other business processes and their outputs.

Unlike the extension and cross-border management paradigms, the questions raised and examined as a result of this worldview add uniquely to business' body of knowledge. It is silent on the assumptions that business is ultimately the same wherever practiced, that business practice will converge, or that the U.S. leads the world in terms of business styles and techniques.[21] Rather, it assumes that business is a process that varies from one social setting to another because of the cumulative effects of culture-influenced learning. Thus, when two or more business processes interact, each will be affected, sometimes radically, sometimes subtlety, but always differently.

Whether business practice is converging or diverging is of interest only to the extent that such trends may shed light on the culture-influenced learning processes of various "cultures" and the consequences of their interaction with other business processes. Also, whether the U.S. leads the world in terms of business styles and techniques is only of interest to the extent that the business leader at any point in time may have a role to play in identifying possibly useful business practices for other societies and their organizations that are ready for change (see, for example, Ozawa 1997).

WHAT IS ADEQUATE LEVEL OF INTERNATIONAL BUSINESS LITERACY?

Of course, as IB scholars we would like to assert that in today's world, an erudite or intellectually learned individual requires more than a nodding acquaintance with the IB literature and its collective and pervasive influence on what he or she does as both researcher and educator. But such an expectation is frankly utopian. It may even be politically unwise at this time to demand a comprehensive and complete commitment to programmatic reform, since such a demand would probably result in immediate rejection by most faculties and administrators of doctoral programs. Either the need for internationalization is not yet sufficiently "obvious" to most members of the business academy for a total commitment to be made, or an internationalized doctoral program has not yet appeared that "captures" the academy's imagination.[22]

A more realistic expectation, given current circumstances, is that most schools will probably seek some "satisficing" level of IB literacy (Simon

1957). Thus, a more pragmatic approach, perhaps, is to ask what body of knowledge and package of skills and tools can be considered essential for a satisficing level of IB literacy.[23]

It should be possible to use the now familiar undergraduate and graduate IB literacy model of awareness, understanding, and competency at the doctoral level.[24] However, undergraduate and graduate business programs are designed to develop future practitioners and most, if not all, doctoral programs are designed to develop future scholars, *not* practitioners. As Figure 1 suggests, doctoral programs are designed to either train researchers (the dominant model), educate educators, or some heroic combination of the two. They also tend to emphasize either unidisciplinary or integration approaches for both research and teaching. Thus, major, significant differences exist among doctoral programs as to the meaning attached to a "satisficing level of IB literacy."

GENERAL RECOMMENDATIONS AND OBSERVATIONS

Before proceeding to make recommendations for the three literacy levels, five general recommendations are offered. They are in response to the external forces discussed earlier: (1) a passion for knowledge; (2) a need for managerial relevance; (3) a need for new research skills; (4) a need for teaching skills; and (5) a need for language capabilities.

A Passion for Knowledge—To incorporate, as suggested earlier, a passion for knowledge from all possible sources combined with a tolerance for "foreign ideas" is not intrinsic to any recommended internationalization model. Moreover, although I believe that such an attitude can be encouraged, it is ultimately a consequence of personal experience and choice. Nonetheless, doctoral students can be given the skills, tools and knowledge needed to seek alternate, even disparate sources (e.g., foreign libraries and journals, internet bulletin boards) for ideas, insights, material, data, etc. To be encouraged to do so, they should be introduced to the writings of eminent foreign scholars (e.g., Hedlund and Mattsson of Sweden, Hofstede of the Netherlands, Pugh of Great Britain, and Redding of Hong Kong). They should also be encouraged to contact scholars at foreign schools, attend and participate in conferences and seminars in other countries, and even take courses of study overseas under the guidance of scholars who have differing views on business reality. Importantly, they need to be introduced to the philosophy of science and business science issues of today (e.g., Casti, Feyerabend and Popper of Austria; Guba, Hunt, and Lincoln of the United States; and Phillips of Great Britain) so that they can determine for themselves the merits of different worldviews. Reasoned disagreement is surely better than ignorant fidelity.

Managerial Relevance—The need for managerial relevance is of growing concern for most accreditation organizations and the business community. Although it should also be of equal concern to those who are responsible for the provision of future business researchers and educators, it does not appear to be the case at many business schools.

How a particular business school decides on the issue of managerial relevance is, of course, central to the purpose, structure and content of its business programs, including its doctoral program. As noted earlier, business schools must attempt to satisfy two constituencies, the business academy and the business community, and apparently by default, most business schools have come down in favor of the former (Leavitt 1993). Instead of stressing the "unscientific" human and synthesizing dimensions of management, or the immediate needs of management, most business schools stress the abstracted, reductionistic science of management and its application. Since graduates of doctoral programs tend to teach what they have been taught and research what they have been told is important, the questions that need to be addressed are (1) why this particular choice, and (2) does the choice have a bearing on the internationalization goal.

Essentially, there are two dimensions to the managerial relevance issue. The first deals with whether management is an art or science. The second deals with whether the purpose of business education is to educate or train. Regardless at which end of each dimension a person chooses to stand, IB as research and education can make significant contributions.

Management as Art or Science—The central question behind "managerial relevance" is whether management is art or science. That is, is there such a thing as a science of management, and can this science be taught and then applied, very much like engineering is taught and then applied. Those who are for greater managerial relevance are probably lamenting the absence of "management as art." If law and medicine can be taught as art as well as science, why cannot business?

The issue of management as science or art has been summarized quite well by Locke (1989:40-41):

The classic definition of what managers do is that they "plan, organize, co-ordinate, and control," in order to optimize. These are rational, analytical actions, which seem to be well suited to the techniques used in scientific management. But as Ian Glover noted, the manager's job is actually "of an unprogrammed character [he or she] . . . is not much concerned with the flow and use of 'hard' information, his information is distorted, incomplete, his job is ambiguous." He is not "primarily a decision-maker, a planner, but an 'inspirer,' a fire fighter, and a rationalizer after the fact." Professor Philippe Nemo has, in France, expressed similar sentiments. "The problem," he writes, "of social practice can be formulated in the following way: to adapt man's actions not to the facts that he knows (that deductive reason can take care of) but to facts that he does not know. Or, how to act best in a given circumstance in which one cannot, in principle, know all the conditions and prospects." Glover and Nemo's views limit the connections possible between science and business studies. They suggest that to the extent that the studies conform to the guidelines of science, their usefulness to the practicing manager diminishes. As Glover phrased it, attempts to 'study' decision making are overly academic, attempts at 'programming' it all seem to be like the search for fool's gold, confusing the academic ballgame of analysis with the executive task of synthesis.

Put differently, "management as art" is a process of constant learning, adaptation, and the skillful application of tools in an unstable, ever changing, and increasingly uncertain context. Thus, the question becomes, can this type of management be taught. The answer, of course, is yes, since graduates of business programs manage to become successful professionals and entrepreneurs. But how do they become these success stories? The answer is by gaining experience and probably by learning to use information and knowledge that is not taught in business schools, but comes from other sources.

The more socio-culturally heterogeneous the business context, the greater the need to place emphasis on the art of management. And, of course, the most heterogeneous business context is the international context. The IB arena is, indeed, very human, very uncertain, and involves an act of synthesizing strands of "soft" information, "feel" for a situation, inductive reasoning that draws on a person's breadth and depth of knowledge, and taxes his or her limited experience. Thus, it is the ideal situation from which to draw examples and cases when incorporating managerial relevance, or that area of management that has not yet yielded itself to scientific management inquiry, into the business teaching process. It is also the ideal situation in which students of management can gain considerably enriched experiences (e.g., internships). At the same time, however, those who choose to emphasize management as science can enrich and broaden what they teach as a consequence of the IB paradigms discussed earlier.

Business Education or Business Training—The central question behind "managerial relevance" when viewed as an educational task, is "do we educate or train future practitioners?" The distinction is important in the United States, since a business school is an integral part of a university, and therefore, bound by its educational traditions.[25] The distinction is not so important in other parts of the world where business schools often evolved separate from universities (e.g., France and Great Britain). Thus, the words educate and training take on subtle, but important differences in the United States. Education is viewed as preparing someone for a yet to be defined future (i.e., emphasis is placed on acquiring and enhancing analytical reasoning with breadth of knowledge). Training is viewed as preparing someone for a known "present" or anticipated future (i.e., emphasis is placed on acquiring skills and regurgitating "facts").

In the U.S., there is support for a more abstracted, science-based, universalistic form of business teaching than is found in other parts of the world (Locke 1989). Supporters of this school of thought would probably argue that today's business practice is somewhat irrelevant, since it is in response to a somewhat transitory situation that will have changed by tomorrow. As a consequence, so the argument would go, the practitioner *educated* in the universal (generalized) aspects of business will have a much better foundation for succeeding in a changing world than someone trained in today's specific (time-bound) practices. A major problem with this argument, of course, is that its adherents tend to be those who persist in using a business knowledge base that is parochial (i.e., U.S.), not global, and often not understandable to the business practitioner.

Whether a doctoral program's faculty favor business training or business education cannot be used as an excuse for not internationalizing the program. As noted elsewhere, tomorrow's U.S. business practice is in the process of being shaped in the international arena, and, because of NAFTA, this arena is now even more a part of the U.S. business arena than before.

Research Skills—Increasingly, that portion of most doctoral programs devoted to introducing students to research strategies and research tools are based on a paradigm predicated on reductionistic assumptions, and stresses an "objective" reality "out there" that is driven by immutable natural laws and mechanisms. Yet, as noted earlier, this paradigm is being challenged on many fronts from within the social sciences, including business. Thus, those in charge of doctoral programs have a responsibility to *judiciously* introduce their students to the issues raised by other worldviews (e.g., naturalistic inquiry, postpositivism). This would help provide them with the knowledge and skills necessary to make rational and appropriate decisions about the ontological, epistemological and methodological issues involved when selecting among alternate worldviews.

Moreover, this emerging need for an expanded and deeper understanding of the relationship between worldviews and research methodologies is congruent with the knowledge and skills that will be required of future literate business scholars. As the academy of business scholars grows and encompasses scholars from different cultures' it is not too far fetched to assume that they may have adopted worldviews that are different from those adopted by Anglo-American scholars. For example, we already have considerable tension in the United States between those adopting quantitative research techniques and those adopting qualitative techniques.

Teaching Skills—Most doctoral programs emphasize research, not education (teaching) (Leavitt 1993). Consequently, doctoral programs are often, if not always, crammed with courses that deal with (1) a particular discipline's literature (theoretical and empirical), and (2) quantitative research methodology. Education and teaching, if acknowledged, are generally treated in a rather superficial, if not cavalier fashion. For example, at a university with which I am familiar, teaching is minimally addressed by requiring all doctoral students, irrespective of discipline, to take a one-week course in pedagogy prior to entering the classroom for the first time. As a minimum, they are also required to teach one faculty-monitored course. The rest of the program deals with (1) acquiring an in-depth understanding and appreciation of a specific, but increasingly narrow body of literature, and (2) developing the skills needed to conduct rigorous research, primarily of a deterministic nature.

The one-week pedagogy course, along with the requirement that all doctoral students teach at least one course, does not include any discussion of the issues related to the teaching of business subjects (e.g., the issue of managerial relevance, touched upon above). Nor does the course include any discussion of those issues raised earlier that are concerned with the need to acquire multidisciplinary team teaching, cross-national team teaching, and interdisciplinary teaching skills, and the pros and cons of business experience.

Given current trends, deficiencies such as those just described must be reduced, if not eliminated. And again, the place to look for solutions is the IB arena where multinational and global enterprises are blurring the traditional functional boundaries. Also, as Beamish (1997) notes, the development of IB cases as a teaching/learning experience for doctoral students introduce them to the difficulties and issues confronted by businesspeople.

Language Capabilities—It is an old saw in the United States that states "It is always good to know another language (and culture)," yet it is also a fact that this saying has been ignored, even relegated to the trash pile in business schools. U.S. citizens, much like their British brethren, have long felt that they were "beyond that." They believed that they are already members of the global community, if not *the* global community. It is, in fact, almost banal to say that English is the language of global business.

Yet, today, an increasing number of universities and colleges require their freshman students have a second language capability. This, of course, is an acknowledgment that the global community is more diverse than generally assumed by Anglo-Americans. More importantly, it is also an ackowledgment that language is an expression of human diversity. However, it places the teacher, the educator, in an embarassing situation. Can the teacher, the educator, or the scholar be more ignorant than the students he or she teaches?

Globalization does not refer just to the globalization of business, it also refers to the globalization of business inquiry and business education. For example, exchange programs are not restricted to undergraduate students. They now include graduate students, faculty members, and will soon (hopefully) include doctoral students. Moreover, we are rapidly approaching an era of global business scholarship, and this era will require a communication ability that goes well beyond the ability to communicate clearly, precisely in one language. The business scholar of tomorrow must be capable of entering into a dialog with his or her foreign colleagues that goes beyond a superficial exchange of ideas, and the experience of learning a second language is a proven technique for enhancing a person's ability to understand the nuances that are part of another culture. Another technique, for example, is to live in another culture for an extended period of time.

THREE LITERACY LEVELS

My purpose here is not to make specific recommendations. Rather, it is to recommend what I believe are the "bare essentials" required to internationalize doctoral programs. These bare essentials are based on the assumption that doctoral programs are designed to produce scholars, not practitioners. Also, a more comprehensive and detailed list of recommendations must take into account the high degree of specialization and socialization that has occurred within the functional areas, and the paradigms, metaphors, constructs and methodologies that they have either adopted or developed, and tenaciously cling to. Even the translation of the "bare essentials" into specific courses of instruction is dependent on the structure and content of a particular doctoral program, the institutional and faculty reasons for its existence, the school's present and future (IB) faculty resources, and the IB paradigm or paradigms embraced by the involved faculty.

Awareness—Awareness is the minimal level of IB literacy. The goal at this level is to insure that doctoral students are at least aware of two things. Firstly, the U.S. can no longer place an exclusive, or even superior claim on the production of business knowledge, either explicitly by commission or implicitly by omission. Secondly, most of the paradigms, metaphors, theories and constructs they will be introduced to in the course of their studies are probably "culture bound."

To gain this type of appreciation of the global nature of business inquiry, doctoral students need to be introduced to the following (either as a separate course or as part of already approved courses[26]):

1. representative samples of the streams of IB and foreign business literature that directly, even indirectly, complement the body of knowledge they are presently required to learn; and
2. representative samples of contrasting orientations, paradigms, metaphors, etc., and their supporting arguments, that can be found in the business, IB, *and* social sciences literature (U.S. and foreign).

They also need to be provided with the intellectual tools and knowledge needed to draw reasoned conclusions concerning the relative merits of differing worldviews, the questions raised by these worldviews, and the methodologies they spawn in answering these questions. As mentioned earlier, this requires introducing them to current philosophy of science and science debates, and to the theoretical and methodological developments occurring in the core social sciences.

Understanding—For most doctoral programs, IB awareness is all that can be expected, at least in the near future. At schools of business with more enlightened faculties, awareness is just the first step in achieving greater IB literacy. IB understanding represents a significantly higher level of learning and a higher level of commitment from the institution and the program's faculty. For example, it is one thing for a doctoral student to be informed of the possibility that expectancy theory might be culture bound; it is another thing for the student to understand the possible reasons for why this might be, and the implications this might have for his or her research and teaching.

IB understanding is probably required of doctoral students who plan to conduct research in other countries, and who expect to teach the international equivalents of their functional courses. It requires that doctoral students build on their IB awareness knowledge and skills by being introduced to at least the following (again, either as a separate course or as part of already approved courses):

1. the issues and problems associated with the conduct of research in and across "foreign" countries (or embedded business processes);
2. the issues and problems associated with cross-cultural team teaching and research using various orientations, paradigms, and theories; and
3. the issues and problems associated with using qualitative research strategies and techniques and those other strategies and techniques required to understand the theoretical and empirical work of their foreign counterparts.

Competency—The goal of competency is the preparation of IB researchers and educators. As such, its takes students well beyond IB understanding by introducing them to the multifunctional wealth of IB knowledge, and provides them with the skills and foreign experience needed to complete IB research of a functional, multifunctional, or interfunctional task within an international context.

I also believe that these students should be made aware of the differing thoughts and arguments on what constitutes business education in other parts of the world, and trained in the basic nuances of teaching business in other countries using different worldviews and metaphors. Whereas a reading ability in at least one foreign language is probably sufficient in the cases of IB awareness and IB understanding, fluency in at least one foreign language should be a requirement at the IB competency level. These students should also be required to spend some time in another country at a non-U.S. company or as a scholar at a foreign institution. As future global scholars, these students should be given the opportunity to interact with foreign scholars, just as U.S. managers are expected to interact with, and compete with, foreign educated/trained managers.

THE POLITICS OF INTERNATIONALIZING DOCTORAL PROGRAMS

The internationalization of doctoral programs will not be easy, not because there is not a recognized need for such revision, but rather because the faculties responsible for these programs do not believe that the international dimension can add significantly to what they are already doing as researchers. In addition, they do not believe that failure to incorporate the international dimension into a school's undergraduate, graduate, and doctorate business programs will adversely affect the school's survivability.

In a recent *Fortune* article entitled "What's killing the business school deans of America?" O'Reilly (1994) answers the question by suggesting that the malady originates with a business school's faculty. As Ross Webber, chairman of the Management Department at Wharton explained, business school faculties have become so isolated from changes in the real world of business that they cannot comprehend the need for reform. "The business world is ahead of the university in promoting teams, cross-functionality, and project groups that bring together disparate elements" (1994:65).

The dean is caught in the middle. He or she wants to bring the faculty into the 1990s and the faculty is refusing to budge from the 1950s, particularly the senior faculty and the narrowly trained, and narrowly focused, research-driven faculty.

Notwithstanding this unattractive situation, the deans are hopeful;[27] perhaps they have to be, since the alternate scenario is unimaginable. As O'Reilly (1994:68) reports:

> Several deans predict that most schools will adapt rapidly—eventually. Few will put themselves through wrenching change or brave experiments until forced. Most, they say, will wait until some other school does something that truly impresses students and recruiters, and shamelessly imitate them if they must to survive.

As cloisters for unabashed, self-serving savants, business schools interested in internationalizing their doctoral programs cannot mandate reform. The deans frankly lack the power to do so. Rather, the approach must be one of persuasion (the most difficult) as already discussed, or isolation. By isolation I mean the creation of specialized doctoral programs that seek to produce intellectually learned graduates who meet the needs, not of research-dominated schools of business, but rather teaching-dominated and mixed-focused schools of business.

CONCLUSIONS AND IMPLICATIONS

This is neither the place nor the time to evangelize for a truly open-ended, passionate system of doctoral training since for the most part it would be speaking to the already converted. Such calls must come from within each of the business disciplines as the increasing sterility and social dysfunctionality of their approaches become more self-evident. As "outsiders," or, at best, fringe members of the various business disciplines (as represented in the power structures of their academies and their schools), IB scholars can only hope that the objectivity and integrity of the business academy at large is such that it will eventually recognize the merits of a passion for knowledge, a tolerance for opposing views and methodologies, and the *systemic* inclusion of the international dimension. That is, the business academy needs to open itself to an appreciation of a broader, more generalized understanding of human expression that is not truncated by some sense of misplaced loyalty to what are at best parochial and arbitrarily defined fields of inquiry.

To inspire students—undergraduate, graduate, or doctorate—is, I believe, an obligation we all accept when we become faculty members or administrators of an institution of higher learning. And, indeed, the growing complexity, diversity, and richness of business practice in what is rapidly becoming a globally integrated world, requires that we truly become global scholars. The opportunity to add another dimension to our doctorate, graduate, and undergraduate students' learning should be both motivating, challenging, and thus exhilarating. And ultimately, this is what the internationalization of the doctoral program is all about. After all, doctoral programs should be at the leading edge of human understanding as it relates to business.

NOTES

1. Essentially, the business disciplines are interdisciplinary fields (e.g., marketing is a synthesis of economics, sociology, and psychology). What is being suggested here and hinted at elsewhere (Dunning 1988 and Toyne 1989) is the redefinition of business functions along lines that more closely approximate what is now occurring within business, and what is being called for by those who advocate a more holistic understanding of business. For a fuller discussion of this point see Toyne and Nigh (1997).

2. The dissemination of knowledge is also done using such media as conferences, journals and books.

3. Partly because of staffing constraints and partly because of faculty biases and training, the research and teaching approaches adopted and emphasized at particular institutions are often identical.

4. Alutto believes that most doctoral programs are producing graduates trained for research/silo enhancer schools of business. He also believes that this type of school is in the minority. According to Alutto, the mixed-focused school appears to be more prevalent.

5. Although the types of research and teaching are identical at most educational institutions, and thus a two-dimensional matrix could be used in many situations, some institutions may use practitioners and visiting professors to augment their tenure-track faculties. Such business schools could emphasize unidisciplinary research while offering undergraduate and graduate programs based on integrated teaching principles.

6. This, of course, assumes that U.S. business scholars tend to be parochial in terms of their interests and the body of knowledge they draw upon for theoretical support—an assumption that has support in the sociology of science literature. Also see Boyacigiller and Adler (1991).

7. For a discussion of these principles, see *The Voice of Liberal Learning: Michael Oakschott on Education*, edited by Timothy Fuller (New Haven, CT: Yale University Press).

8. Courses concerned with commerce were offered at Oxford, but subsequently dropped in the 14th century.

9. Upper levels of the business process can be viewed as contextualizing, informing, selecting from among possible behaviors, governing, regulating, or controlling the results of lower-level processes (see, for example, Salthe 1985:84). These constraining attributes (which include the creation of appropriate organizations) can be viewed as stable when the rate at which they change is slower than the rate at which the focal-level process changes.

10. For purposes of explication, national business process and social-embedded business process are used interchangeably. However, it is recognized that in the same way that using national borders to define cultural groupings is not correct, defining social-embedded business processes by national borders may be equally wrong.

11. For example, at the undergraduate level, the AACSB has increased the number of credit hour devoted to non-business topics by reducing from sixty to fifty percent of the maximum number of semester credit hours that can be devoted to business top-

ics. Also, the Graduate Management Admissions Test now requires the completion of a written examination that allows examiners to evaluate the communication and analytical reasoning skills of applicants.

12. A factor not covered here is the faculty-sapping cutbacks in operating budgets that most state schools have experienced in the last few years. While such cutbacks may result in entrenchment, and thus strengthen resistance to change, they may also provide administrators an opportunity to more carefully evaluate their future faculty needs (e.g., specialists versus integrators or generalists).

13. Why, for example, did the Academy of Management find it necessary to have as its 1994 annual meeting theme "Reducing Barriers to Understanding" if there were no concern for, or recognition of, a breakdown in communications among the sub-parts of the discipline?

14. At some U.S. business schools the administrators, or directors of functional doctoral programs have agreed to replace the "minor" with a "cognate." This, of course, provides these administrators with complete authorization over the content of specific doctoral programs. For example, an administrator of a Ph.D. program with a concentration in Consumer Behavior might require a Psychology cognate that is selected by the Marketing faculty, not the Psychology faculty.

15. See, for example, the work done on networks, strategy, organization design, and marketing at the Stockholm School of Economics. Possibly because of linguistic limitations, but more likely because of training, U.S.-based business researchers rarely, if ever, cite the work of their "foreign-based" peers.

16. It is, perhaps, more correct to say that "national cultures" are manifestations of different collective perceptions of reality.

17. With the help of such scholars as Shelby Hunt, marketing has done quite a good job in this area.

18. The paradigmic roots of IB inquiry are discussed more fully in Toyne and Nigh (1997, Chapter 1).

19. This is based on the widely held belief in this country that business is economically driven.

20. Learning is bounded in that a person or organization has limited information, knowledge, and experience to draw on at any particular point in time.

21. The truth of these assumptions is not questioned or challenged by this paradigm. They are not needed.

22. The Master of International Business Studies (MIBS) program at the University of South Carolina is an example of an IB educational model that has been unabashedly copied by other institutions.

23. Such an approach could open Pandora's box. Since most IB scholars are actually unidisciplinary scholars who just happen to be interested in international topics, it might be difficult, if not impossible, to get general agreement.

24. The three-level literacy approach to the internationalization of business programs was first used by Jeffrey S. Arpan at John Carroll University. Descriptions of these levels can be found in Arpan (1993) and Toyne (1992).

25. Thunderbird, for example, has recently been emphasizing business training by promoting "the application of theory." It is able to do this because it is not a part of a university and its traditions.
26. The pros and cons of various approaches for the insertion of this material into a doctoral program can be found in Cavusgil (1993).
27. The senior faculty may actually be more responsive to a more holistic interpretation of business than are research-driven faculty who have probably been socialized more recently.

REFERENCES

Alutto, Joseph A. 1993. "Whither doctoral business education? An exploration of program models." *Selections.* (Spring): 37-43.

Anon. 1994a. *Report on the International Symposium on Higher Education and Strategic Partnerships.* Vancouver, BC, Canada: Inter-American Organization for Higher Education (Quebec) and the Open Learning Agency (Vancouver).

Anon. 1994b. "The Discreet Charm of the Multicultural Multinational." *The Economist.* 30 July, 57-58.

Arpan, Jeffrey. 1993. "Curricular and Administrative Considerations—The Cheshire Cat Parable." Cavusgil, S. Tamer (ed.). *Internationalizing Business Education: Meeting the Challenge.* East Lansing, MI: Michigan State University Press.

Beamish, Paul. 1997. "International Business Education vis the Case Method." In Toyne, Brian and Douglas Nigh (eds.). *International Business: Institutions and the Dissemination of Knowledge.* Columbia, SC: The University of South Carolina Press.

Bedeian, Arthur G. 1989. "Totems and Taboos: Undercurrents in the Management Discipline." Presidential Address, Academy of Management Meeting, August.

Boddewyn, Jean J. 1997. "The Conceptual Domain of International Business: Territory, Boundaries, and Levels." In Toyne, Brian and Douglas Nigh (eds.). *International Business: An Emerging Vision.* Columbia, SC: The University of South Carolina Press.

Boyacigiller, Nakiye and Nancy J. Adler. 1991. "The Parochial Dinosaur: Organizational Science in a Global Context." *The Academy of Management Review.* 16(2): 262-90.

Boyer, Ernest L. 1990. *Scholarship Reconsidered: Priorities of the Professoriate,* Princeton, N.J.: The Carnegie Foundation for the Advancement of Teaching.

Casson, Mark. 1997. "Economic Theories of International Business: A Research Agenda." In Toyne, Brian and Douglas Nigh (eds.). *International Business: An Emerging Vision.* Columbia, SC: The University of South Carolina Press.

Casti, John. L. 1989. *Paradigms Lost: Tackling the Unanswered Mysteries of Modern Science.* New York, NY: Avon Books.

Cavusgil, S. Tamer (ed.). 1993. *Internationalizing Business Education: Meeting the Challenge*. East Lansing, MI: Michigan State University Press.

Daft, Richard L. and Arie Y. Lewin. 1990. "Can Organization Studies Begin to Break Out of the Normal Science Straitjacket? An Editorial Essay." *Organization Science*. 1(1): 1-9.

Dunning, John H. 1997. "Micro and Macro Organizational Aspects of MNEs and MNE Activity." In Toyne, Brian and Douglas Nigh (eds.). *International Business: An Emerging Vision*. Columbia, SC: The University of South Carolina Press.

Dunning, John H. 1988. "The Study of International Business: A Plea for a More Interdisciplinary Approach." *Journal of International Business Studies*. 20(3): 411-36.

Fayerweather, John. 1986. "A History of the Academy of International Business from Infancy to Maturity: The First 25 Years." *Essays in International Business*. Columbia, SC: The University of South Carolina, No. 6.

Feldman, Daniel C. 1997 "When Does Demonstrating a Difference Make a Difference? An Organizational Behavior Perspective on International Business." In Toyne, Brian and Douglas Nigh (eds.). *International Business: An Emerging Vision*. Columbia, SC: The University of South Carolina Press.

Fuller, Timothy (ed.). 1989. *The Voice of Liberal Learning: Michael Oakeschott on Education*. New Haven, CT: Yale University Press.

GMAC. 1990. *Leadership for a Changing World: The Future Role of Graduate Management Education*. Los Angeles, CA: Graduate Management Admission Council.

Glover, Ian. 1978. "Professionalism and the Manufacturing Industry." In Fores, Michael and Ian Glover. *Manufacturing and Management*. London: HSMO.

Gould, Stephen Jay. 1981. *The Mismeasure of Man*. New York, NY: W.W. Norton & Company.

Granovetter, M. 1985. "Economic Action and Social Structure: The Problem of Embeddedness." *American Journal of Sociology*. 91: 481-510.

Kotkin, Joel. 1992. *Tribes*. New York, NY: Random House, Inc.

Leavitt, Harold J. 1993. "The Business School and the Doctorate." *Selections*. (Winter): 12-21.

Locke, Robert R. 1997. "International Management Education in Western Europe, America, and Japan: An Historian's View." In Toyne, Brian and Douglas Nigh (eds.). *International Business: An Emerging Vision*. Columbia, SC: The University of South Carolina Press.

Locke, Robert R. 1989. *Management and Higher Education Since 1940*. Ithaca, NY: Cornell University Press.

Nemo, Phillippe. 1984. "Les Enseignements Nontechniques dans les Grandes Ecoles de Gestion." *Revue Francaise de Gestion*. (Nov.-Dec.): 16-27 (quoted in Locke 1989, Locke's translation).

O'Reilly, Brian. 1994. "What's Killing the Business School Deans of America?" *Fortune*. 8 August: 64-68.

Ozawa, Terutomo. 1997. "Images, Economies of Concatenation, and Animal Spirits: Dependency vs. Emulation Paradigm." In Toyne, Brian and Douglas Nigh (eds.). *International Business: An Emerging Vision*. Columbia, SC: The University of South Carolina Press.

Pfeffer, J. 1987. "Bringing the Environment Back In: The Social Context of Business Strategy." In Teece, D.J. (ed.). *The Competitive Challenge: Strategies for Industrial Innovation and Renewal*. Cambridge, MA: Ballinger Publishing Company.

Porter, Lyman W. and Lawrence E. McKibbin. 1988. *Management Education and Development: Drift or Thrust into the 21st Century?* New York, NY: McGraw-Hill Book Company.

Porter, M.E. 1990. *The Competitive Advantage of Nations*. New York, NY: The Free Press.

Salthe, Stanley N. 1985. *Evolving Hierarchical Systems: Their Structure and Representation*. New York, NY: Columbia University Press.

Simon, Herbert A. 1957. *Administrative Behavior* (2d ed.). New York, NY: Free Press.

Thurow, Lester C. 1985. *The Zero-Sum Solution: Building a World-Class American Economy*. New York, NY: Simon and Schuster.

Toyne, Brian. 1997. "International Business Inquiry: Does it Warrant a Separate Domain?" In Toyne, Brian and Douglas Nigh (eds.). *International Business: An Emerging Vision*. Columbia, SC: The University of South Carolina Press.

Toyne, Brian. 1993. "Internationalizing the Business Administration Faculty is No Easy Task." In Cavusgil, S. Tamer (ed.). *Internationalizing Business Education: Meeting the Challenge*. East Lansing, MI: Michigan State University Press.

Toyne, Brian. 1992. "Internationalizing Business Education." *Business & Economic Review*. 38(2): 23-27.

Toyne, Brian. 1989. "International Exchange: A Foundation for Theory Building in International Business." *Journal of International Business Studies*. 20(1): 1-17.

Toyne, Brian and Douglas Nigh. 1997. *International Business: An Emerging Vision*. Columbia, SC: The University of South Carolina Press.

Vernon, Raymond. 1964. "Comments." In Robock, Stefan H. and Lee C. Nehrt (eds.). *Education in International Business*. Bloomington, IN: Graduate School of Business, Indiana University.

Zysman, J., and L. Tyson (eds.). 1983. *American Industry in International Competition: Government Policies and Corporate Strategies*. Ithaca, NY: Cornell University Press.

WILL GLOBALIZATION PREEMPT THE NEED FOR INTERNATIONALIZING DOCTORAL PROGRAMS? IF NOT, WHAT THEN?

Robert G. May

INTRODUCTION

I believe that beginning around the mid-1980s, business faculty began to see the point of internationalizing undergraduate and masters curricula. World events coupled with some on-going trends finally got everyone's attention. In particular, there was the late-dawning realization in the U.S. that our economy no longer dominated the world. U.S. business people, who thought they discovered competition long ago and had perfected the art, found that others had developed a more profound level of competition. We business educators used to congratulate ourselves on providing a superior product too, based on the success of American business worldwide. Interestingly, when American business people fell off their pedestals, they got up angry. In addition to a certain amount of whining, they began to question why they were not prepared for this new level of competition and why we were not producing the kind of talent that could help them. Vociferously, they have demanded more capable as well as knowledgeable graduates from our programs, and a global perspective is close to the top of their lists of essential characteristics of business graduates. Add to this the end of the Cold War, making global business a real possibility and placing greater emphasis on economic power relative to political/military power, and the realization that the Europeans actually are going to succeed in coalescing into a workable economic community. Even the most parochial faculty member, if shown enough writing on the wall, can get the message. Requiring international exposure in undergraduate and masters programs in business is no longer controversial.

How to accomplish that exposure and to what extent are still subject to much debate. In my opinion, to date there is very little, if any, momentum for a degree of infusion of international content across the curricula that would *require* doctoral level international training of all business doctoral students. As Arpan, Folks and Kwok (1993) report, infusion into existing required and elective courses is the most common method of introducing international perspectives into the curriculum. The other popular methods are: a required course in international business; a required international course in the major field; and a course from a menu of international courses. I submit that all of these methods represent acceptable curriculum requirements *because* they do not require profound knowledge of international issues by the vast majority of faculty. Under the infusion approach, individual faculty merely bring some interesting international dimensions into their existing courses. This requires only superficial expertise at most. Under all of the other methods, accomplishing the objective is delegated to specialists.

As we look ahead, I see major resistance, but some glimmers of hope for ultimately including international dimensions in all doctoral programs. First, there is the potential excuse that globalization will preempt the need for internationalization. Next, there is a traditional set of barriers embedded in the faculty culture that has evolved since World War II. Although there are some hopeful trends, major intervention will be required to change doctoral education within twenty years or less.

THE EXCUSE OF GLOBALIZATION

Globalization is a much-used but ill-defined term. It is used by so many segments of the population to encompass so many different concepts that some other term will have to be invented for precise discourse. Let me define what I believe is the ultimate vision of globalization. It is a vision of strictly non-national (and, especially, non-nationalistic) business entities rationalizing production, distribution, and financing activities worldwide, completely unconstrained by national policies, institutions, and customs. Presumably, such rationalization would be optimized globally, based on absolute (global) comparative advantage rather than relative (local) comparative advantage.

In such an environment, political entities would exist only to provide local security within a network of global law-enforcement and, more importantly, to develop their populations into highly competitive work forces, capable of high productivity and, therefore, prosperous standards of living. Businesses would have incentives to aid in this development and to keep it well distributed across the global business patch, because segments of the patch that do not prosper do not make good markets for goods produced by other segments. The locales of the global village would have incentives to eliminate all artificial economic frictions, including any idiosyncratic regulations, taxes, tariffs and cultural distortions of purely "rational" business practice, lest they create an artificial comparative advantage for another locale in what would otherwise be their most productive endeavors. What necessary frictions are retained would be completely harmonized across locales so that businesses would find dealing with one virtually the same as dealing with another. Culture would still count in doing business, but only in areas such as consumer marketing strategy.

Should this vision ever come to pass, business would finally be *just business*. No modifiers such as "global," "multi-national," or even "international" would apply. For example, dealing with cross-cultural marketing globally would be merely an extension of dealing with demographic-based market segmentation in a locale.

CULTURAL BARRIERS TO TRUE GLOBALIZATION

Will the vision ever be a reality? Perhaps it will one day, but not in our lifetimes. Locales (countries) have too much to lose in the short run to rapidly harmonize their economic infrastructures with global standards. Arriving at standards alone takes decades and reflects the separate countries' resistance to sacrificing local short-run welfare for the mostly abstract benefits of harmonization. Among the greatest sacrifices countries will have to make to achieve globalization is suppressing cultural influences on business practices. Yet, unlike the U.S. that has been built on a melding of diverse cultures with the effect of diluting them all, many societies today are still very culturally homogeneous and tight-knit. Acceptance of non-local behavioral norms is much resisted.

An example is the anti-Franglaise movement in France as well as the French determination to protect its agricultural interests in its negotiations within the EC–principally, I believe, for cultural as well as political and economic reasons. My impression is that the French people support their system of protected regional "brands" that have been established through centuries of cultivation and refinement of traditional production methods. They believe in the French way of life and will protect it at all costs. Since the traditional ways are not necessarily the most efficient ways, cultural preservation implies economic protection.

Japan is another example. The Japanese Government and the Bureaucracy argue that Japan's manufacturing markets are more open than the U.S. markets because Japan actually has much lower import tariffs. They argue that American business should *just be competitive* and make the necessary long-term commitments to penetrate Japanese markets as Japanese businesses have done to penetrate U.S. markets. Many U.S. businesses that have succeeded in Japan echo this "no whiners" attitude.

However, when challenged about what it takes to be competitive, the Japanese will readily admit that it is more than price and quality, and includes on-time delivery, after-sale service, and long-term relationships. The American people have no sympathy for businesses that whine about price, quality, delivery, or service. The problem seems to be relationships (and certain remaining regulations). The Japanese prefer long-term, stable, predictable relationships to any kind of one-off deal, no matter how economical. Their behavior and preferences are a reflection of their culture of harmonious cooperation and are reinforced by the practice of cross-ownership and business groups (*keiretsu*). In other words, the culture favors established insiders and tends to exclude outsiders.

The U.S. has an abundance of anti-discrimination laws. Thus, we have something of an environment that supports subordinating cultural preferences to efficiency (and equity). Whereas, in more homogeneous cultures, it is almost unthinkable to subordinate culture to anything. It is simply the way things are done and the results are not thought to be discriminatory. Thus, many Japanese business persons are perplexed by our attitude. They never asked that our markets be opened. We opened them because we wanted them open. By implication, theirs would be open if they wanted them open.

Cultural, and therefore international, factors are going to be a substantial part of doing business for a long time to come. The true global village is a long way off. Thus, business graduates must be well acquainted with international business in general and the international dimensions of their specializations.

So, if the demand side is not going to go away, what about the supply side?

FACULTY CULTURE AND THE SUPPLY OF INTERNATIONALIZED PH.D.S

A number of aspects of faculty culture make me pessimistic that internationalization of all Ph.D. programs will come about before the end of my career (in fifteen to twenty years). First, the overall faculty culture exhibits a low opinion of international business research. I have worked and studied at four major doctoral-granting research institutions. On all four campuses, international business has struggled against prevailing faculty attitudes. Some faculty feel that international business is not a separate discipline, but an applications-oriented specialty within the other disciplines. Faculty members who do research in such specialties do so at their own risk, because their colleagues do not rate the specialty journals as highly as main-stream journals in the disciplines. In addition, the quality of international research is often denigrated as largely descriptive of institutional and behavioral differences that merely complicate the practice of business but do not change it in fundamental ways.

Second, since World War II, business disciplines and faculty have been drifting more and more to basic research. Journal editors seem to prefer internal validity of research over its richness of context, including institutional and behavioral context. Thus, in preparing doctoral students for future careers, faculty emphasize research methodology and workmanship over context-oriented subject matter in doctoral seminars.

Finally, as Stopford (in this volume) opines, it is unwise " . . . to conceive of internationalisation [sic] of doctoral training as implying a substitution of work: it is additive." Yet, the agendas of most doctoral programs are perceived as overly full, there is pressure to downsize and streamline them, and there is competition for any shift toward international requirements. The methodology of research has become ever more complex, requiring many years of study before students meet the high standards of workmanship expected today. In addition, many schools have become more customer-driven in response to criticism of MBA programs by employers and national rankings of MBA programs, based in part on student and employer satisfaction. They want an outstanding educator as well as an outstanding scholar when they hire even a rookie faculty recruit. Hence, doctoral programs have of late begun to place greater emphasis on building teaching skill than they have for at least two decades.

In light of the above, I foresee a gloomy outlook for faculty support for a required international component in business doctoral programs. However, I do see some hopeful trends as well. More of our faculty are traveling and teaching overseas. Most of them return with a more worldly view of their disciplines and at least some anecdotal knowledge of the international dimensions of their disciplines. I find such faculty to be more favorably oriented toward international education in general. In addition, several disciplines are becoming more international in focus, for example, marketing, finance, and strategic management. When given encouragement, more faculty (at least at

The University of Texas) are embarking on international research and academic development projects. Encouragement comes in many forms, including prearranged visits to and teaching assignments at partner schools abroad, ready access to participation in international executive education opportunities, and money to develop international courses and conduct international research. Finally, thanks in part to the influence of the AACSB, deans are showing respect for international research and academic development. In some cases, they have let it be known that international activities and expertise will be valued in the merit reviews and promotion decisions affecting all faculty. While these trends are encouraging, the rate of progress in converting the majority of business school faculty is glacial.

CONCLUSION: MAJOR INTERVENTION IS NEEDED

Globalization is not going to preempt the need for internationalization of business education any time soon. Thus, there is an ongoing need to internationalize curricula and a derived demand to internationalize faculty through doctoral education. However, for a variety of reasons, business faculty are unlikely to rally to the cause of internationalizing doctoral education. Thus, I conclude that major intervention is needed.

Faculty are curious about a wide variety of questions within their disciplines. Left without any special incentives, they will do work that interests them and is aligned with the priorities of major journals. If given enough financial support, however, faculty will alter their portfolios of inquiry. I have seen first-hand evidence of this behavior. Auditing is a sub-discipline within accounting. For many years it languished and attracted few distinguished tenure-track faculty from doctoral-granting institutions. It was considered punishment to be assigned to teach auditing. However, in the early 1970s the international accounting firm of Peat Marwick Mitchell, now KPMG Peat Marwick, initiated its Research Opportunities in Auditing Program which funded hundreds of auditing research projects over two decades. The result has been a dramatic increase in the quantity and quality of faculty engaged in auditing research and education. A new journal was founded that now is accorded "A" status at many quality institutions.

Other examples of financial intervention include the Ford Foundation's Doctoral Fellowship program of the 1960s. It attracted many outstanding candidates to business doctoral programs who otherwise might have pursued different careers or different disciplines. It also encouraged the writing of doctoral dissertations that were based on new approaches to business research.

I believe that the incentive effects achieved by the KPMG Peat Marwick Foundation and the Ford Foundation could be achieved in international scholarship by one or more benefactors. The CIBER program (supporting Centers for International Business Education and Research) of the U.S. Department of Education is a step in the right direction. However, the objective of internationalizing the vast majority of business faculty is formidable. More benefactors are needed.

Once a much larger segment of the faculty are engaged, they will come to appreciate and support preparing future faculty to make international teaching and scholarly contributions. Moreover, I do not foresee any other effective force for change short of administrative coercion (which I definitely do not recommend).

REFERENCES

Arpan, Jeffrey S., William R. Folks, Jr., and Chuck C. Y. Kwok. 1993. *Internationalizing Business Education in the 1990s: A Global Survey.* The Academy of International Business.

Stopford, John M., "International Issues as a Context, Not a Discipline." in this volume.

Internationalizing Doctoral Education in Business: Cost-Benefit Considerations

Lyman W. Porter

Introduction

That doctorate-producing business schools around the world, and certainly including those in the United States, should "internationalize" their doctoral programs is hardly arguable. There are simply too many forces and developments all pointing in the same direction that make this a necessity. Therefore, the overarching issue, it seems to me, is not "whether?" but "how?" and "to what extent?" Attempts to implement this objective will not be easy and are likely to encounter a number of formidable obstacles or potential "costs" that will need to be dealt with effectively. The purpose of this position paper is to explore briefly some of these particular issues from a cost-benefit perspective.

First, though, it may be useful to make a few observations about several important situational factors that will affect the consideration of these matters:

The Context for Internationalizing Doctoral Education in Business

The state of the world: Exogenous, world-wide developments are clearly the driving forces that are impelling U.S. business schools to face up to the necessity of internationalizing all of their programs, even that last bastion of resistance to reform, doctoral programs. The rapid explosion of activity in global business and finance, the technological advances that result in virtually instantaneous electronic communication around the world, and the increasing speed and scope of international transportation are just a few of the more obvious factors that constitute the array of irresistible forces. Only in the global political arena (Bosnia, Northern Ireland, parts of the Middle East, etc., come to mind) are advances somewhat slower and more problematical. Even here, however, developments of the past ten years or so, such as the demise of the Cold War and some progress on reducing Arab-Israeli tensions, seem to point to a more universally positive climate for internationalizing any type of activity.

The state of U.S. business school education: In my view, the past few years have seen more changes in American business schools, particularly with respect to their undergraduate and MBA programs, than any time in the past 25-30 years. There are probably many reasons for this, but, again, undoubtedly the most significant are those developments outside of business schools, namely, changes going on in business and how it is conducted. However, there are also endogenous forces within the business school community, such as self-reflective critical reviews of current policies and practices and, in particular, recently adopted major changes in AACSB accreditation standards. These external and internal developments make this an especially propitious time to examine how increased internationalization of business school doctoral programs might be accomplished.

The state of doctoral education within business schools: Of all the areas of business school activities—including bachelor degree programs, MBA programs, teaching, faculty research, and relations with the corporate community—the one area that probably has received the least concerted attention and, not coincidentally, the one that has changed the least during the past several decades, is the education and preparation of doctoral students. Until the most recent major changes that were adopted in 1991, AACSB accreditation Standards never mentioned nor incorporated doctoral education in the overall accreditation process or review. The new (1991) Standards do refer to doctoral programs, but only briefly and in a very general way. However, that small step is significant because, for the first time, a school's basic approach to its doctoral program (if it has one) and where that program fits in in relation to its other degree programs will be examined as part of the total review of the school's activities vis-a-vis its mission. The 1991 Standards thus provide a small wedge for taking a look at what we are doing in this realm of higher education for business. Consequently, while business school doctoral programs have shown relatively little change for many years, the time appears to be ripe for opening up, at least to some extent, the black box of Ph.D. education, including how it can incorporate global components.

BENEFITS AND COSTS

BENEFITS: WHAT COULD BE GAINED?

There are a number of obvious benefits that could be gained if U.S. business schools were to internationalize their approach to doctoral education. It is not necessary to elaborate on those here, but a couple of the most evident advantages might be mentioned: For the schools themselves, it would help them to keep up with "where the action is." If business competition is becoming more global, so is business school competition. By internationalizing their doctoral programs, U.S. schools would be better positioned to meet their worldwide competition in all respects. For U.S. doctoral students in business, especially those born and raised in this country, the primary advantage would be that they would be better prepared for coping with the teaching and research challenges of the 21st century. Greater internationalization of their doctoral programs would help them gain a more global perspective and cosmopolitan orientation and simultaneously help reduce any tendencies toward ethnocentrism.

There are also some less obvious and more subtle benefits that might be gained if U.S. business schools were to make internationalization of doctoral programs a higher priority. One is that such an attempt might help schools more clearly define their mission and demonstrate improved implementation of it. For those schools claiming a strong global emphasis in their mission, internationalizing their Ph.D. programs would reinforce their other efforts, such as MBA and undergraduate curriculum changes, in this direction. A second indirect benefit could be a strengthening of cross-functional approaches to courses and research activities. Since international business problems seldom come packaged in a single functional area, a focus on internationalizing a school's doctoral programs would almost certainly require more cross-disciplinary efforts by the faculty. Another less directly-intended advantage that a school might gain by this type of change in doctoral education would be stronger links with other campus units that could contribute to the revised programs. Language departments and area studies units come to mind as possibilities. Anything that provides additional bonds of the business school to the larger campus would seem to be a plus.

COSTS: WHAT COULD BE LOST?

Those business school faculty members who support the internationalization of doctoral programs are prone to view the issue only in terms of its benefits, such as those described above and others. However, it is also extremely important to look at potential costs, obstacles and problems. Many of these, in my opinion, involve very legitimate concerns and should not be minimized or dismissed out of hand. A few of the more consequential are the following.

The Add-On Problem—That is, this (internationalization) plus everything else. If a doctoral program is going to insist that some or all of its students demonstrate some form of internationalization competence, what gets dropped? Or, is the new competence simply to be added on to what is already there in the program? If it is the former, and assuming that all the elements of the current program are essential, then something is clearly going to be lost. If it is the latter, which is probably more likely, then there will be additional time required for completion of the degree, which means that several different kinds of increased costs will be incurred.

The Specialist/Generalist Dilemma—The doctoral degree, at least the research-oriented Ph.D. degree, is inherently a specialist degree. Unless one were to conceive of the doctorate as simply an advanced (generalist) MBA degree, then it is imperative that specialized knowledge be obtained at the Ph.D. level. Therefore, would the added requirement of internationalization competence in any way interfere with acquiring the necessary specialization competence? This issue is obviously related to the "add-on" problem mentioned above, but here the question is more one of divided attention rather than one of added time *per se*. There is, obviously, no inherent reason why an internationalization requirement would interact negatively with a specialization requirement. Rather, the potential problem is that the greater the extent that internationalization competence forms part of the overall requirements for the granting of the degree, the more likely it is that a student will pass up opportunities to gain extra cutting-edge specialization competence. That is, some of the latter opportunities may be traded-off in order to fulfill the former requirement. The outcome, at least in some instances, may be the gain of a "mushy generalist" at the loss of a razor-sharp specialist.

Finding Qualified Faculty—If internationalization were to be made a doctoral program requirement, finding qualified faculty to instruct doctoral students in this regard would not be an issue ten or twenty years from now. The problem is one of getting from here (now) to there (then). If a magic wand were to be waved and all U.S. business school doctoral programs were to be internationalized starting next year, would well-qualified faculty resources be available to implement this new requirement? The answer is undoubtedly "yes" for some schools and definitely "no" for others. Assuming that there are at least some (probably many) schools in the latter category, then the issue is how such a requirement could be effectively implemented in the near term.

Faculty Resistance—Not all (and perhaps only a minority) of current faculty in business schools are going to be wildly enthusiastic about revising doctoral programs to include an internationalization requirement. Some faculty members are certainly going to see it as a move that will weaken doctoral education rather than strengthen it (for some of the reasons outlined above). Thus, if such a requirement were to be put into effect rapidly and/or on a total scale, it is reasonably predictable that there would be a fair amount of faculty resistance or, at best, reluctance. Overcoming such resistance or foot-dragging reluctance represents a potential cost that should be taken into account up front and directly.

Coping with the Potential Costs—There are no easy or simple solutions for dealing with the types of costs listed above. My own view is that if business school doctoral programs are to be internationalized, the preferred approach should be one of "targeting." That is, it is my belief that, at least initially, not all schools offering doctoral programs should instantly internationalize those programs, not all doctoral students within a school's program should be required to meet the same level of "internationalization competence," and not all faculty instructing in doctoral programs must be "internationalized" to the same extent. This stance is probably heresy to those who believe that the need to internationalize doctoral programs is so great and so urgent that it must be done quickly and on a near universal basis. However, I do not think that is either desirable or feasible. I would much rather see some schools take the lead on internationalizing their Ph.D. programs and show other schools how this can be done and what the positive effects are. Prominent and successful examples, I contend, will have more impact than any sort of bludgeoning requirements. Thus, for the immediate future I favor targeting efforts rather than a blanket approach as a way to maximize benefits and minimize costs.

Conclusions

It seems to me to be clear that doctoral-granting business schools need to be involved in "consciousness-raising" about the extent to which their doctoral programs should be internationalized. I am convinced that not enough attention has been given to this issue up to now and it is, therefore, time to do so. Comprehensive schools that include doctoral-level along with master's-level and (in some cases) undergraduate education cannot afford to ignore where they stand on this issue, especially since they are turning out many, if not most, of the future educators of business school students.

A second need is for doctoral-granting schools that do intend to include a global or international emphasis as a major part of their overall educational objectives to make sure that their doctoral programs are consistent with the stated mission. It would not seem appropriate for programs at one level (e.g., master's) to support the mission and at another level (i.e., doctoral) to be indifferent to it.

Finally, any attempts to internationalize doctoral business programs will require very skillful efforts and a great deal of care in implementation. The goal is virtuous and one that is easy to grasp, but is virtually certain that implementation will provide a perfect illustration of the adage: "The devil is in the details."

III. Institutional Arrangements to Enhance Faculty Competence and Involvement

INTRODUCTION

S. Tamer Cavusgil

The ability to internationalize a doctoral program in business is a function of university rules and regulations, the pro-active stance of the dean, the foresight and empowerment of individual program directors, the commitment of faculty, and the interests of students. Key to institutional supports are the opinions and attitudes of the faculty. Are there appropriate incentives for faculty to become engaged in international research and teaching? In this section, this and many related questions are explored.

Edwin Miller advocates a strong partnership and/or close cooperation between administration and faculty. Faculty should develop individual international professional development plans and administration should provide support for the implementation of these plans. Administrators must provide appropriate incentives and rewards to stimulate and entice faculty to expand their discipline-based limits to incorporate the international body of literature into their research and teaching, and to consider conducting international and/or cross-cultural research in business. In addition, both administration and faculty must develop criteria for judging international competence in business and assist doctoral students in developing appropriate pedagogical practices not only to include international topics, but also to address the cultural learning needs of international students.

Ben Kedia addresses the deficiencies in Ph.D. education in his presentation of survey research findings on the international capabilities of faculty. He challenges faculty to reconsider their narrow specializations in light of the cognitive, affective and behavioral change needs students must meet in order to achieve pedagogical excellence. He constructs a learning theory model that both faculty and students must take into account in order to internationalize doctoral programs.

John Daniels puts a practical face on these models by outlining the thrusts the CIBER and Indiana University have implemented to assure that each Ph.D. student in business is equipped upon graduation to be able to teach his/her courses from an international perspective.

Readers of this section will gain a distinct appreciation for the key role faculty play in internationalization and for the support system, especially incentives, that administrators must provide to faciltate the changes needed in doctoral programs.

HELPFUL INSTITUTIONAL ARRANGEMENTS FOR INTERNATIONALIZING DOCTORAL EDUCATION IN BUSINESS ADMINISTRATION

Edwin L. Miller

INTRODUCTION

It is well known that a major sea change is occurring within American colleges and schools of business administration, and educational leaders are becoming aware of their responsibility to prepare students to live and work in a world that is rapidly becoming interdependent and multicultural. This major paradigm shift in business education is likely to produce the following educational and administrative consequences: (1) integration of an international perspective into the academic programs at the undergraduate, graduate and doctoral levels that will result in students' expanded educational perspectives; (2) development of criteria for judging which issues will be incorporated into the academic programs; (3) development of opportunities that will enhance the international competence of the faculty; (4) establishment of outreach programs that will integrate an international perspective into the institution's culture and day-to-day life; and (5) development of programs of research that will be grounded in the international arena.

The movement from a domestic to a global perspective, the demise of communism, the spread of capitalism, the surge in cross-border travel, and the explosion of electronic communications have combined to shape a world that is becoming borderless in its orientation. These forces are creating an impact on most of the nation's political, social and economic institutions including higher education. If America is to compete successfully in the global marketplace, higher education will be challenged to enter a "game of educational catch-up." The process for transforming academic and research programs places heavy demands upon faculty and administrators. However, there will be opportunities and rewards to be gained by participating in this critical undertaking.

It is fashionable for senior administrators in business schools to describe their institutions, their academic programs, and their faculties as being international in perspective and their graduates as possessing an international or global orientation. As attractive, appealing and important as these attributes are, one must recognize that internationalization and its consequences are frequently misunderstood and incorrectly applied. The process of internationalizing an academic program is complex, relative, and institution specific because internationalization and the resulting international perspective of students, faculty and administration will vary by institution and time. For example, critical variables in the internationalization equation include the following: (1) the relevance of internationally oriented materials for specific academic or functional areas; (2) the faculty's commitment and motivation to incorporate an international perspective into their teaching and research agenda; (3) the skill and ability of administrators to manage the internationalization process; and (4) the dynamic character of the internationalization process and the definition of international or global competence.

The means by which a business school, its faculty and administration go about developing and implementing a plan for internationalizing themselves, the curriculum, the research enterprise, the student body and the institution's culture is a complex management process. For the faculty member or administrator responsible for directing the process, it will require skill in managing internal politics, identifying administrative and faculty leadership, obtaining faculty commitment and participation, and allocating financial resources. These tasks represent some of the most critical challenges and potential problems confronting even the most astute administrators and faculty members. Simultaneously, they will have to cope with the task of: (1) developing a definition of internationalization and an overall strategy which will provide the vision and foundation required to successfully integrate an international perspective in the teaching and research missions and the administrative responsibilities of the institution; and (2) designing a plan for managing the change process for successful incorporation of an international perspective throughout the school and most certainly the doctoral program. Accomplishment of this twofold task will require administrators and faculty members to understand the dynamics of the change process and the exercise of skill and professional confidence to manage this major shift in American business schools.

SOME PRELIMINARY THOUGHTS ON INTERNATIONALIZING DOCTORAL
EDUCATION

Where does the administrative and faculty leadership begin if it believes that an international dimension should be integrated into its doctoral program? At the outset, let me say that an institution's commitment to internationalize the faculty and curriculum cannot be limited to a specific degree program or faculty group. The commitment is all-inclusive and it impacts faculty development, each of the academic programs, the nature of the research enterprise and the institution's environment. Rose (in this volume) divides the internationalization of business Ph.D. programs into micro and macro categories. The micro category includes such educational activities as individual classes, courses and seminars, and development opportunities for faculty and students. The macro category highlights the range of activities that stress the need to internationalize departments, colleges, and other academic units within a college or university. It is a mistake to assume that a mandate to incorporate an international perspective in doctoral education will result in a uniform approach to program structure, research direction, and faculty development across departments or institutions.

Business schools and their leadership may be disappointed if they fail to consider the reasons for incorporating an international perspective, the resources that will be required, and the positive as well as negative consequences associated with such an endeavor. The institution will be courting failure if it quickly moves to adopt a currently popular model and means for developing and implementing an international initiative simply because other business schools or colleges are marketing their doctoral programs as international in orientation and their graduates as internationally or globally competent. "Keeping up with the Joneses" is not justification for adopting an internationalization program because the school or college may be starting a program "for all the wrong reasons."

Business schools have different missions, different goals, different resources, different constituencies, and different perceptions about the intellectual and professional measures of internationalization to be achieved in their academic and research programs. It is critical for an institution's faculty and administratiion to devote time to the serious task of defining internationalization in terms of the institution's mission, resources, and constituencies, and, consequently, what its internationalization program will realistically be able to accomplish in the short and long terms. For example, internationalization of the academic and research programs at one of the nation's leading research business schools, which possesses significant financial and human resources, will be different than at a business school or college, supported by very limited financial and human resources, and whose mission is to offer an excellent undergraduate educational program. The overriding institutional requirements are clearly (1) that the institution do the very best it can with the resources that it is able to devote to the internationalization process, and (2) that the faculty and administration commit themselves to the goal of *continuous* and *incremental* gains as it designs and implements its internationalization program.

APPROACHES TO THE INTERNATIONALIZATION PROCESS

There are at least three models or approaches to the internationalization process that come to mind, and it might be helpful to briefly discuss each one. First, internationalization can be viewed as nothing more than an expression of the faculty and administration to internationalize themselves and the doctoral program. From this perspective, internationalization is defined in terms of the faculty and administration's statement reflecting their desire to prepare doctoral students to live, teach and engage in research in a world that is becoming interdependent and multicultural. For some faculty members and administrators it will be enough to have expressed their intent to internationalize the faculty, the curriculum, and the institution's culture. Nothing more will be expected or done to implement their expressed intent.

Second, internationalization is a process for designing a plan that will be useful for: (1) developing internationally oriented materials for all appropriate courses in the doctoral program; (2) developing the professional competence of the faculty to design high quality internationally oriented research and for addressing international issues wherever and whenever they are appropriate in the academic program; (3) recruiting a doctoral student-body that possesses international experiences or wants to engage in internationally oriented research; and (4) acquiring and allocating funds that will be necessary to accomplish the above set of activities.

Third, internationalization can be defined as the behavior, the perspective and the knowledge that a Ph. D. graduate will possess as a consequence of successful completion of his or her doctoral program. To paraphase the statement that today's business leaders must "think globally, act locally," the Ph.D. graduate is expected to be sensitive to the dynamics of international business and how they affect the graduate's field of expertise while simultaneously grasping the interaction between the dynamics of international business, management practice, and functional area theory. It is unacceptable for doctoral programs to graduate students who are ignorant of the international dimensions associated with their professional fields of expertise. The goal will be to produce graduates from a doctoral program who are judged to be globally or regionally competent by their faculty, by their students, by themselves, by prospective collegiate employers, and by their peers.

FACULTY AND ADMINISTRATIVE COMMITMENT TO INTERNATIONALIZATION

As a corollary to the discussion and resolution by the faculty and administration concerning what international means within the school or college context, it is essential that the faculty and administration publicly commit to the overarching goal of incorporating an international dimension throughout the institution's teaching and research programs and culture. Without such an endorsement there is only a small probability of successfully achieving the internationalization goal. Flowing from this public expression of intent to incorporate an international perspective into the doctoral program, it will be critical for the faculty to recognize the importance of developing international content that will permeate their teaching and research as well as the framework for viewing issues and problems associated with their respective fields of expertise. Simultaneously, the institution's administration must be prepared to dedicate multiple forms of financial resources to support the internationalization process because it is abundantly clear that internationalization will be a costly undertaking and that the goal of internationalization will be dynamic in its character. The faculty and administration must strive to develop a clear understanding of what will be entailed in the internationalization process including the magnitude of the resources being committed, the trade-off between programs and activities that will be supported, and the expected level of faculty participation. Furthermore, there must be realistic expectations about the likelihood of ever internationalizing the faculty and curriculum. These are necessary but not sufficient conditions for internationalization because in the final analysis, it will be the commitment and participation of the faculty and administration that will be the determinants of success.

Internationalization of doctoral education is much more than a quick fix and then on to the next administrative and educational problem confronting an institution's faculty and administration. The faculty and administration's commitment to incorporate an international perspective throughout its doctoral program will not guarantee immediate and noticeable content changes in the institution's teaching and research programs. One will be disappointed if immediate results are expected because it will take time to reallocate resources, gain faculty involvement and participation, reorient faculty recruitment efforts, design faculty development programs, restructure the doctoral program, and include internationally related materials in appropriate doctoral level courses. There are some activities that can be quickly and easily undertaken, and they will result in noticeable consequences in the short term. Other actions and activities will require constant attention over a longer period of time, and it may take several years before there will be a noticeable impact on the doctoral program and the international competence of the students.

THE CALCULUS OF INTERNATIONALIZATION OF DOCTORAL EDUCATION

What are some of the key variables that must be included in an institution's plan for internationalizing its doctoral program? Although it may seem obvious to the reader, I would like to stress that it will be administrators and faculty members who will develop and carry out the program for internationalizing doctoral education. Internationalization of doctoral education can be considered to be a management problem and successfully coping with the politics of change will represent an assignment of considerable importance. For additional insight into this management problem, the reader is encouraged to examine several other articles appearing in this publication: Toyne (1994) explores the politics of change; Daniels (1994) reports on the approach and his experiences while leading the program to internationalize Indiana University's doctoral education; and from the perspective of a senior academic administrator, Schmotter (1994) offers some important guidelines for members of the dean's office or faculty members responsible for guiding an institution's internationalization program.

In the remainder of this paper the actions and behavior of two major academic and administrative constituent bodies will be highlighted: (1) senior level administrators; and (2) faculty groups and their members. For purposes of discussion each of the institutional arrangements will be classified on a short and long term basis of impact. The short term will be up to two years in length, and the long term will range from two to four years.

Senior Level Administrators—Internationalization of the faculty and its teaching and research programs will require aggressive action and skilled leadership from the dean's office including the dean and his or her senior level administrators. It is absolutely critical to the internationalization process that the dean and his or her staff help to establish and interpret the international vision of the institution, participate in faculty personnel decisions, and allocate scarce resources to operationalize the spirit of the goal that has been articulated. The dean occupies a boundary-spanning position between the business school and the multiple external constituencies that share some relationship with the institution. Given the nature of their positions, the dean and the senior administrative staff will play pivotal roles in the internationalization process because of their public expressions of support for internationalization of the teaching and research programs and their commitment to the internationalization of doctoral education. The allocation of financial resources to internationalize the doctoral program will be a clear example of the institution's commitment to internationalization of the academic programs, especially doctoral education. It is the dean who will provide the intellectual leadership in the development and interpretation of the vision of internationalization as it relates to the institution and its academic and research direction. It is the dean who will help to shape the mission statement. It is the dean who will challenge the faculty to develop their respective international competencies. It is the dean who will help to appoint members to faculty committees and shape the committees' charges. It is the dean who will allocate resources to support committee recommendations and faculty appointments.

What are some of the specific actions that a dean, as the administrative leader, may undertake in order to guide an institution and its doctoral program toward internationalization? Faculty development remains the key to the internationalization of a school, its academic programs, and its research enterprise. The most fundamental and perhaps the most difficult action is that of creating conditions in such a way as to enable faculty members to achieve their professional goals best by directing their efforts toward expanding their professional competence. For the individual faculty member as well as for the faculty as a whole, the anticipated outcome will be a better grasp of the international dimensions of their field or fields. It will be necessary to offer the faculty member a wide array of rewards as he or she strives to acquire the professional competency and confidence to incorporate an international dimension in the doctoral level courses and the initiation of internationally oriented research projects. As a consequence, doctoral students will come to have an expanded perspective of their field of expertise and an appreciation for the international ramifications for research, theory development, and management practice.

What if there is a weak dean in terms of power and influence vis-a-vis the faculty, or who is uncertain about the merits of incorporating an international dimension throughout the academic program? It is difficult to imagine that a dean would be insensitive or indifferent to the need for incorporating an international element into the curriculum because of the pressures coming from the business community, the AACSB, the business media, the faculty, the academic community at large, and the student body. If such a situation were to exist, strong faculty leadership would be required to identify ways for winning a dean's support for the internationalization efforts. One wants to avoid the situation in which the dean becomes an obstructionist in terms of the internationalization efforts, and that may require serious thinking about strategies for including the dean in any international program that is about to be launched. In some measure, this situation becomes an internal political problem, and the Organizational Behavior literature and knowledge focusing on overcoming resistance to change, managing the change process, faculty empowerment, and team building are relevant to this lack of administrative leadership support.

Financial Incentives—Money is the most commonly available and powerful tool that a dean has to influence a faculty member's behavior and international expertise. Before any funds are allocated to support an institution's internationalization program, especially the doctoral program, there needs to be a thoughtful discussion about internationalization. The following are examples of questions that the faculty and administration will address: (1) How international should the faculty be? (2) What functional areas in the doctoral program should be emphasized? (3) What does internationalization have to do with the intellectual direction and content of doctoral education? These are far-reaching questions, but they will help focus in yet another way the school's intention to internationalize itself. Once this discussion has been completed the dean will be in a much stronger position to utilize monetary rewards to influence faculty behavior: in the short and long term.

In the *short term*, monetary resources can be used to affect faculty behavior and course content in the following ways. (1) Financial support can be provided to those faculty members who want to become engaged in a program to enhance their professional competency in the international arena. Participation in professional development activities designed to expand the faculty member's competence to understand how internationally oriented issues affect his or her field of research and teaching is an obvious first example. There are several excellent internationally oriented summer programs designed to expose faculty members to the international dimensions of his or her field of expertise, and they represent a relatively painless way to acquire an exposure to international. Prior to the faculty member's participation in such a program, the faculty member and the institution should agree that upon his or her return, they have the assignment of becoming a change agent for internationalizing course content or program design within their respective departments. (2) Faculty release time to audit relevant internationally oriented courses that will expand the faculty member's professional competency is another avenue to be explored. For example, the faculty can be encouraged to enroll in internationally oriented courses that will expand their perspective as they relate to their area of specialization. From another direction, faculty members can be encouraged to participate in selected executive education courses in which there is a significant proportion of the material that is international in content or a large number of the participants who come from abroad. The exposure to new ideas, new ways of looking at a field or its problems and sharing ideas with others promises intellectual growth and development.

From the institution's perspective, summer development programs and release time arrangements are among some of the more effective and efficient means for producing impact in the short term. It is expected that the faculty member will have expanded his or her perspective, acquired the professional confidence to incorporate internationally oriented materials into those doctoral seminars where it is appropriate and provide the faculty member with the foundation for critically judging the contribution of internationally grounded research as it pertains to his or her field.

In the *long term*, financial resources can be allotted in such a way as to affect faculty recruiting, faculty personnel related decisions, and enrichment of the institution's overall environment. The dean may influence faculty recruiting in at least two ways. The first is by requiring faculty groups to seek out and hire faculty candidates who have an international orientation associated with their functional areas of expertise. The second is by adding new positions whose job requirements include international expertise. These may be considered to be opportunities for faculty groups to expand in size, breadth of course offerings and sources for infusion of an international expertise throughout the courses. Furthermore, these positions come at little or no cost to the faculty groups or groups.

Merit increases, release time, and summer support represent some of the ways that a dean can reward those faculty members who are conscientiously and successfully striving to incorporate an international dimension into their sphere of professional expertise. Encouragement of faculty to develop internationally oriented research projects and to publish the results of those projects in mainline academic or international journals is a relatively effective way for the dean to use the institution's financial resources and redirect the research orientation of the faculty.

Incorporating a requirement of international competence and activity as a criterion for promotion of tenure track faculty represents an important and effective way to introduce an international orientation into the fabric of the faculty, and ultimately the institution's overall environment. By this means, the dean will play an important role in helping to move the traditional structure and promotion criteria of the faculty. However, this administrative process will require the dean to possess highly developed political and leadership skills because there will likely be faculty uncertainty and resistance.

Resources can be directed toward doctoral student recruitment, support of student or faculty-initiated internationally oriented research, and assistance for international business units such as the federally funded Centers for International Business Education. Building cooperative relationships with other units of the university by means of joint appointments for faculty members, and limited financial contributions to critical but under-enrolled internationally relevant doctoral level courses in other units of the university represent still other ways to affect doctoral programs in business administration.

The Skillful Use of Personnel Decisions—In the *short term*, perhaps one of the most effective means to affect doctoral education is by the timely and skillful use of joint appointments with faculty members from other units of the university. Drawing upon the expertise and perspectives of faculty members whose contributions to the academic or research programs of the business school or college represents a relatively easy way to enrich the international capacity of the institution. Such appointments could include teaching a course or courses throughout an academic year, or by offering membership in an academic department within the school.

Business school faculty who possess an international expertise to teach cross-functional doctoral seminars will positively affect doctoral programs. When courses are team taught, the consequences will be a manifestation of the institution's desire to internationalize doctoral education, cross-pollinate various academic areas and stimulate faculty development. Several courses that can be team-taught, cross-listed or jointly offered include business policy, corporate strategy and organization theory, organizational behavior and human resource management. Rather than focusing on specific courses, it is much more valuable to consider functional areas that are candidates for collaboration. These include corporate strategy, finance, marketing, and organizational behavior. Encouraging representatives from these functional areas to begin exploring the international content overlap between their functional specialities and the possibility of designing cross-functional courses to include an international dimension will result in the enhancement of international exposure and understanding by students and faculty members. Most seductive to the dean and the administration will be the relatively minimal cost outlay. The overall result will be a clear example that the institution is serious about internationalization, and it is prepared to take rapid, decisive action.

A long term consequence of cross-functional seminars is the erosion of barriers that separate departments or functional areas on the basis of specialty. Team teaching or jointly offered doctoral seminars help to identify those areas where there are common interests for study and research. There are numerous examples of subject matter overlap and different models and perspectives for addressing similar issues, and when these are highlighted in joint seminars the results will be a much more integrated perspective and approach to one's field of study and the development of doctoral theses that reflect the expanded orientation of the student and faculty members. The seminar becomes the lever that enhances the quality of research and teaching in both functional areas, and it begins an active and vibrant interchange between faculty groups. An unexpected benefit will be the influence that doctoral students will have upon internationalizing the institution's doctoral program. Enrollment in cross-listed seminars, development of cross-functional term papers, framing of internationally oriented theses topics and inclusion of thesis members from disparate functional groups are examples of how students may be an integral variable in the internationalization of doctoral education. The doctoral students may lead the faculty in such matters.

In the *long term*, such personnel decisions as promotion, tenure, and merit pay increases can represent another sphere in which the dean can exert some modicum of influence on the internationalization of the doctoral program. The dean, as the senior administrator and hopefully one of the institution's influence leaders, can help to shape the general criteria for promotion, tenure, and merit pay increases by recommending that internationally oriented activities be factored into the overall evaluation of each faculty member. Internationally oriented research projects, the publication of articles that address international or comparative management issues, the incorporation of international content in doctoral seminars, the supervision of doctoral theses containing an international contribution, and participation in scholarly or corporate related activities are examples of various activities that can and will have a long term impact on the international environment within a business school or college.

A clearly *long term* consequence, will be the recruitment of business school faculty members who possess a regional or international perspective. A highly focused recruiting program will be a powerful tool for redirecting a curriculum, reshaping course content, and a clear indicator of support of an international commitment throughout the institution. Selecting new faculty members who have a regional expertise or a general interest in international combined with their functional competence has proven to be a critical tool in the internationalization of doctoral level courses, the overall internationalization of the business school, and the development of business school strategies for reaching out to other parts of the university, the business community, and peers in other academic institutions.

These are just some of the helpful ways for the dean and the administration to influence the internationalization of doctoral education. Obviously, there are other techniques and practices available, but these stand out as some of the more powerful means to be found at the dean's level. It must be stressed that internationalization is a joint venture requiring the cooperation between the senior level administrators and the faculty of a business school or college. The administration cannot do it alone, and in most instances it will be difficult for the faculty to accomplish the task without administration support.

THE FACULTY GROUP AND ITS MEMBERS

Assessment of International Competence—International or global competence represents an important starting point for any comprehensive and viable plan for faculty development and involvement in internationalizing its doctoral program. It will be administratively and academically important if the faculty can agree upon the meaning and measurement of global competence in terms of faculty expertise, course content, student knowledge and acquired skill base. If a faculty agrees upon the need to incorporate an international dimension in their doctoral level courses, what level of international competence should the faculty member possess, and should each faculty member develop some measure of competence? At the very least, there are two criteria of international competence. First the faculty member will have an understanding and appreciation of the dynamic commercial, political and social interrelationships between the U.S. economy and the rest of the world, and a grasp of what international business is and how U.S. firms compete in the global market place. Second, the faculty member will be expected to have acquired an understanding of relevant international business theory and current international business practices as they relate to his or her area of professional expertise. These are important and meaningful criteria, and they represent the basis for a faculty development program.

In a similar manner, each course that is considered to be a candidate for incorporating an international perspective must be evaluated in terms of its learning objectives, the amount of international material to be included in the course, and the measures that will be employed to judge the knowledge acquisition. Finally the faculty must seriously examine its expectations concerning the level of knowledge that must be acquired by the student by the time that she or he has completed their doctoral program.

Faculty Development: The Master Key—Faculty development is the ultimate key to the internationalization of doctoral education, faculty and student research projects, and the overall orientation and commitment to the institution's international outreach. It is the faculty member as teacher and scholar who will introduce his or her doctoral students to the international dimensions of the field and specialty within that field. The intellectual and administrative challenge becomes that of building competence in a faculty who may, at the outset, be uncertain about extending itself to include new perspectives, new bodies of knowledge, and new demands on an already overly extended set of job requirements and job demands. There are two caveats that should be highlighted. First, it is clear that an international dimension is not appropriate for all functional areas included in the academic program. For those functional areas where internationalization is inappropriate, steps to internationalize the course content will be perceived as contrived and irrelevant. Second, some faculty members will feel threatened by the thought of incorporating an international dimension into their professional competence; others will resist all efforts to embark on any plan for globalization of doctoral level courses or research; and another segment will eagerly participate in the school's internationalization and globalization program.

What are some of the possible practices for nurturing faculty development? At the outset, it is important to recognize that development programs will cost money, and it will be the dean's assignment to locate ways to fund this critical human resource activity. For that group of faculty who are eager to participate in the school's internationalization and globalization program, involvement will be relatively easy and participation will be cost efficient. The challenge of overcoming faculty resistance among those faculty members who are at best neutral to any program designed to develop their international competence represents a much more complex challenge.

How might one go about coping with such a challenge? A necessary first step will be to try and understand why the faculty are resistant. In discussions with them, it will be important to communicate that the intellectual task of understanding the international dimensions of their respective fields of expertise is not to be equated with the challenge of earning a Ph.D. degree in international business. One can turn to the resistance to change literature and the strategies and techniques offered by scholars and management practitioners, and the organizational behavior faculty members aware of this literature will be able to provide vital help to the leader of the internationalization program.

The design and implementation of activities that will remove the threat of faculty failure or embarassment will play an important role in overcoming resistance to change. What are some of the techniques and skills that a dean can use to overcome the resistance exhibited by faculty members? Several of the better understood and implemented strategies include: (1) faculty involvement in a task-force whose goal is to identify approaches and techniques to internationalize courses; (2) encouragement and financial support of selected faculty members to accompany internationally experienced faculty colleagues on some of their overseas trips; (3) nomination and financial support of specific faculty members to join international trade missions sponsored by state or related trade and professional groups; (4) development and financial support of faculty internships with corporations engaged in international business; and (5) encouragement of faculty members to apply for release time to acquire international expertise.

Faculty development will have short and long term consequences for the institution's internationalization program and its direct impact on the doctoral program. Faculty development represents a two-way street that requires continuous reevaluation and upgrading. Developing faculty skills and competence will be an ongoing activity covering the career span of the faculty member, and it is anticipated that one's professional competence will grow throughout a career. However, returning to the two-way street example, on one side of the street each faculty member will be responsible for designing a plan for his or her professional development. That personalized development plan will be faculty member specific, and it will reflect one's professional capabilities and interests in terms of teaching, research, and community involvement. The faculty member will then be responsible for working the plan in order to achieve the objectives that he or she established. On the other side of the street, it will be the school or college, generally reflected by the dean, that will seek to develop a supportive environment that will enable the faculty member to capitalize upon those opportunities.

International Competence of Doctoral Graduates: The Criteria—What is it that the faculty expects their students to have mastered by the time they have graduated? If the faculty believes that international business and global competition are relevant to their specific fields of study then such topics will enter into the composition of the doctoral program. Drawing upon Jeff Apran's (1994) discussion of global competence it seems valuable to identify and highlight the following set of criteria. For example, a faculty group may require its doctoral students to have an appreciation of how one's national economy and its people are connected to the rest of the world. This may be sufficient and nothing more will be required. Such a criterion can be met by being familiar with the *Wall Street Journal* or the *Economist* and their internationally oriented articles. At a more advanced level, the criterion will be somewhat more demanding and complex. The student will be expected to have "a grasp of the technical dimensions and vital links between one's economy and its people and the rest of the world, what causes international business, how international business affects domestic business economic growth and the standards of living." At the most advanced level, the doctoral student will be expected to be thoroughly grounded in the body of knowledge in his or her field, have a firm grasp of the technical dimensions of his or her field of study as it relates to international business, and a grasp of how cul-

ture affects the management process. That is, the student will be expected to
be able to demonstrate a possession and application of specific skills and
techniques about foreign markets and the ability to apply this knowledge
and skill base in their doctoral research. In this publication several of the
authors have highlighted these complex issues. Kedia and Toyne (both in
this volume) have contributed excellent papers which address the problem of
defining and measuring global competency. Duhan (in this volume) provides
some very insightful observations about the task of preparing doctoral students to become tomorrow's professors of business administration.

From a slightly different perspective, a faculty may consider the pace of
acquiring international competency to be measured throughout the tenure
of the doctoral student's enrollment in the program. Acquisition of international competence may range along the continuum from the short through
the mid to the long term. For example, developing an appreciation of how
one's national economy is connected to the rest of the world can be acquired
in the *short term*, and such a level may be quite appropriate for certain functional areas or at certain stages in one's doctoral program. It is probably to be
expected that doctoral students will possess such an understanding when
they are admitted to the program, and their doctoral program of study will
build upon this basic foundation.

In the *mid term*, doctoral students will be expected to have acquired a
grasp of the vital links between one's economy and the rest of the world,
including an understanding of what international business is and how it
works. The acquisition of such a knowledge base will challenge the faculty as
well as the student to moderate the disciplinary pressure to narrow one's
intellectual perspective to a functional area and a specialization within that
field and exclude international and global forces affecting the field. The
problem becomes that of developing a doctoral program that stresses depth
in a common body of knowledge while integrating international content
into it.

In the *long term*, doctoral students in specific functional areas will be
expected to have acquired the technical skills and understanding that will
enable them to engage in high quality research that can be internationally
oriented and contribute to the developing body of knowledge. Such expertise is apt to be inappropriate for certain functional fields and for certain students. However, decisions concerning the level of competence should be
individually specific and not left to chance.

Preparing the Doctoral Student: The Role of Teacher—Today's doctoral students in business administration will be entering a job market significantly different from that of their faculty members and doctoral advisors. Porter and McKibbin, in *Management Education and Development: Drift or Thrust Into the 21st Century*, document the changing environment for business education and educators who will be providing that education. One of the major educational imperatives is that of preparing students who will be joining firms competing in the global marketplace, and these graduates will require the very best business education that can be provided them. Today's doctoral students will be bearing a heavy responsibility for educating this cadre of future managers, and doctoral programs in business administration have a pivotal role to play in the preparation of tomorrow's educators. Porter, in this volume, provides an interesting perspective to the internationalization process when he questions the costs and benefits associated with different orientations of doctoral programs. Specifically, he addresses the relationship between an institution's mission and goal and the direction of its doctoral program. He cautions that before an institution embarks on a doctoral program or the restructure of its doctoral progam serious thought should be given to its educational mission and the cost and benefit of internationalizing the structure and content of all of its academic programs.

Throughout this manuscript I have been emphasizing the centrality of scholarship in doctoral education, and that is as it should be. However, attention must be devoted to the role of teaching and the means whereby the doctoral student acquires some measure of competency as a teacher and a communicator of knowledge. This means more than a course on pedagogy. It will require doctoral students to develop a broadened perspective of their functional fields to include an international perspective relevant to the existing body of knowledge and for their development as a teacher and scholar.

The education of doctoral students to be teachers represents a joint venture between the administration, the faculty, and the students themselves— the administration to provide the financial resources to underwrite seminars, the faculty to develop educational and research experiences that will provide the environment for doctoral students to broaden their functional orientations, and doctoral students to consider how international business and management affect their functional area of expertise and bring that perspective into the classroom. The consequences of this joint venture will probably begin to appear as early as a year or two after its initiation.

Where does one begin? Faculty members leading doctoral seminars may want to devote some time during the seminar to the relevance and implications of international business and management to the core content of the seminar. Integration of an international dimension into the appropriate functional areas will not occur by osmosis or noble thoughts. The faculty must devote time and serious discussion to the means for integrating international issues and transmitting that knowledge to students wanting to have careers in business administration.

From a more practical dimension, doctoral students will need to gain teaching experience, including course development. Perhaps as a first step, doctoral students may be required to develop a course outline for the beginning course in their functional field, and they will be expected to include an international dimension in the outline. The next step would be to teach the course. The consequences would be the acquisition of pedagogical skills and a better understanding of how internationally oriented topics affect the core content of a functional area.

CONCLUSION

It is time for the business school faculties to reexamine the goal, structure and substance of doctoral education. The "winds of change are blowing," and doctoral programs will be coming under closer scrutiny in terms of their goals and the means for achieving those ends. We as academics and administrators will be well advised to devote valuable time and resources to respond to the challenges facing business schools, the evolving role of teacher and scholar, and the academic preparation that will be necessary to prepare the next generation of academics.

I have attempted to highlight the necessity for close cooperation between the administration and the faculty and some helpful institutional actions for operationalizing that cooperation. Without such commitment and cooperation, we as educators will be shirking our responsibility for adequately preparing the next generation of professors to teach in business schools and colleges, and educating those business students who will be joining firms competing in the global marketplace. We are faced with a twofold problem: upgrading the international business knowledge and competency of today's business school faculties and educating today's doctoral students to become tomorrow's teachers and scholars. As academics, we are in the knowledge business, and intellectual excellence should be our hallmark in terms of teaching and scholarship. We must expect nothing less in our doctoral programs or from the graduates of those programs.

REFERENCES

Arpan, Jeffrey. 1993 "Curricular and Administrative Considerations-The Cheshire Cat Parable." in S. Tamer Cavusgil (ed.). *Internationalizing Business Education: Meeting the Challenge.* East Lansing, MI: Michigan State University Press.

Daniels, John D. "Internationalizing Doctoral Programs in Business: The Indiana University Experience." in this volume.

Duhan, Dale F. "Some Thoughts on the Internationalization of Doctoral Education in Colleges of Business Administration." in this volume.

Kedia, Ben. "A Pyramidical Approach to the Internationalization of Doctoral Business Education." in this volume.

Porter, Lyman. 1988. "Internationalizing Doctoral Education in Business: Cost-Benefit Trade-Offs." Porter, Lyman W. and Lawrence E. McKibbin. *Management Education and Development.* New York: McGraw-Hill Book Company.

Rose, Peter S. "A Dual Approach to Internationalizing Business Ph.D. Programs." in this volume.

Schmotter, James. "Lessons for Doctoral Education from Successful International Companies." in this volume.

Toyne, Brian. "Internationalizing Business Scholarship: The Essentials." in this volume.

A Pyramidical Approach to the Internationalization of Doctoral Business Education[1]

Ben L. Kedia

Introduction

A major goal of the Center for International Business Education and Research (CIBER) at The University of Memphis has been to establish a specialized International MBA (IMBA) program that integrates foreign language training, cultural and area studies, and international internships with internationally focused business administration courses. We are entering the second year of operation of this program and currently enroll 45 students. Due mainly to our preoccupation with the IMBA program, so far we have invested limited energy in the internationalization of our Ph.D. program. While we have in excess of 100 students enrolled in our Ph.D. program, we lack an agreement among our faculty regarding how to internationalize the program. However, recognizing the importance of internationalizing our doctoral program, we are beginning to pay more attention to this objective. This paper discusses some of our initial thinking regarding the internationalization of our doctoral program. Business education in general and doctoral business programs in particular have come under increasing attack in recent years. Some of these issues will also be discussed, as they are unlikely to disappear. The internationalization of the doctoral program affords an opportunity to examine these issues and avoid potential future criticisms and concerns.

Recent events have shown that nations are moving toward a greater economic interdependence, driven by continued growth in international trade and investment. Countries have been integrating international and regional economies through cooperative commercial relations. These arrangements go by a plethora of acronyms (EU, NAFTA, ASEAN, Mercosur, Andean Pact, LAIA, ECOWAS, and GATT) all of which evidence the growing interdependence

135

among nations. As a result, world trade has been growing faster than world GDP. Foreign Direct Investment has been growing four times faster than trade since 1982, despite a recent downturn during the recession. Deregulation of capital markets has fueled an equal boom in cross-border financial flows (United Nations 1993). These trends will shift the nature of competition from existing industries to continual creation of new businesses (Prahalad 1990). The expansion of international trade and investment, increasing globalization of industries, and the changing nature of competition will continue to have a profound effect on the managerial agenda. However, the academic agenda of business schools in the US has remained largely unaffected by these changes (Barnett 1990; Prahalad 1990).

DEFICIENCIES IN DOCTORAL BUSINESS EDUCATION

Against this background of change, questions have been raised about the relevance of much of business education (Cheit 1985; Daniels 1991; Porter and McKibbin 1988; Rehder, Porter and Muller 1990). Many (e.g., Alluto 1993) argue that schools of business have an obligation to bring to their teaching and research a multidisciplinary focus most appropriate for practice. However, we must recognize that business education is shaped by the professional attitudes and values of business school faculty. These attitudes and values are developed in a significant manner during doctoral education. Most faculty were trained in an earlier mileau with a focus on a more domestically oriented agenda. However, if the teaching and research agenda of the business school faculty is to provide enhanced relevance for global management, the training of our current and future generations of doctoral students needs to be structured to support these missions.

Strongly influenced by Gorden and Howell (1959) and Pierson (1959), modern business education and research is based on the Ford-Carnegie paradigm. The result has been training that:

1. emphasizes disciplinary fragmentation and analytical rigor at the expense of practical relevance;
2. de-emphasizes (even penalizes) teaching while emphasizing empirical (data dependent) research;
3. emphasizes specialization among Ph.D.s and perpetuates departmentalization;
4. socializes faculty members into narrowly-focused departments whose members are internationally illiterate.

In its application, the paradigm has resulted in an education-research system whose outcome (education) has become increasingly irrelevant for those being educated. Moreover, the academic system has become isolated from external influence. Another unintended consequence of the paradigm is its tendency to divide the faculty into younger, research-oriented faculty and older, practice-oriented faculty (Leavitt, 1993). Unfortunately, this leaves future Ph.D. education almost entirely in the hands of research-oriented faculty. According to Leavitt (1993), each new batch of Ph.D.s emerge more oriented toward academia than toward practice. He argues that this trend would not be so alarming, were it not for the fact that these same Ph.D.s will later be expected to teach MBAs how to become effective managers.

Compounding this problem is the lack of internationalization of faculty. Based on the AIB's fifth benchmark survey, Arpan, Folks and Kwok (1993) reported that in US business schools, 68% of the faculty had minimal international business education/training, or none at all. Another 22% have only moderate education and training (p. 18). Nor does the future look any better. Of the 68 U.S. business schools reporting objectives for their doctoral programs, only 1 in 10 (7 schools in total) have an objective educating their doctoral students in the international dimensions of their chosen field. Further, only 18% (12 schools) sought to develop an expertise in the international dimension of business in their doctoral students. From this, it is obvious that doctoral programs lack commitment to the internationalization of their students.

Critical of the existing system, the Graduate Management Admission Council (GMAC 1990), made the following recommendations:

1. Fundamental changes are required in the content of business programs and the way this content is taught.
2. Schools need to develop a balance between academic rigor and managerial relevance.
3. Schools need to develop more appropriate approaches to the recruitment and development of faculty members, including new models of doctoral education which emphasize knowledge, skills, attitudes, and values required of future faculty members.
4. Schools need to upgrade and re-orient existing business administration faculty to be more responsive to the emerging needs of practitioners.

DIRECTIONS FOR CHANGES IN DOCTORAL BUSINESS EDUCATION

Doctoral business programs must first address certain fundamental issues with respect to (1) relevance and (2) internationalization. A fundamental issue involved in doctoral business education is whether it should be entirely academic, related to professional practice, or provide a balance between the two. On one hand, schools such as MIT, Carnegie, Chicago and Stanford are largely dominated by academic, research-oriented models of doctoral education (Leavitt 1993). In these institutions, faculty members value colleagues who are narrowly trained in core disciplines and have little concern about thinking in a holistical manner about the professional application of their basic disciplines. On the other hand, some schools appear to be a bit more professionally oriented. In fact, some of these schools award a DBA (e.g., Harvard, Indiana) rather than the Ph.D. to demonstrate their professional orientation. The philosophy behind this orientation is that in other professional schools, such as law and medicine, faculty scholars primarily train lawyers and physicians, and that business faculty scholars train managers. Thus, faculty should be grounded in both the basic disciplines and the reality of professional practice (Alutto 1993).

Nonetheless, the academic model appears to be favored for doctoral education on most American campuses. Yet, Howell (GMAC 1992) has observed:

> Except where there is research, the training of most professors is completely orthogonal to the job at which they spend most of their time-teaching students who themselves are not going to be scholars.

It was noted by the GMAC (1992) report that "this observation is especially compelling in light of recent evidence suggesting that 75 to 90 percent of those who earn doctorates from American universities do absolutely no research thereafter that is published."

Few question that the Ph.D. degree should be related to scholarship, research, and abstract thinking. No one is suggesting the Ph.D. be awarded for education that is based almost entirely on professional practice. The real question is that since business doctorates will be required to train MBAs, should business doctoral education incorporate some dimensions of professional practice; if so, what and how much? If doctoral training continues to be dominated by narrow discipline-based considerations, we shall continue to produce educators with (1) limited knowledge of matters outside their field of specialization, and (2) distorted views of the appeal, importance, and implications of their special fields (Bossard and Dewhurst 1931). This perpetuates conflicts between classical research and modern professional viewpoints (Baker and Tyack 1956).

The relevance of classical business school research is also being increasingly questioned. For example, Dean Scott S. Cowen of Case Western Reserve University was quoted as saying, "As much as 80% of management research may be irrelevant" (Byrne 1990). In this regard, Sullivan's (GMAC 1992) three-part question is particularly insightful. Are curriculum and research mutually supportive? Is research in doctoral programs grounded in issues important to business? Are research results being translated into understandable formats for general audiences? While implying that many would answer all three questions in the negative, Sullivan suggested that it largely defines the respondents' view of doctoral business education.

INTERNATIONALIZING DOCTORAL BUSINESS EDUCATION

If the current course of specialization and socialization in narrowly focused disciplines in doctoral programs is continued, and if teaching and research relevance issues are overlooked, it will be extremely difficult, if not impossible, to internationalize doctoral business programs. International business does not fit neatly into the disciplinary fragmentation of a collegiate business school. As a result, international issues and topics must be integrated into existing academic disciplines. This means that future doctoral education will have to be expanded to include an international dimension. However, faculty trained in a traditional discipline are at best indifferent to and, at worst, openly hostile towards internationalization. Consequently it will take either heroic leadership or a significant change in reward system to effect the change. Notwithstanding the difficulties, successful approaches to affect such changes are possible (Miller 1992; and Steers and Ungson 1992).

The first step in successfully internationalizing a doctoral program is to establish the learning goals for students. In preparing students for university teaching and research in a traditional academic discipline (e.g., accounting, finance, management, marketing), the time and attention that can be devoted to internationalization will be limited unless the program length can be significantly expanded. Attempts to internationalize doctoral education at the expense of a traditional disciplinary focus will be resisted by many functional faculty. The internationalization learning goal for each student would also depend on the international knowledge, experience and expertise the student brings to his/her doctoral program. Since most students lack an international background, the internationalization goal should be modest.

Given the constraints on opportunities for internationalization, programs must concentrate more on the essential objective of internationalizing. Bennett (1986) differentiates between cognitive (knowledge), affective (attitude), and behavioral (action) learning goals or the type of competency one is attempting to create. Cognitive goals relate to a change in what is known and the amount of information one has on a given subject (i.e., how much is added to a person's body of knowledge). Affective goals relate to a change in one's attitudes and feelings toward something or someone. Behavioral goals pertain to a change in one's ability or the skill to do something. In the context of internationalization, this means that each doctoral program must decide whether the objective is to provide students with (1) international knowledge (cognition), and/or (2) to provide an intermediate level of knowledge with a meaningful second foreign language and international experience (affective), and/or (3) to provide an advanced level of international knowledge with a second foreign language and international experience (behavior) that would affect the change desired. This may have to be determined individually for each student based on his/her international background.

In business schools, the intellectual classroom activities of reading, lectures, and discussions accomplish primarily cognitive goals. Affective goals, on the other hand, are facilitated by such classroom experiential activities as international case problems, videos, exercises and foreign language learning, as well as experiential activities outside the classroom, such as study abroad programs, internships abroad, domestic internships with multinational companies, and teaching and research abroad. Behavioral goals are accomplished through a combination of activities that reinforce both cognitive and affective goals. Although, any given activity can contribute to the attainment of one or more of these goal areas, their predominant contribution is usually toward either cognitive or affective, while behavioral goals are typically met through a combination of complementary and supportive activities.

Learning goals associated with internationalizing doctoral business education, vary according to the levels of international competencies desired. The first level of competency pertains to that needed by all academics in order to prepare them to handle the international component of the core discipline they will teach (e.g., principles of management or principles of marketing). This basic level of the international education can be achieved by requiring at least one course, such as a seminar in international business, of all doctoral students. The University of Memphis has adopted such an approach but only for students specializing in business strategy.

A second level of competency pertains to those academics who will teach international courses at the undergraduate or master's levels, but may have limited involvement in international research. Achieving this level of competency requires a minor in international business. The University of Memphis has made such a minor available to all of its doctoral students regardless of their major. It is highly desirable that these students be encouraged to acquire some foreign language ability and international experience. However, adding such a requirement to the doctoral program may not be realistic or practical, given limited university resources and the length of the typical doctoral program.

The third and highest level of competency is for those academics who will have major responsibility for research and teaching in the domain of international functional areas. These are the international business experts of the highest order, those who will need to major in international business. In addition to appropriate courses, these students must possess a second foreign language competency and should have significant international experience.

KOLB'S LEARNING CYCLE

For understanding the role of various kinds of learning for internationalizing doctoral business education, we turn to David Kolb's (1974) experiential learning theory. Kolb conceived of the learning process as a cycle consisting of four stages, through which individuals progress as they learn. These stages include (1) getting involved actively in new experiences (Active Experience), (2) making reflective observations on these experiences (Reflective Observation), (3) integrating observations to build models and theories to explain and predict outcomes of future actions (Abstract Conceptualization), and testing theories to make decisions and solve problems (Active Experimentation). Kolb's learning cycle is shown in Figure 1.

This description of the cycle implies that concrete experience is the natural starting point, and active experimentation is the natural ending point, of the process. What is important is that for learning to be meaningful, comprehensive and integrative, one needs to move through the entire cycle. In an international context, sending students overseas for study, internship, cultural and language training, teaching, or research provides a different case

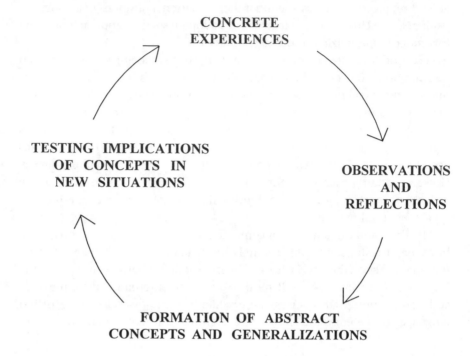

Figure 1. A model of Learning Process
Source: David Kolb (1984), *Experiential Learning*, Englewood Cliffs, NJ: Prentice Hall.

of learning new experiences. Not only does a student take more responsibility for his/ her own learning, but s/he must do so in an ambiguous and unfamiliar cultural environment perhaps with inadequate foreign language skills.

The principal distinguishing feature of Kolb's model is its greater emphasis on the necessary contributions of the experiential (i.e., active experimentation and concrete experience) sides of learning. While it is undoubtedly true that a degree of understanding is attainable solely through the traditional intellectual classroom activities that rely primarily on abstract conceptualization and reflective observation, it is only by travelling through the entire learning cycle that one obtains the kind of deeper, fuller understanding referred to as insight.

The learning cycle can also be related to our discussion of learning goals: abstract conceptualization relates to cognitive goals; active experimentation and concrete experience relate to affective goals; and reflective observation leading to reformulation of abstract conceptualization relates to behavioral goals. The learning process will not only awaken intrinsic stimuli within the students but will help generate willingness and interest to learn "how to learn" for continued internationalization. Kolb (1984) suggests that the cycle "involves integrated functioning of the total organism-thinking, feeling, perceiving, and behaving." Thus, if one goes through the entire cycle, the relevance of international business education will be enhanced.

A PYRAMIDICAL APPROACH

Human cognitive development leads to expanded use of abstraction and reflection, and the subsequent diminution of the reliance on active experimentation and concrete experience for learning. This is not to say that one ever reaches a stage in which the active and concrete aspects are unnecessary. Active experimentation and concrete experience remain important for understanding new situations or problems. In all stages of life, all four aspects are necessary parts of learning and understanding.

We can conceive of higher educational learning as a pyramid with a quadrilateral base with each side representing one of the four aspects of Kolb's learning cycle, with the rising pyramid representing the stages of educational levels in terms of degrees awarded: baccalaureate; master's; and doctoral. At the foundation level of education, the role of active experimentation and concrete experience are important for application and self-understanding. However, as one progresses to higher levels, the roles of abstract conceptualization and reflective observation grow in importance. It is necessary to realize, as the pyramid displays, that without the proper groundwork of experimentation and experience, the other dimensions of the pyramid are not as established. This pyramidical representation is shown in Figure 2.

The significance of the pyramid for business education lies in its implications for the types of educational activities necessary to prepare business academics for the international aspects of their respective tasks. Formal international coursework will be necessary to achieve three levels of international competence for business academics: for Ph.D. (cognition); IB minors (affective); and IB majors (behavior). This kind of abstract and reflective learning needs to be supplemented by concrete experiences and active experimentation that will provide useful insights in terms of what is really different about international business. Thus, in relating these ideas to the

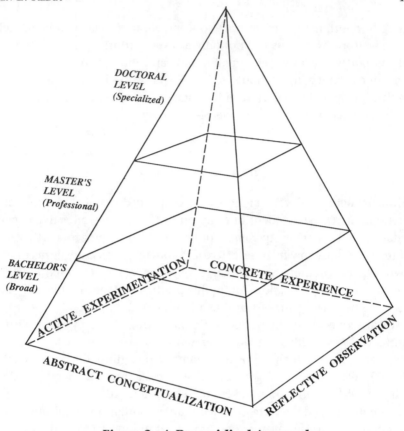

Figure 2. A Pyramidical Approach
Learning Process and International Education
Source: David Kolb (1984), *Experiential Learning*, Englewood Cliffs, NJ: Prentice Hall.

pyramid, international experience and foreign language training are necessary tools for achieving higher level of competence in international education. Once these types of experiences are gained, then the requisite roles of
abstract conceptualization and reflective observation become more significant. In this context, one need not think of internationalization of doctoral
education in isolation, but conceive of building upon international knowledge and expertise acquired during the master's and bachelor's degree programs. One can also see that it is difficult to begin at the Ph.D. level to gain
a high level of competence without first having acquired some type of
preparatory skills.

Of the activities already mentioned, some are best pursued at the bachelor's or master's level; namely, international case problems, videos, exercises, area studies, foreign language learning, study abroad programs, and internships. Given the rigid requirements in most doctoral programs, it is unlikely that room can be made to incorporate such experiential and experimental-based activities. As discussed previously, doctoral students minoring or majoring in international business should have already obtained these experiences before entering the Ph.D. program. For example, language learning is an integral component to the understanding of a culture. Similarly, learning about specific geographic areas or countries provides context to international business courses. Likewise, international internships will help students learn about successfully operating and managing abroad. Through such foreign experiences, students will gain a sense of relevance for abstract conceptualization and reflective observation and obtain insights in order to prepare themselves better as international business researchers and teachers. For students who lack such an experiential base, teaching or research abroad early in their academic career can make up for this deficiency. Still, the length of time required and the rigor of the doctoral program make it difficult to allow for such activities.

Summarized in Table 1 are the strategies for achieving international competence in the Ph.D. program. As discussed above, the strategy employed to attain a certain level of competence will depend on the base of experience the Ph.D. student has upon entering the program. A doctoral student entering the program with no language skills, no area studies and negligible foreign experience can undertake the necessary steps for achieving cognitive competence through various structured activities in the doctoral program. However, for this type of student achieving the highest level of competence, proficiency in international teaching and research is difficult. Moving downward along the diagonal of Table 1 from cognitive competence to behavioral competence requires additional time and effort that may not be feasible within the confines of a doctoral program. However, as illustrated in the table, for those students who have a high level of international preparedness, competence for specializing in international research and teaching can be realized. Thus, for those doctoral programs offering this type of specialization, incoming students should be required to have a certain level of previous international expertise and experience.

Table 1 Strategies for Achieving International Competence During Ph.D. Program

Level of Preparedness for Incoming Doctoral Student	Cognitive Competence	Affective Competence	Behavioral Competence	Competency Outcome
No language No area studies No foreign experience	Seminar in Int'l. Business Integrate Int'l. topics into existing courses Int'l. colloquiums	International Minor Study and Internships Abroad	International Major Teaching and Research Abroad	Teach international component of core courses
Some language or area studies Some foreign experience	Seminar in Int'l. Business Integrate Int'l. topics into existing courses Int'l. colloquiums	International Minor Study and Internships Abroad		Teach international courses at undergraduate/ masters level
Second language Area studies Foreign experience	Seminar in Int'l. Business Integrate Int'l. topics into existing courses Int'l. colloquiums			Specialize in research and teaching of international subject matter

CONCLUSIONS

Business education and research is increasingly perceived as irrelevant. It is also regarded as "parochial" when it comes to the international domain. These concerns have significant implications for the future training of doctoral students-the next generation of educators. Based on Kolb's learning cycle, this article suggests that incorporation of all the four learning styles in international contexts will both enhance relevance and internationalization of business doctoral programs. However, the entire international aspect of education based on the four styles need not be (and cannot be) incorporated during the doctoral phase of education. Some of them are best pursued at the master's and bachelor's levels. Doctoral education needs to build on this knowledge and experience. Finally, changing a doctoral program requires faculty and administrative recognition and support. While the move toward the internationalization of doctoral programs is increasingly recognized as necessary and relevant, obtaining support remains a challenging and daunting task.

NOTE

1. The author would like to thank Peter Davis, Jeff Krug, O. C. Ferrell, Bob Berl, Bettina Cornwell, David Kemme, Emin Babakus, John Francis, and Edith Busija for their helpful comments on this article.

REFERENCES

Alutto, Joseph A. 1993. Whither Doctoral Business Education? An Exploration of Program Models. *Selections.* (Spring): 37-43.

Arpan, J. S., W. R. Folks, and C. Y. Kwok. 1993. *International Business Education in the 1990s: A Global Survey.* University of South Carolina.

Baker, G. and D. Tyack. 1956. *Faculty Requirements and Standards in Collegiate Schools of Business.* AACSB Arden House Report.

Barnett, Carole K. 1990. "The Michigan Global Agenda: Research and Teaching in the 1990s." *Human Resource Management.* 29(1): 5-26.

Bennett, Janet Marie. 1986. "Modes of Cross-Cultural Training: Conceptualizing Cross-Cultural Training as Education." *International Journal of Intercultural Relations.* 10: 117-34.

Bossard, J. H. S. and J. F. Dewhurst. 1931. *University Education for Business.* Philadelphia, PA: University of Pennsylvania Press.

Byrne, J. A. 1990. "Is Research in the Ivory Tower 'Fuzzy, Irrelevant, Pretentious'?" *Business Week.* (3185): 62-66.

Cheit, E. F. 1985. "Business Schools and Their Critics." *California Management Review.* 27(3): 43-62.

Daniels, John D. 1991. "Relevance in International Business Research: A Need for More Linkages." *Journal of International Business Studies.* 22(2): 177-86.

GMAC. 1990. *Leadership for a Changing World: The Future Role of Graduate Management Education.* Los Angeles, CA: Graduate Management Admission Council.

GMAC. 1992. "Current Issues in Business Doctoral Education: A Report on the Dallas Invitational Conference." *Selections.* (Autumn): 9-26.

Gorden, R. A. and J. G. Howell. 1959. *Higher Education for Business.* New York NY: Columbia University Press.

Kolb, David A. 1974. "On Management and the Learning Process." In Kolb, David A., Irwin M. Rubin, and James M. McIntyre (eds.). *Organizational Psychology: A Book of Readings.* 2d ed. Englewood Cliffs, NJ: Prentice Hall.

Kolb, D. A. 1984. *Experiential Learning.* Englewood Cliffs, NJ: Prentice Hall.

Leavitt, Harold J. 1993. "The Business School and the Doctorate." *Selections*. (Winter): 12-21.

Miller, Edwin L. 1992. "Internationalization of the Michigan Business School: A Letter from the Front." In Alan M. Rugman and W. T. Stanbury (eds.). *Global Perspective: Internationalizing Management Education*. Vancouver, Canada: Centre for International Business Studies, Faculty of Commerce and Business Administration, University of British Columbia.

Pierson, Frank Cook. 1959. *The Education of American Businessman*. New York, NY: McGraw-Hill.

Porter, L. W. and L. E. McKibbin. 1988. *Management Education: Drift or Thrust into the 21st Century*. New York, NY: McGraw-Hill.

Prahalad, C. K. 1990. "Globalization: Intellectual and Managerial Challenges." *Human Resource Management*. 29(1) (Spring): 27-37.

Rehder, Robert R., James L. Porter, and Helen J. Muller. 1990. "Challenging the Management Education Monster: The Learning Alliance MBA." *Selections*. (Winter): 13-25.

Steers, Richard M. and Gerardo R. Ungson. 1992. "In Search of the Holy Grail: Reflections on the Internationalization of Business Education." In Rugman, Alan M. and W. T. Stanbury (eds.). *Global Perspective: Internationalizing Management Education*. Vancouver, Canada: Centre for International Business Studies, Faculty of Commerce and Business Administration, University of British Columbia.

United Nations. 1993. *World Investment Report 1993*. New York, NY: United Nations.

INTERNATIONALIZING DOCTORAL PROGRAMS IN BUSINESS: THE INDIANA UNIVERSITY EXPERIENCE

John D. Daniels

The CIBER at Indiana University (IU) commenced 1 October 1992. One of its major thrusts has been to internationalize the doctoral program. The objective is to assure that each Ph.D. student in business is equipped on graduation to be able to teach his or her courses from an international perspective. We believe that we are the first major business school to have made this commitment; therefore, our experiences to date may serve to help guide other schools that wish to make similar commitments.

NATIONAL RATIONALE FOR INTERNATIONALIZATION

In 1973 the AACSB Standards Committee added three key words, "domestic and worldwide" to the purpose of the curriculum for all students. These words were added because of the growing international interdependence of the United States, the need for companies to make international operating adjustments, and the traditional domestic focus of U.S. business school programs. It is within this framework that there is rationale for internationalizing doctoral programs. Basically, most Ph.Ds in business go into teaching; therefore, they need to be proficient in the international aspects of their areas if they are to be able to add the "worldwide" dimension to their courses.

As early as twenty years ago, there was a realization that most U.S. business school faculty nationwide had difficulty in adding international content to their classes. There are several reasons for this, such as a belief that there is already too much crammed into their courses, i.e., the adding of an international dimension would necessitate dropping other materials that they consider to be more essential. But an important factor is that many faculty members lack the training and/or experience to feel confident about adding international content to their courses. Business programs have responded by trying to re-tool faculty in two ways. First, they have sent professors to various workshops, such as those offered by the AACSB, the AIB, the Academy of Management, the University of South Carolina, and the University of Hawaii. Second, they have sent faculty abroad, for example, to teach in executive programs in foreign countries or to accompany students on study abroad programs.

Although these programs have been substantial, they have been insufficient. In a CIBER conference here in 1991, Lee C. Nehrt presented statistics that painted a dismal picture of how far AACSB member schools have gone in internationalizing their faculty. He concluded that less than ten percent of faculty members are sufficiently trained internationally and that the number of faculty members attending workshops is less than the number of Ph.D. students graduating without international training; therefore, the overall situation is deteriorating rather than improving.

RATIONALE FOR IU

When we were preparing our proposal for funding as a CIBER, we perceived a national need for globally trained doctoral students. Our perception of need was based on the same trends that led the AACSB to add an international standard in 1971, along with our own observation that most new doctoral students lacked training in the global aspects of their disciplines. We additionally saw this area to be a niche in which we could take a leadership position inasmuch as most CIBER institutions had put most of their emphasis on master's programs.

We also reasoned that we were in a good position to make a national impact. Our doctoral program had approximately one hundred students and was ranked by the AACSB as the nation's nineteenth largest. This ranking is significant because the 53 largest U.S. doctoral programs in business produce about 92 percent of all doctoral graduates. We knew of no studies to compare the quality of these programs; however, there was sufficient anecdotal evidence to indicate that we had a generally high and national reputation. Further, our graduates were being placed in every type of institution—large versus small, teaching versus research emphasis, domestic versus foreign, and in all parts of the country.

We reasoned that our efforts among doctoral students would help to internationalize our other programs as well. For example, a high portion of undergraduate courses are taught in whole or part by doctoral students; therefore, we could achieve some "trickle-down" effect by concentrating on the Ph.D. program.

In the process of preparing our CIBER proposal, we conducted a fact-finding interview survey of over one hundred IU School of Business faculty and doctoral students who had taught during Fall 1991. This survey determined the background and international experience of instructors, the extent that they cover international materials, the obstacles they perceive for their own and the school's increase in international coverage, their opinions on different types of international thrusts for the school, and their advice on serving undergraduates, MBAs, and doctoral students. This survey served both to confirm the need to serve doctoral students and to give us direction on how to structure and implement our plans.

BUILDING SUPPORT AND MINIMIZING OPPOSITION

As we all know, change usually comes slowly within universities. Business schools are no exception. This is evidenced by the slow progress toward training students for worldwide responsibilities; therefore, we had no reason to be optimistic that we could easily implement changes if CIBER funding were received. We reasoned that legitimate arguments could be made against any proposal to internationalize the doctoral program. Further, there were probably some disincentives for faculty either to accept change or to do the work necessary to effect the change. Given this reality, we decided to take a number of steps before and after writing the proposal. These included most of the advice one finds in change-agent literature: (1) minimizing loss of autonomy; (2) promoting participation; (3) sharing of rewards; (4) making changes incrementally; and (5) using opinion leaders. We had little control over another change-agent technique, timing changes for least resistance, but we have been fortunate in this respect.

Minimizing Loss of Autonomy—Indiana University's School of Business is like many other business schools in that doctoral programs are administered de facto among highly autonomous departments and by highly autonomous faculty within those departments. Programs are often jealously guarded and individualized. The ceding of autonomy is difficult, even for research methodology courses. Faculty members typically are willing to take on doctoral supervision as an overload, and they typically want to turn out students whose research profile resembles their own—sort of a reproductive function. Given this reality, we decided early that each department or major area would have almost unlimited autonomy in deciding how it would go about internationalizing its students. This decentralization also made sense because of the different nature of the areas to be internationalized. For example, there is more of a need to change content for the internationalization of marketing than for decision science, i.e. decision science tools are more universalistic, even though the reliability of data inputs differs from country to country. Further, some of our areas, such as policy/strategy, had already become quite international; whereas others, such as accounting, had not.

Promoting Participation—Before writing the proposal, I met with our faculty academic council, a group made up of department and program heads and deans. They endorsed the concept provided that funds would be forthcoming and that decision-making would be at the departmental level. The specific arguments made to them are included in the section on timing.

After we received notification of funding, CIBER sponsored a one day retreat in which more than twenty faculty members participated. Representatives from each department with a doctoral major were present. There was some overlap with the members of the faculty academic council, but for the most part this involved different people and those with the most departmental responsibility over doctoral programs. After short introductory remarks by the director of the school's doctoral program and by one of the international business faculty members, the attendees broke into four groups to discuss questions I had prepared and disseminated in advance. Doctoral students from different departments served as rapporteurs. They summarized discussions that were then distributed to all faculty members in the business school. Although little consensus was reached on any question, this meeting served to broaden participation and commitment, to educate faculty on the domain and needs of international business, and to allow for a cross-fertilization of ideas by faculty from different departments. To date, the answers to these questions have not been resolved, and some may never be resolved. Nevertheless, the questions and summary report have served as a basis for discussion (1) as different departments have moved differently to internationalize and (2) as the school has debated whether to require a common international business seminar for all doctoral students in business. The specific questions discussed were:

1. What do/should we mean by internationalizing our Ph.D. program? What are differences between our end objectives versus means to reach these objectives? Why do we need to internationalize?

2. There are three common approaches for training managers for international responsibilities. These are:
   (a) *content specific:* e.g. by function, geographic area,
   (b) *tools:* e.g. where to get information, foreign language proficiency, and
   (c) *adaptability:* e.g. through sensitivity training.
   Can any of these approaches be used as a model for Ph.D. training? If so, which? If so, should our doctoral students be exposed to some specific combination?

3. Do we need to assess where we now stand in the internationalization process? How do we factor in areas that have universal applicability? Should we explicitly delineate for doctoral students those areas that do and do not have universal applicability?

4. Do needs differ by doctoral field? If so, how and why? Are there, nevertheless, areas that all doctoral students should know about? If so, what? If so, can we develop a common means of delivery?

5. How do we link what we do in the Ph.D. program with the undergraduate and MBA programs? If we manage to infuse adequate international dimensions to the undergraduate and MBA, will this lessen what we need to do at the Ph.D. level? Can we combine any Ph.D. and MBA classes/activities specifically to gain economies in our international efforts? Can we take measures to assure that doctoral students will add international dimensions to the undergraduate courses they teach?

6. What are the advantages of separate international courses versus infusion of international into existing courses? Are there short and long term differences? Are there differences by field?

7. What costs, including trade-offs with other learning objectives, might we have to incur to reach our international objectives? Will students need more time to complete a program?

Sharing of Rewards—Although there are few rewards to be shared, we have spread them as much as possible. For example, if a department is using funds to bring in speakers or to make faculty grants to develop new materials, we have encouraged them to involve as many departmental members as possible. We have also stressed that the change in doctoral qualifications reflects positively on the department, rather than on the CIBER or international business group.

Making Changes Incrementally—By not starting with a master plan to encompass the entire college, we have encouraged departments to make initial changes that seem less threatening to them. Our actions have partially been a matter of luck. When our funding was less than we originally requested, we scaled back departmental allotments. Our expectation was that future funding would allow us to add future departmental increments. This has resulted in departments thinking incrementally and developing further ideas for the future. (Some specific departmental activities are summarized in this paper.)

Using Opinion Leaders—We have worked with different major areas for different years. One of the two groups we chose for year one was the finance department. It is a department that often leads the way for change within the school. For example, shortly before our CIBER start-up, the finance department changed the credit hours for its courses; and this action was quickly emulated by other departments. Further, we have worked with departments so that their invited speakers on international topics are credible to faculty because of their research and the institutions they represent.

Timing of Changes—Although we had no control over the timing for proposing the internationalization of the Ph.D. program, we were fortuitous. In 1991, when we were writing our proposal, many students were having difficulty in being placed in tenure track academic appointments. This was the first time that many faculty members had witnessed such a situation. Further, resources were becoming much more scarce, especially those for summer research or course development stipends. We were able to seize on those two situations in our discussions with the faculty academic council by offering hope that our proposal would help alleviate both problems.

SPECIFIC CIBER ACTIONS

Although we have promoted departmental autonomy, we have, nevertheless, left some activities to be administered through the CIBER office. These include the awarding of pre-dissertation awards to business students and dissertation awards to both business and non-business students.

Pre-dissertation Travel Awards—We have been able to offer travel awards on a competitive basis. The purpose of these awards is to encourage students to consider international options at an early point in their programs. This should make them more likely to undertake a dissertation with high international content, an important consideration in that faculty members often follow a similar research stream throughout their careers. The research may also lead to dissertation topics, help students get published before graduating, and provide for needed research (such as case writing) that faculty members are reluctant to undertake. Some of the topics funded thus far are a comparison of gift purchase behavior in Japan with behavior in the United States, the impact of culture on U.S. companies' operations in the United Kingdom and Thailand, a case study of a joint venture between Statoil of Norway and the Danish Underground Consortium, a case study of the environmental impact of Xerox's direct investment in India, and a comparative study of manufacturing processes between AC Rochester plants in the United States and Brazil.

Dissertation Awards for Business Students—We have given competitive awards to enable students to collect data that might otherwise be impossible to attain. We are giving maximum publicity to this award so that students will think early within their program about the possibility of doing research on an international topic. For example, the first award we gave is for a study on the antecedents to and outcomes of international joint ventures. Interestingly, this study does not require foreign travel.

Dissertation Awards for Non-business Students—Undergraduate business students take about half their credits outside business schools. Other undergraduates take even fewer business courses. We reasoned that one of the purposes of the internationalization process is to help students become informed citizens about the role of international business; therefore, objectives to meet this purpose must eventually be partially met in courses outside business schools. Because of this we are making competitive merit awards for non-business students so that they add a significant international business dimension to their dissertation proposals. The first year that we had such an award, we frankly did not know whether we would receive any applications. We ended up with six, all from different departments. We made an award to a history student, who wrote about the internationalization of the champagne industry. We hope, eventually, that awards will become well enough known so that more non-business students will add international business dimensions to their research. In turn, this should lead to more references to international business in non-business courses.

DEPARTMENTAL ACTIONS

When we began our process, we had ten different majors within our doctoral program. We presumed that the international business major was already internationalized; therefore, our proposal called for actions in the other nine. Our original plan was to deal with three of these each year. As discussed earlier, our funding was less than we requested; therefore, we cut the amount of stipends and lengthened the time for instituting major-by-major changes. We concentrated on two areas per year at about half our originally proposed level. This situation may actually have long-term benefits. For example, the finance department worked on CIBER-supported international projects in the first year. By observing what other departments do over the next few years, the finance department may develop new ideas that will hopefully receive future infusions of CIBER support.

In the first year, we concentrated on the areas of finance and policy/strategy, the former because it served as an opinion leader and the latter because it offered quick results and quick trickle down effects into the undergraduate program. In the second year we concentrated on business economics and operations management, mainly because they were the two areas that seemed most eager to make changes. As expected, the approaches thus far have been quite diverse from one department to another. This diversity has occurred not only in how funds have been spent, but also in how faculty have been involved in decision making. In each case, my main contact has been the department chairman, who works with his or her faculty members. Experiences are summarized below.

Finance—The department is large, and it relied on a committee comprised of five faculty members who teach doctoral seminars to propose a plan to CIBER. The department's main thrust has been to infuse significant international materials into five doctoral seminars taught by each of the faculty members on the committee. CIBER support also went for sponsorship of two visiting lecturers, an award for a doctoral student writing the best paper on an international financial topic, and support for a summer study group composed of faculty and students who sought ways to add international dimensions to courses.

Policy/Strategy—The number of faculty members in this group is small; and within this group faculty were already fairly internationalized when

CIBER funds became available. The group has used CIBER support to present a showcase workshop that was attended by all policy/strategy faculty and doctoral students at Indiana University, as well as faculty and/or doctoral students from ten other institutions. Two keynote speakers came from other universities, and we distributed the proceedings widely. Support also went for faculty acquisition of and orientation to new materials.

Business Economics—This is a large department. Many business economics courses have had a heavy international component for some time; and a cadre of faculty with long-term international exposure spearheaded a proposal on how best to use CIBER funding. This department has used funds to support a foreign scholar in residence, to provide materials and data bases to doctoral students, and to add international materials to existing seminars.

Operations Management—This is a small department in which one faculty member was delegated responsibility to devise a plan. Funds have gone for support of a guest lecturer seminar and for the writing of cases to use by doctoral students. The case writing process was tied to another international grant that paid transportation for faculty members to teach in Slovenia and Hungary. CIBER supported an extension of the faculty visits abroad so that they could write the cases. The operations management department also used CIBER support to pay for all its faculty members and doctoral students to go by van to attend a seminar in Baltimore on internationalizing operations management.

CAVEATS

Since we are effectively plowing new ground, we have learned that we must be flexible. We have seen this with the need to respond to unexpected funding decreases. We have seen it with unexpected opportunities, such as the Baltimore seminar. We have seen it with departmental differences I would advise not to develop rigid plans to be applied uniformly to all departments.

My experience is that international business faculty may sometimes be an obstacle to international activities that might occur outside what they see as their domain. We were fortunate at IU in that there are only three IB faculty members on the Bloomington campus where the doctoral program is housed. Two of us see no threat because of our age, i.e. we'll likely be retired before any infusion is complete; and all three of us see a long-term demand for what we teach. I would advise that any international business faculty be given useful and status-enhancing roles in the change process.

In working with departments, I have encountered some tendency for proposals to be too short-term. (We hold out on complete departmental autonomy by approving proposals that departments must submit.) For example, one proposal called simply for supporting research of existing doctoral students, but this would leave no means of serving students in later years. We insist that funds be used in a way that assures continuity. For example, if there is a guest lecturer, the faculty should attend the presentation so that they can then transmit the content to future doctoral students. (We insist on a commitment up-front.) We also refuse to give funds for a faculty member to attend a conference to present a paper, believing that such funds should come from other sources.

THE FUTURE

From an IU perspective, the most encouraging event is that the faculty has approved and begun the offering of a required international business seminar for all business majors in the Ph.D. program. Support for this has come largely from people who have been involved with the internationalization process during the first three years of CIBER support. But, there are still obstacles, such as a lack of support by all faculty. There are two seminars from which students may choose, one dealing with public policy issues and one with company operations. CIBER has supported the development of these courses in exchange for eliminating further support for specific majors The international business faculty will be heavily involved. As a trade-off, we have already eliminated new admissions for the international business major in our program, concentrating instead on support for international business minors and for infusion of international content into other courses.

An uncertainty involves the market for future graduates. As business school enrollments level-off or decline, there are fewer demands for new Ph.D.s in business. The elimination of mandatory retirement may further temper demand. Lower demand for new Ph.D.s may harbinger a need to concentrate more on re-tooling faculty members, rather than putting emphasis on changing the profile of new Ph.D.s. IU, like many other institutions is responding to market conditions by down-sizing its Ph.D. program to about half its present level. Therefore, we shall be supplying fewer internationalized

Ph.D.s than we anticipated at the onset. This environmental change further underscores the need for flexibility in plans for internationalizing doctoral programs.

PART IV: APPROACHES TO INTERNATIONALIZING DOCTORAL PROGRAMS

INTRODUCTION

S. Tamer Cavusgil

Targeted in this section are several variations on internationalization developed at many of the institutions represented at the Roundtable. The chapter begins with several overview articles that outline conceptual models for internationalization and then details the internationalization programs implemented at several institutions.

Dale Duhan asserts that internationalization should occur through changing the values and culture of the institution and the faculty. The topics and content of research and teaching must also be internationalized through infusion and specificity, i.e., having students take classes explicitly focusing on international issues. Teaching and research methods need to be reconsidered as well as in which journals faculty and student publications appear.

Peter Rose sets out the parameters of internationalization to include both macro and micro levels. His article first sets out a working definition of internationalization. He then goes on to outline the micro level issues in internationalization, including class and course activities, as well as teaching, research and service activities. Moving on to the macro level, he asserts that internationalized institutional goals, administrative support, and the designation of one person who holds primary responsibility for internationalization must all be present if the change endeavor is to work and be sustainable.

Richard Lutz asserts that changing doctoral program is like "herding cats" because each faculty member has a sense of autonomy and individualism. He cautions that Ph.D. programs in business, as in other subjects, are bastions of the status quo where faculty seek to reproduce themselves in their students. What is needed, he argues, is a strong incentive-based model of internationalization in which outcomes are measured in terms of student placement.

Paul Beamish details the internationalization experiences of the Western Business School, Ontario, Canada, highlighting the use of international field experiences (including case writing, teaching abroad, and thesis research) and a unique set of components within the international business course that all doctoral students are required to take. He cautions that the Western way should not be viewed as prescriptive as each internationalization plan must be developed to fit each institution.

Daniel Ondrack, asserting that "the only business is international business," outlines the internationalization experience of the Faculty of Management at the University of Toronto. He argues that internationalization should provide added value to students and should provide options to enhance the types of learning students demand, i.e., awareness, knowledge, emotions and skills. He describes each of the programs and courses developed in the internationalization process.

Reijo Luostarinen reports on a study he undertook on a number of European international business programs, and provides details on his program at the Helsinki School of Economics and Business Administration. He outlines the concepts and contents of internationalization as they are applied to the curriculum, the faculty, the student body, and to the institutional context. He then sets forth the dynamics of internationalization at Helsinki and other European institutions. He concludes his paper with policy recommendations for public policy makers and academic institutions.

The reader of this section is guided through several conceptual and actual approaches advocated or taken at different institutions in the U.S., Canada, and Europe. Several authors have developed conceptual schema to be viewed as guidelines for any institution to utilize in designing an internationalization effort. Others offer the plans that were adopted at their own institutions with the warning that their programs should not be translated automatically to other institutions because the culture, commitment and support system will vary with each institution.

THE INTERNATIONALIZATION OF DOCTORAL EDUCATION IN AMERICAN COLLEGES OF BUSINESS ADMINISTRATION: PRESERVING OUR PROFESSIONAL LEGACY

Dale F. Duhan

INTRODUCTION

The mission of the academic profession is the *creation and dissemination of knowledge*. All professions have their unique roles within society, and as academicians we are the trustees of knowledge. Every generation of professionals leaves a legacy that is specific to them and can take many forms. Our legacies include the knowledge that we have accumulated over the centuries, the institutions that we have created to make that knowledge available to society in general, the benefits (or detriments) that society realizes from the availability of that knowledge and, most importantly, the new generation of people who we bring into our profession to replace ourselves. This new generation is the most important legacy because it is the means by which the value system for the creation and evaluation of knowledge is kept alive. Our doctoral programs are the means by which we create that most important legacy.

The mission and activities of our profession are generally structured around the activities shown in figure 1. The doctoral programs that train new members of our profession are also generally structured around these same activities, although not necessarily in this order. For instance, doctoral programs generally require that course work and major exams are completed prior to proposing and defending a dissertation. Thus the first task in doctoral programs is typically teaching, which is followed by research (the dissertation), which is in turn (hopefully) followed by publications.

Doctoral programs enormously influence the legacy that is left by our profession in three ways. First, in the process of training new professionals, the *values and culture* of the academic profession are transferred from one generation to the next. How future members of a profession evaluate the work

Figure 1   *The Mission of the Academic Profession*

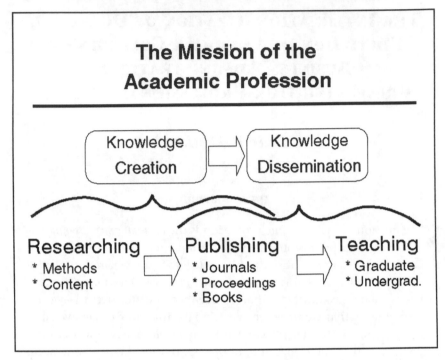

of their peers is rooted in these values. Second, doctoral programs strongly influence the *topics and content* of future research and teaching. The training of new members of the profession is necessarily selective in the knowledge that is emphasized. Doctoral courses cannot possibly include all of the knowledge within even narrowly defined disciplines, therefore selectivity is unavoidable. This selectivity in content strongly influences the knowledge that is disseminated in the future (we teach what we know). Additionally, the choice of dissertation topics is frequently influenced by course content, and dissertations often are the genesis of research streams that individuals pursue for most of their careers. Third, the doctoral programs also provide the new members of the profession with training in the *methods and skills* required for researching, publishing, and teaching.

These three forms of influence and the basic missions of our profession provide a framework for discussion (presented in fig. 2) of the internationalization of doctoral education in business administration. Additionally, there are many administrative issues that are important to internationalizing doctoral education.

Fig. 2   **The Tasks of Doctoral Education**

Doctoral Program Components	Professional Mission		
	Teaching	Researching	Publishing
Values & Culture			
Topics & Content			
Methods & Skills			

INTERNATIONALIZATION AND THE TASKS OF DOCTORAL EDUCATION

VALUES AND CULTURE (THE RATIONALE FOR INTERNATIONALIZATION)

Above all else, our profession values the **sanctity of knowledge.** If the quality of the knowledge provided to society is not good then our profession loses its value to society. In light of that we in the academic profession have established standards for the quality of knowledge to which we expect members of our profession to strive. These standards are based in the widely held belief that it is best to produce knowledge through scientific methods. As a result, one of the most important standards is that knowledge should be *generalizable* across time and contexts. This requirement of generalizability dictates the need for the internationalization of knowledge creation and dissemination in business administration. In some academic fields, such as physics or astronomy, it can be argued legitimately that the international context is irrelevant to the quality of the knowledge in those fields. This is not so in business administration, because business activities must be conducted differently in different jurisdictions and cultures. Moreover, this aspect of business is becoming more prominent as the world shrinks through the advances of technology. Consequently, to uphold the most basic value of our professional culture we must internationalize the processes and the institutions through which we create and disseminate knowledge in business administration.

The requirement that *knowledge* be generalizable is a value that should strongly influence all aspects of our profession and should be instilled into our doctoral students. As we work to train doctoral students, the literature upon which our *teaching* is based should have the benefit of international verification.[1] *Research* should be designed to consider an international dimension regardless of the basic issues being investigated. Indeed, perhaps it should be an *expectation* that research proposals (whether for dissertations, grant applications, etc.) include an international issue. Time and financial burdens may preclude doing research in more than one country, but international issues can be included even if only in the form of comparisons of the research done to similar research from other contexts. In all of the opportunities to influence publication work (as reviewers for journals and research proposals, as editors or track chairs, etc.), we should seriously question whether research that lacks (or would lack) the international dimension should have included that dimension. If the international dimension is not included, then the burden of proof should be placed on justifying why it does not.

INTERNATIONALIZATION THROUGH TOPICS AND CONTENT

The recent Academy of International Business (AIB) survey on international business programs reported that "infusion," the blending of international issues into existing courses, is the most common method for the *internationalization of curricula* (including doctoral curricula). The other approaches that the survey identified can be classified as "specificity," that is, having students take classes explicitly focusing on international issues. One of the difficulties associated with the specificity approach is that it lowers the likelihood that international topics will be included in other courses. Indeed, there have been many instances in which professors have been discouraged from encroaching on the "turf" of other departments or courses when they "infuse" new topics into their courses. On the other hand, it is often difficult to insure that "infusion" occurs. If the topics are not explicitly put into a separate course and made the responsibility of specific faculty members, those topics may not be covered at all. Both instances call for greater coordination and communication among faculty.

In the case of doctoral education, both infusion and specificity should be used with respect to international business. All courses should examine the generalizability of the knowledge within that course by considering the international context of that knowledge. Additionally, there should be courses that are explicitly international and that differ in their content from the "infused" international content by providing more focus on particular topics and/or regions of the world. For instance, infusing international issues into a seminar on Consumer Behavior leads to including in the course literature that explicitly uses "culture" as a contingency variable for Consumer Behavior theories and research. This infusion would enhance the value of other courses that explicitly explore specific cultures. Recently, I heard a presentation on dissertation research entitled "Communications Strategies and Behavioral Adaption in Intercultural Channel Relationships." The course work that would be necessary to prepare a doctoral student for this research would probably include (1) courses that addressed international issues in channels of distribution, communications, and buyer behavior, as well as (2) courses that provided an in-depth view into the cultures that are used in the research. So both infusion and specificity are necessary to adequately prepare a doctoral student for this line of research.

The internationalization of research topics in doctoral programs (primarily dissertations) may well be the easiest and fastest approach to the internationalization of both doctoral education and our profession. Requiring an international dimension in the topics of dissertation research focuses the creative and intellectual efforts of doctoral candidates beyond our own borders. It compels them to read and digest the literature regarding some international aspect of business research. It creates demand for the resources needed to do the research (e.g., an internationally oriented literature collection). It provides an incentive for faculty to remain current in at least some international issues. It fosters expertise among doctoral candidates who then share it among themselves. Like the ripples from a rock thrown into a pond, the internationalization of dissertation research can influence all of the aspects of the conduct and culture within a doctoral program to the benefit of all concerned.

The internationalization of publications by doctoral students is similar in many ways to the situation regarding teaching and course work. International issues can be "infused" into manuscripts submitted for publication in journals that are not themselves internationally focused. Alternatively, the manuscripts can be positioned so that they are appropriate for journals that are internationally focused. Likewise, the ripple effect of including an international dimension in dissertation research extends to the publications that result from the research.

INTERNATIONALIZATION OF METHODS AND SKILLS

Beyond the issue of curriculum content, doctoral education should address teaching business in international contexts. As we train doctoral students in the process of teaching classes, we should include consideration of the influences of cultural differences in classroom learning. For instance, some pedagogical techniques common in the U.S. (e.g., the use of case analysis) are very foreign and not always well-accepted in some cultures. American teaching styles are relatively informal compared to much of the world where it is more often considered rude for students to interrupt a professor with questions or comments. In these cultures students can be very uncomfortable with having part of their evaluation based on class participation. Indeed, while teaching outside of the U.S. I have had students come to me and apologize for what they perceived to be the rude behavior of other students in the class when they spoke up with questions or comments during my presentation. I had been pleased with the questions and took them as an indication of the student's interest in the topic and understanding of the material.

Although the basic criteria for evaluating research (the quality of knowledge) is no different in the international context than it is in the U.S. context, there are great differences in the performance of many research tools in many international contexts. For instance, in many Asian countries a cultural phenomenon called "courtesy bias" or "social acquiescence bias" can significantly influence responses to questionnaires in that respondents are reluctant to use the negative end of a questionnaire scale item. In their cultures there seems to be a reluctance to openly or publicly disagree with or be negative about statements made by someone else. Another example is the greater inclination of U.S. respondents to use the extreme points on questionnaire response scales.

One of the most important skills that we can impart to doctoral students is how to write manuscripts effectively for publication. All too often, the process of transferring these skills to doctoral students is left to "osmosis" rather than explicitly teaching them how to do it. This process can broadly be delineated into making the case for *why* the research is needed (or why it makes a contribution to knowledge), and *how* the research should be done. Making the "why" case for the research involves reviewing the literature and presenting the theory that is the rationale for the many decisions that must be made in the gathering of evidence. It is more difficult than many doctoral students realize to develop good theory and to present it well. Often our doctoral students are trained well in the measurement and analysis skills needed for good research, but they have difficulty in expressing the reasoning behind the research process explicitly and clearly. The process of teaching doctoral students publication skills, especially the development of generalizable theory, should lead them to recognize the importance of the international dimension of business research. That, in turn, will encourage the inclusion of international topics and issues in their manuscripts.

ADMINISTRATIVE ISSUES AND INTERNATIONALIZATION

In addition to the various tasks of doctoral education described above, there is the important matter of administering the process. The key areas of administrative concern are the resources needed by faculty and doctoral students to teach, conduct research, and publish (e.g., libraries, computers, etc.), policies regarding admissions to programs, and the staffing of courses.

INTERNATIONALIZATION OF RESEARCH RESOURCES

It is impractical to expect faculty and doctoral students to work with international issues if they do not have the appropriate tools. For internationalization to become a reality, doctoral students and other researchers must have access to the necessary research literature and databases. This includes domestic journals that report internationally-oriented research as well as journals devoted entirely to international research. Unfortunately, this need increases the demands on university libraries at a time when many of those libraries are suffering from budget cuts and rising costs for periodicals. Some libraries are finding that they can resolve some of these difficulties by using CD-ROMs or other data base tools that provide abstract and even full text services for many more journals than the library could ever afford to keep on the shelf. Also, many researchers are solving this problem by accessing resources outside of their own libraries via Internet. This shift in media on the part of many libraries and researchers actually offers an opportunity for the addition of many more international sources, even in the face of budget difficulties.

INTERNATIONALIZATION THROUGH ADMISSIONS POLICIES

Doctoral programs are the gatekeepers of the academic world. Much of the internationalization in academia has occurred as a result of the selection of individuals with international backgrounds as students and candidates. This mode of internationalization is important and beneficial, but it cannot be relied upon as a primary strategy for the internationalization of doctoral programs. It is unreliable because a person's decision to apply for admission to a particular doctoral program is outside of the control of doctoral program administrators. Even if it were possible to control for these factors, the presence of individuals in the profession from various backgrounds does not guarantee that international issues are the focus their research and teaching. Additionally, regardless of their backgrounds, people who enter doctoral programs need training in the knowledge and research methods that can be used across a variety of cultures and contexts. Thus, even though international students add a valuable dimension to their respective doctoral programs, the student selection process is not a reliable approach to the systematic internationalization of doctoral education.

INTERNATIONALIZATION THROUGH STAFFING

Perhaps the single most effective approach to the internationalization of doctoral training is to internationalize the faculty who teach doctoral courses and who supervise the research of doctoral students. This approach can be termed "internationalization through staffing;" that is, choosing faculty with international research interests to teach doctoral courses. This approach will naturally increase the likelihood that international topics and methods will be infused into doctoral classes. Indeed, faculty should be encouraged to include their international research in the classes that they teach. A further benefit to this approach is that it increases the likelihood that international topics and international methods will be used in doctoral dissertations. Doctoral students generally select their dissertation committee members from among the faculty with whom they have had classes. As a result, this approach can increase the international content (and hence the generalizability) of the research that will be done to increase the body of knowledge in business administration. This approach can be operationalized in many different ways, such as:

1. the use of present members of a faculty with international research interests and activities;
2. the use of short term "visiting scholars;"
3. the use of longer term "guest professors;"

4. the hiring of new faculty with international research interests and activities; and

5. increasing the level of international orientation of present faculty.

The use of faculty from institutions outside of the U.S. as either visiting scholars or guest professors can stimulate greater interest in international issues in a variety of ways. Short term visits of a few days can be very helpful in improving the international content of doctoral courses. They can provide a "sense of event" around a particular topic, a focus on a particular block of literature, and/or an opportunity to discuss a topic with someone who has a different frame of reference. Longer visits can be much more influential. For instance, longer visits from international faculty are more likely to result in joint research with both faculty and doctoral students that continues after the guest professor returns to his/her home institution.

Several factors make the use of guest professors a practical approach to internationalizing U.S. doctoral programs. For example, many business schools in other countries have faculty members trained in the U.S., and who are familiar with courses taught here. Thus when they are invited to our schools these individuals can easily fit into our curricula, while bringing with them a perspective from an international environment. Additionally, there are tax treaties between the U.S. and many countries that make it possible for guest professors to exempt their earnings from U.S. taxes, making financial arrangements easier to manage.

The complement to bringing professors from other parts of the world is to send professors from U.S. institutions to teach and do research abroad. This type of experience, especially if it is of a longer term, can significantly increase the level of faculty involvement in international issues, research, and teaching. It also can provide a basis for faculty exchange programs with other institutions. Again, this process is facilitated by tax treaties that allow tax exempt status for academic professionals. Exchanges of this nature can be particularly productive if the institutions continue the exchange relationship over a long period of time. An extended exchange relationship allows faculty from each institution to become familiar with and involved with the research programs of the other institution.

There are a number of undergraduate and masters student exchange programs that have developed in recent years. One such program with which I have had experience is the Consortium of European Management Schools (CEMS) Program. This program is built around a core of CEMS faculty at the major business schools in 12 European countries. These 12 schools have agreed upon course requirements and course content for a CEMS masters degree. Students have to complete a portion of their course work in a country other than their own, forcing them to have an international experience. It also creates the opportunity for relatively easy faculty exchange since the content for specific courses (e.g., marketing research) is interchangeable among the 12 institutions. Since it is generally the case that faculty who teach doctoral courses also teach other non-doctoral courses, this type of an exchange program provides an excellent opportunity for faculty exchange at the doctoral level. Many U.S. business schools have developed exchange programs for their undergraduate and masters students. If these programs are carefully crafted, they provide the basis for faculty exchange programs that can have an important influence on the internationalization of doctoral education. The key to obtaining this benefit from these programs is to get the doctoral faculty to participate.

Conclusions

The rationale for internationalizing business education is generally presented as a necessary response to increases in demand for more international skills in the market place. The case that is made here focuses instead on the responsibility of academic professionals as the stewards of knowledge within society. However, the academic profession is not the only segment of society that produces and distributes knowledge. Therefore we need to concern ourselves with what it is that makes us different from other knowledge professions such as marketing researchers, journalists or librarians. We are different in the standards that we apply for assessing the quality of knowledge and the types of knowledge that we strive to produce. In business administration we must internationalize the knowledge that we create and disseminate it in order to meet the generalizability requirement for high quality knowledge. It is in the process of educating and acculturating new members of our profession that we can have the greatest impact on the future level of internationalization in our profession.

Notes

1. All of our teaching can benefit from the inclusion of international contexts so that the generalizability of the knowledge we are presenting is obvious. Indeed, international verification of knowledge in business administration is parallel to intersubject certification.

A Dual Approach to Internationalizing Business Ph.D. Programs

Peter S. Rose

Introduction

If we are to make real progress toward internationalizing business Ph.D. programs, it is important for us to define as precisely as we can what is meant by "internationalizing." Only then can we set realistic goals and adequately measure the progress of each business school towards the ultimate goal of a truly international school of business. "Internationalizing" as used here may be defined to mean exposing doctoral students and graduate faculty (and through them, the students they teach) to the similarities and differences across nations and across broad regions of the globe in: (a) business institutions, practices, and methods; (b) legal and regulatory policies affecting the business sector; and (c) the variety of cultures that surround the business sector. In other words, Ph.D. students must be encouraged and stimulated to investigate how business decisions, business institutions, and cultural and regulatory environments differ from one nation, region, and continent to another, how they are similar to one another, and how and why those differences and similarities affect the performance and welfare of businesses themselves and of the customers they serve. The "internationalizing" process should stimulate and encourage business doctoral students to seek an understanding of how international forces affect the individual business firm and, in turn, how individual firms and institutions can operate more efficiently within an increasingly global market environment.

I firmly believe that, to be really effective, the process of "Internationalization" for a business doctoral program must proceed, simultaneously, along *two* different levels:

A. The *micro level*, in which individual class meetings, courses, and seminars have their coverage expanded to include international business issues and problems and these issues and problems are fully integrated into the whole fabric of individual courses and seminars. Relatedly, individual graduate faculty members should be provided with adequate incentives to strengthen the international dimension of their research, teaching, and service activities.

B. The *macro level,* in which whole curricula, degree programs, and the administration and content of all business school activities and programs are infused with significant international material. Moreover, personnel appointments, promotions, and responsibilities within collegiate schools of business should be made, at least in part, on the basis of international business or academic accomplishments and experience.

I contend that *no* business Ph.D. program can be internationalized successfully, and certainly will not remain successfully internationalized for very long, unless internationalization proceeds at *both* micro and macro levels, so that *reinforcing synergistic benefits* are attainable across the multiple dimensions of each business school's programs. As Edwin L. Miller (in this volume) has noted, progress toward internationalization of business programs requires the active involvement of administrators, faculty, and students across the entire business school. If internationalization is not viewed as a high priority item for a college or university's undergraduate or master's business program, internationalizing the business Ph.D. program is also unlikely to receive sustained support from a university's administration or from its faculty.

Moreover, it seems logical that the internationalization of business schools should begin with the Ph.D. program, rather than with masters' or undergraduate programs, because, if the past is any indication of future trends, business Ph.D. programs are the primary source of future business faculty. As new professors emerge from business Ph.D. programs that are infused with sufficient international content, those new Ph.D. recipients are more likely to integrate international business material into the undergraduate and graduate courses they teach, gradually spreading the internationalization process throughout a business school's whole curriculum.

INTERNATIONALIZATION AT THE MICRO LEVEL OF INDIVIDUAL BUSINESS COURSES, SEMINARS, FACULTY, AND STUDENTS

As we noted above, internationalizing business doctoral programs at the *micro* level refers to integrating international business content into individual classes and courses and into the research, teaching, and service functions of the individual faculty member. We begin by talking about internationalizing Ph.D. coursework and then, at a later point, discuss how to aid graduate faculty in further internationalizing their professional activities. Exhibit 1 provides a summary outline of the essential steps that must be taken, in the author's view at least, to fully internationalize business Ph.D. programs.

THE PH.D. SEMINAR

If a business Ph.D. program does not have a Ph.D. seminar in each major sub-field of international business (international finance, marketing, etc.), the creation of such a seminar may be a helpful first step toward full internationalization of the Ph.D. program. Alternatively, international material can be added in the form of an international component to existing doctoral seminars. If the international seminar approach is taken, at least one international seminar should be *required*, not optional, coursework for all business Ph.D. students.

For example, at Texas A&M University where I teach, Ph.D. students in finance are all required to take four semester-long seminars in investments, corporate finance, financial institutions and markets, and international finance in order to complete their coursework and take preliminary examinations (see especially the recently published description of A&M's international finance seminar currently taught by Arvind Mahajan [1989]). At Texas A&M University the international finance doctoral seminar is regarded as *equal* in importance to all of the other seminars in the Texas A&M finance Ph.D. program. Moreover, when preliminary examinations are given at the end of the student's coursework, international finance questions are always included on the comprehensive exam along with questions on investments, corporate finance, and financial institutions and markets. This is especially important because most Ph.D. students in business enter teaching careers when they graduate and, if they are trained in international business, they will find it easier and less costly from the standpoint of professional time (especially time taken away from pursuing their individual research programs so vital to achieving promotion and tenure) to internationalize the courses that they teach. Thus, through well-conceived and frequently offered internationally oriented doctoral seminars, the benefits of internationalizing the business Ph.D. program may be conferred upon the next generation of business faculty.[1]

EXHIBIT 1 Internationalizing the Business Ph.D. Program at Micro and Macro Levels

Micro Level (Individual Classes, Courses and Seminars and Individual Faculty Members and Students)

* Developing Ph.D. seminars in international business across all major business disciplines or adding significant international components to existing doctoral courses.
* Expansion of Master's level courses in international business and economics to help in the training of Ph.D. students.
* Creating international fellowships for Ph.D. students.
* Providing financial support through grants, gifts, and other sources for bringing international speakers to campus, for preparing multinational business cases, and for acquiring international journals, data tapes, etc.
* Encouraging the use of internationally-oriented textbooks in courses at all undergraduate and graduate levels.
* Requiring travel abroad and demonstrated skill in one or more foreign languages before a Ph.D. student graduates or as a prerequisite for entering a doctoral program.
* Developing off-campus international seminars, conferences, or tours abroad or programs focused upon major international centers that are accessible to all business faculty and doctoral students.

Macro Level (Curricula, Degree Programs, Departments, and Colleges)

* Including international objectives and evidence of progress toward internationalizing curricula, programs, and administrative leadership measures in the business school's annual and long-range plans.
* Developing faculty and student exchange with other internationally-oriented business education and research programs.
* Establishing chairs, professorships, and faculty fellowships in international business disciplines.
* Appointing international leadership to key positions within the business school.
* Basing at least some portion of faculty salary increases, promotions, and tenure decisions on progress toward the business school's international goals.
* Encouraging the development of foreign language skills within the business school through special courses, travel, and selective hiring of faculty.

* Encouraging or requiring business school administrators and faculty to periodically travel, work, and study abroad.
* Reshaping business school admissions of both graduate and undergraduate students in order to encourage international diversity and interactions among different cultures.
* Establishing and promoting the use of an International Business Library for both *students and faculty.*

USING EXISTING COURSES TO PROVIDE PH.D. STUDENTS WITH EXPOSURE TO INTERNATIONAL MATERIALS

A possible alternative to the special doctoral seminar in international business or to adding significant international components to existing seminars is to require Ph.D. students to enroll in one or more master's level courses in international economics or in international business. As Jeff Madura (1991) has noted, this has the advantage of accessing existing courses and instructors already on staff, thereby minimizing the resource demands that the business school might otherwise be obligated to meet if it offered specialized seminars for doctoral students alone.

One disadvantage to this approach is that master's level courses tend to be more focused on multinational business practices rather than upon research methodologies and international theory. The primary aim of these particular courses is to better prepare MBA students who, arguably, have a greater need for more practical business material rather than a large block of theory and concepts. Moreover, many business Ph.D. programs are already crowded with required courses in the major field as well as in supporting fields (such as statistics or economics) so that the addition of a *new* course requirement may mean dropping other courses or demanding that Ph.D. students stay longer to complete their programs, placing additional strain on school budgets.

Ultimately, some tough decisions must be made concerning the limits of available resources and about which courses and programs are essential and which would be "nice" to have in order to offer a well-rounded program, but are simply not essential. Given the speed with which business markets are internationalizing today, business schools and their faculty may face some difficult choices about what must go to make room for expanded international business coverage or run the risk of increasing educational irrelevancy.[2]

Let us hasten to add, however, that not everyone in the international field agrees that the internationalization process mandates adding more courses. It may be possible within existing courses to replace individual readings, cases, or problem assignments that have a domestic-only focus with those that center upon international issues. Moreover, as Lutz (in this volume) observes, foreign students already enrolled in Ph.D. courses can be enlisted pro-actively as contributors to the cultural education of domestically oriented doctoral students. Still, it is the faculty who must play the major role in sensitizing their students to global issues and in encouraging students to think in global terms. As Myers and Omura (in this volume) note in their extensive survey of doctoral program directors in the United States and Canada, the most urgent need, and probably the greatest challenge as well, is to internationalize business faculty if we are ever going to effectively internationalize business schools.

Faculty Incentives—Most business faculty will not automatically begin to internationalize their research, teaching, and service activities without adequate economic incentives and resource commitments. It is in this area that the International Programs Office, Center for International Business, or other internationally-oriented campus unit can make a significant contribution to the internationalization process inside each school. International business centers can serve as the focus of fund-raising efforts to support a grant program that offers business faculty financial support for internationalizing their courses, funding such activities as bringing international business speakers to campus, preparing case problems devoted to managerial decision-making within multinational firms, publishing international research or tutorial materials, conducting surveys of multinational business needs, acquiring tapes containing international business and economic data to support research programs and classroom projects, acquiring international professional journals, trade magazines, and newspapers so that the search costs for faculty and students in acquiring international information are reduced as much as possible, and funding faculty for at least one semester or term of international research, enrollment in business courses abroad, or study at domestic colleges and universities that already have well-developed international business programs.

Upgrading Textbooks—Academic leadership in the business school should encourage faculty to use textbooks and readings that contain significant international material and, for those faculty who write textbooks, to expand their coverage of international topics. This will help to overcome a current problem in most business disciplines: *few standard textbooks today appear to include significant international material*, which makes it more costly in terms of faculty time to develop suitable global material for the classroom.

Foreign Travel and Study—Another potentially useful step for internationalizing business Ph.D. programs at the micro level is to develop and offer an off-campus seminar in international business for Ph.D. students organized by one or more faculty in the business school, but providing for travel to a site where international business experts in teaching, research, and foreign business practices and regulations are available. This off-campus program may include travel to London, Tokyo, Singapore, Hong Kong, New York, and other important centers of international commerce and finance. One or more business schools may be able to combine resources (and share the cost) to offer an effective off-campus (and, preferably, offshore) experience for their doctoral students. Travel of this sort may be feasible at a low marginal cost by allowing doctoral students and faculty to join existing study abroad programs or tours, but following a somewhat different itinerary that meets their special informational needs.

Alternatively, the business school can *require* doctoral students in international business to travel abroad and/or stay abroad for a stipulated period (perhaps for a semester or term) in order to better experience at least one foreign business environment and culture. A foreign language probably should be required, either as a prerequisite before entering a business Ph.D. program or as a curriculum requirement to be completed before a Ph.D. student pursues required study abroad or graduates. Historically, most university Ph.D. programs required demonstrated competence (usually translation skills) in one or more foreign languages; however, in recent years many graduate programs appear to have substituted other (frequently labeled "more practical") requirements, such as statistics or programming languages, in place of the more traditional foreign language requirements. Moreover, the foreign language skills needed by business school graduates today may be more of the "spoken" variety rather than the simple "translation" of text material.

Gaining International Teaching Experience—As recommended recently by Jeff Madura (1991), doctoral students who are expected to teach during their doctoral programs should be strongly encouraged (if not required) to teach at least one undergraduate or master's level course in international business or economics or to present a series of guest lectures in another professor's course devoted to internationalization in marketing, finance, or other business discipline. The object here is to ask Ph.D. students to not only learn international business concepts and practices, but to reinforce that learning by explaining international business principles to their students.

Offering Fellowships and Other Incentives—An excellent investment for most business graduate programs would be to offer fellowships to doctoral students who choose international business as their major field or dissertation project area. The school may also wish to offer rewards for the best internationally-oriented papers and/or dissertation(s) prepared each year by business doctoral students. Significant awards might also be extended to those doctoral teaching assistants who have been judged by their students and by the faculty to have had the most success in internationalizing the content of the business courses they teach or with which they assist faculty members.

INTERNATIONALIZATION OF BUSINESS PH.D. PROGRAMS AT THE MACRO LEVEL

A necessary supplement to internationalizing individual faculty members and doctoral courses is to internationalize entire departments, colleges, and other administrative or academic units within a college or university. Progress at the micro level must be reinforced by a plan to internationalize business education, research, and service *as a whole*.

GOALS AND PROGRESS MEASUREMENT

This process should logically begin at the *macro* level by encouraging academic units within colleges and schools of business to adopt *internationalization* as one of their principal goals. Those goals should be spelled out *in writing* and made a part of the business school's annual and long-range plans. Moreover, the measures of progress toward internationalizing business schools at the *macro* level need to be spelled out in a school's plan as well in order to evaluate and monitor each unit's progress toward its international objectives. Possible quantitative measures include:

1. how many courses offered each year have been revised or updated to include significant international content as a proportion of the whole business school curriculum;
2. what proportion of all the faculty's articles, research papers, and books that appear each year contain significant international content;
3. what proportion of the dollar volume of research grants received each year involve international issues;
4. what proportion of annual travel budgets have involved international journeys;
5. what proportion of the school's invited guests and visiting faculty come from international settings;
6. what proportion of all budgeted expenditures can be directly related to the business school's internationalization efforts; and
7. what proportion of all masters' theses and doctoral dissertations written each year involve significant international issues, hypotheses, and/or data.

Ideally, each of the foregoing measures should display a significant upward trend from year to year.

EXCHANGE PROGRAMS

Administrative leadership within the college should pursue opportunities to exchange faculty and students with business schools and colleges overseas and with domestic business schools that already have well-established international programs so that schools that are behind them on the international "learning curve" can benefit as well.

Moreover, where adequate resources can be found, the business school should establish chairs, professorships, and faculty fellowships in international marketing, finance, management, accounting, and economics that recognize and reward outstanding faculty scholars with demonstrated accomplishments in the international field. Frequently foreign firms have an interest in sponsoring relationships with U. S. colleges and universities, providing supplemental funding for endowed positions as well as for guest speakers and case material that aid each school's globalization efforts.

ADMINISTRATIVE ASSIGNMENTS

Within the administrative area of a business school selected personnel should be designated with primary responsibility to encourage the globalization of research and teaching programs at the doctoral level. These administrative appointments may be centered around an Associate or Assistant Dean for International Programs, a Department of International Business, a graduate International Business Committee, or some other appropriate unit.

Salary and Promotion Incentives

Certainly the clearest signal of the importance of internationalization that can be sent from a business school's administration to its faculty is to announce that salary increases, promotions, and tenure decisions will include a review of the progress and contribution that each faculty member has made toward internationalizing his or her courses, research, and service output. Equally important, this strategy must be carried through into decisions and actions clearly observable to all business faculty and followed consistently each year.

Foreign Language Skills and Travel

Internationalization at the macro level can be further encouraged by stimulating an interest in acquiring foreign language skills among faculty and students. This will require the business school to work with language departments on campus or in neighboring schools to offer special language classes in the evenings, on weekends, or between semesters to minimize the cost in time and inconvenience to faculty and students who choose to acquire working knowledge of a second language.

Academic and administrative leadership within the school of business should set an example for faculty and students by themselves traveling abroad and visiting foreign business and governmental institutions. Moreover, a business school's administrative leadership must address the problem of how to provide adequate funds for foreign travel. The cost of foreign travel has become prohibitive to many faculty and students, particularly during those periods when home currency values are falling against other convertible currencies. Enthusiastic participation of faculty and graduate students in programs and projects overseas often hinges on a school's willingness to provide supplemental funding for foreign travel. If, in this era of tight academic budgets, university-supported foreign travel becomes prohibitive, then electronic links should be pursued in order to establish joint seminars by cable, satellite, and computer networks with other schools and with international business experts speaking to faculty and doctoral students from remote locations.

The Admissions Process

To the extent that the student admissions process can be regulated at public and private business schools, administrators should encourage international diversity in admissions in order to achieve a mix of students from various international backgrounds and to promote the exchange of cross-cultural ideas and concepts in classrooms and in other business school programs where students and faculty exchange research and teaching ideas. This may require a break from the traditional "wait and see who shows up" approach to student recruiting and the adoption instead of a pro-active recruiting stance that pursues the type of doctoral students we would like to have in our graduate programs.

Enhancing International Library Collections

Finally, but certainly not least, the business school should work to find financial support to establish an *international business library* and encourage faculty and students to use it for both research and for expanding the international content of class lecture material. Particularly important is the building of a collection of international journals for research at the doctoral level—a step that can be aided significantly by developing electronic networks between libraries that house key international journals. Exhibit 2 provides an illustration of a basic research journal library collection in international business that some schools may find helpful as they expand their library holdings in international business education and research.[3]

CONCLUSIONS

Internationalizing the business school has recently become a higher priority item on the long-range agendas of many collegiate schools of business around the globe. Some business schools have adopted globalization or "global competence" as a priority goal because of pressure from accreditation agencies that often require that some minimum number of course hours be offered in the international field. Other schools have internationalized simply out of recognition that their students increasingly will be working for companies and governmental agencies active in international markets. After all, business schools must respond to the shifting dynamics of the business and academic marketplace or risk becoming irrelevant to the external constituencies they serve.

Effective globalization will require simultaneous work at the micro level (that is, within individual courses and in the minds of individual faculty members) and at the macro level (that is, across the entire curriculum and throughout universities, colleges, and departments). Synergistic benefits are possible if internationalizing decisions by individual faculty members and students are reinforced by academic and administrative leadership toward globalization throughout the business school. Business faculty will not automatically pursue internationalization without adequate incentives and adequate resources. Leadership within the business school must work to gather additional financial resources and to invest in an expanding base of human capital in order to fully support the internationalization process.

Exhibit 2. A Suggested Basic International Business Library of Journals to Support the Research and Teaching Functions of Graduate Business Schools
(Publisher or Sponsoring Organization Shown in Parentheses)

Accounting

Journal of International Financial Management and Accounting (Blackwell)
Journal of International Accounting — Education and Research (University of Illinois at Urbana- Champaign)
Advances in International Accounting (JAI Press, Greenwich, Conn.)
European Accounting Review (Routledge)
Journal of International Accounting, Auditing and Taxation (JAI Press, Greenwich, Conn.)

General Business

Journal of International Business Studies (Academy of International Business, Western Ontario University)
The Economist (Economist Newspaper Ltd., London)
Columbia Journal of World Business (Columbia University, New York and Pergamon Press)
Euromoney (Euromoney Publications, London)
Studies in Corporative International Development (Rutgers University, New Jersey)
Journal of Teaching in International Business (The Haworth Press, Inc.)

Finance

Journal of International Finance (Utex Corp.)
Journal of International Financial Management (Basil Blackwell)
Journal of Banking and Finance (North Holland)
Journal of International Money and Finance (Butterworth Scientific Limited)
Global Finance Journal (JAI Press, Greenwich, Connecticut, and London, England)
Journal of International Financial Markets, Institutions, and Money (Haworth Press)
The Banker (Financial Times Business Information, Ltd., London)

Marketing

Advances in International Marketing (JAI Press)
Banca Nazionale del Lavoro (Banca Nazionale del Lavoro Economic Research Dept.)
Journal of International Marketing (Michigan State University Press)

Management

Organization Science (The Institute)
Strategic Management (Wiley)
Asia-Pacific Journal of Management (National University of Singapore)

NOTES

1. We do not raise the issue here (though Alutto [1993] does so clearly) about the apparently increasing mismatch between the skills conferred on business Ph.D. students by many doctoral programs, which tend to stress research methods and research productivity, and the skills demanded by schools hiring Ph.D. students as faculty, which seem to stress mainly teaching and service. A weakening market for business Ph.D. graduates in academia has forced many research-oriented schools to rethink how they should be preparing their doctoral graduates for the academic job market. Frequently today even strongly teaching-oriented schools seek out doctoral graduates who can teach international problems and issues to undergraduate and masters' level students and to executive MBA programs. Too often, new Ph.D. graduates of research-oriented business schools appear to be ill-prepared for such a task by their schools' doctoral programs. Thus, newly hatched Ph.D.'s from strongly research-oriented business schools become harder and harder to place in meaningful academic positions.

2. One of the more difficult issues for the future will be the decision of how to integrate issues and problems stemming from the adoption and evolution of NAFTA into the

business school curriculum. Mexico has nearly 150 universities and Canada, close to 90 and both appear to have a desire to establish closer educational linkages with U. S. institutions of higher education. As recently as 1992 there were nearly 26,000 Canadian and Mexican students studying at U. S. institutions of higher education, but just over 7,200 U. S. students pursuing their education in Canada and Mexico (as noted in Cooper and Gaspar [1993]). These numbers, relatively small as they are today, seem likely to expand significantly in the future, offering ample opportunities for international diversification among those business schools able to position themselves to take advantage of NAFTA's continuing evolution. A substantial NAFTA higher-education network is already emerging through the Office of Academic Programs and the Trilateral Task Force on North American Higher Education Collaboration, both supported or co-sponsored by the U. S. Information Agency in Washington, D. C.

One major uncertainty for the future centers around the availability of future financial support for USIA, the U. S. Department of Education, and other federal programs that affect higher education and especially graduate business schools. More stringent funding policies seem likely, in the near future, forcing business schools to manage their available funds more carefully and to seek out new funding options. Private industry and industrial foundations, both foreign and domestic, will need to be pursued more vigorously in the future. Often foreign firms have reacted favorably to requests for support from U. S. business schools in an attempt to develop closer relationships with U. S. educational programs, both as a source of new managerial talent and as a vehicle for the continuing education of their current managers.

3. Barbara Pierce and Garnet Garven (1994) from the Western Business School of the University of Western Ontario have recently prepared an exhaustive list of journals currently publishing articles in international business. These two graduate researchers offer a number of helpful insights to faculty interested in placing their articles with these journals.

REFERENCES

Alutto, Joseph A., 1993. "Whither Doctoral Business Education? An Exploration of Program Models." *Selections*. (Spring): 37-43.

Cavusgil, S. Tamer (ed.). 1993. *Internationalizing Business Education: Meeting the Challenge*. East Lansing, MI: Michigan State University Press.

Cooper, S. Kerry and Gaspar, Julian E. (eds.). 1993. *Proceedings of the Roundtable Conference on Trilateralizing Business Education*. Houston, Texas (published by the Center for International Business, Texas A&M University, November).

Donovan, Jerry J. 1991. "International Trade and Finance Information Sources: A Guide to Periodical Literature." *Economic Review*. Federal Reserve Bank of Atlanta, July/August: 55-64.

Foggin, James H. 1992. "Meeting Customer Needs." *Survey of Business*. (Summer): 6-9.

Lutz, Richard J. "Adapting the Ph.D. Program to Ecological Imperatives: How to Herd Cats." in this volume.

Madura, Jeff. 1991. "Internationalizing the Ph.D. Program." *Journal of Teaching in International Business*. 3(1): 21-26.

Mahajan, Arvind. 1989. "A Model for Developing a Doctoral Seminar in International Finance." *The Journal of International Finance I*. 1 (Fall): 99-132.

Miller, Edwin L. "Helpful Institutional Arrangements for Internationalizing Doctoral Education in Business Administration." in this volume.

Myers, Mathew B. and Omura, Glenn S. "The Internationalization of Doctoral Programs: A Survey of Program Directors." in this volume.

Pierce, Barbara and Garven, Garnet. 1994. "Publishing International Business Research: A Survey of Leading Journals." Western Business School, The University of Western Ontario, Working Paper No. 94-22, September.

Siler, Charles. 1992. "School Consultants Get an 'A' Grade." *International Business*. September: 76-77.

Adapting the Ph.D. Program to Ecological Imperatives: How to Herd Cats

Richard J. Lutz

Introduction

In recent years, a number of environmental forces have caused Ph.D. programs in business schools to move toward a more planful approach. Downsizing Ph.D. enrollments in the face of declining demand, enhancing pedagogical training, exploring cross-functional integration to pursue topics such as Total Quality Management, increasing the representation of cultural minorities, and incorporating topics such as ethics and globalization into the Ph.D. curriculum are among these challenges. Though these topics span a relatively broad array of concerns, they share a common feature that inhibits effective management of the change process required to bring Ph.D. education more in the line with environmental imperatives: faculty resistance.

The Ph.D. program is, in my experience, the arena that tends to evoke the most emotional and outspoken responses from faculty whenever an outside force (e.g., the dean's office) threatens it. Faculty engage in vigorous and prolonged debates about alterations to the MBA or undergraduate curriculum, but these debates pale in comparison to the discussions generated by any proposal to alter the Ph.D. program. After all, as one dean noted, Ph.D. programs are how faculty reproduce themselves.

It is natural for faculty to attempt to produce self-clones in the Ph.D. program. Generally, the faculty member is a successful scholar who knows what it takes to succeed in academe. Often, the student has been attracted to the school at least in part due to the faculty member's reputation, and the student is likely to seek to emulate his/her mentor's worldview. Furthermore, faculty are best equipped to train students in what they know, i.e., their area of expertise, rather than venture into less familiar territory. Ph.D. programs are bastions of the status quo.

191

Unfortunately, the status isn't quo in the environment surrounding Ph.D. education. The average full professor who supervises Ph.D. students was probably trained sometime in the 1970s. Society, global competition, and business school curricula and constituencies have changed markedly over the ensuing two decades, necessitating a concomitant adjustment in the nature of Ph.D. education.

Due to its scholarly emphasis, much Ph.D. education rests on the one-to-one mentoring provided by the faculty member to the student. This is inherently a very personalized process and is not guided by a school-wide strategic plan. As one wit once observed, try taking 80 to 100 fiercely independent, supremely self-assured, and, oh yes, tenured, faculty and lead them in a single strategic direction: you would be more successful trying to herd cats!

THE NEED FOR PROGRAM PLANNING

In the face of these various pressures, the University of Florida has adopted a more *planful* approach to the Ph.D. program. Faculty resistance has been rather high at times, but ultimately the centralized budgeting authority won the power struggle. In essence, the dean's office, through the director of graduate studies, created an incentive-based approach to managing the Ph.D. program. Using this approach, we have been able to accomplish a "rightsizing" of Ph.D. enrollment at 75 percent of its historical level, increase the representation of cultural minorities threefold, and substantially enhance the amount of pedagogical training attendant to the "core" Ph.D. curriculum. The current thrust is with respect to improving the placement quality of our Ph.D. graduates in the academic market.

To date, the Ph.D. program has not addressed substantive curriculum-related issues such as TQM, entrepreneurship, ethics, or globalization. Thus, despite what we judge to be some initial success under our "planful" program approach, we are nevertheless very much in the role of novice when it comes to globalizing Ph.D. studies. However, consistent with our approach to the other challenges recounted above, our initial thinking on the matter entails a two-pronged approach:

1. Educating faculty regarding the globalization imperative and waiting for them to "internalize" the message; and
2. Creating incentives for Ph.D. students to pursue global aspects of their chosen field.

The first feature merely recognizes that nothing will change in Ph.D. education unless the faculty are fully invested in the process. As discussed above, the intensely personal nature of Ph.D. education dooms to failure any "outside" initiative that fails to capture the hearts and minds of the faculty mentors who are the engines driving the Ph.D. program. Clearly, a more globalized faculty cadre is more likely to produce globalized Ph.D. graduates, if by no other process than osmosis. Indeed, one of the primary activities of most CIBERs, and most enlightened business school deans, is the creation of programs designed to raise the global consciousness of faculty and encourage more international activity. Until that necessary condition has been met, any attempt to globalize the Ph.D. curriculum will be futile.

Incentivization—The second feature—incentivization—is an approach that has served us well at the University of Florida in meeting other environmental imperatives. Essentially, each academic unit begins with a "base" budget that allows it to maintain only a minimum-size ("critical mass") Ph.D. program. Securing additional resources that permit program expansion is contingent on the unit's performance vis-a-vis agreed-upon performance criteria. Although at this time the incentive-based system we have adopted does not incorporate explicit attention to issues of globalization, it certainly could in principle. To date, the University of Florida has treated globalization in a more informal fashion, which is probably appropriate to our current level of faculty acceptance of the need for globalization.

In the paragraphs to follow, I will describe our incentive-based planning system for Ph.D. education. This model has proved extremely useful and, by presenting it, I hope that other schools may be able to adapt it to their own needs. I will offer examples of how globalization activities could be built into the planning model at such time as the faculty are prepared to accept globalization as a priority.

The University of Florida Ph.D. Planning Model

Mission—The mission of the University of Florida Ph.D. program is to provide students with advanced training in research methods and substantive knowledge such that they are qualified to assume faculty positions in research-oriented universities or pursue other research careers at the highest levels. Although it is expected that most graduates will pursue academic careers, some may elect to accept research-oriented appointments in industry or government.

Objective—The current objective of the Ph.D. program is to improve overall program quality, as measured primarily by the quality of the initial positions accepted by Ph.D. graduates. The measurement standards are both absolute and relative, i.e., in comparison with the placement records of designated peer institutions. Placement quality is ranked as follows:

1. Top tier university (above peer institutions)
2. Peer institution
3. University with Ph.D. program in the student's discipline
4. Research-oriented university with no Ph.D. program
5. Strong teaching-oriented university
6. Well-regarded foreign university
7. High-level State, Federal or foreign government research post
8. High-level industry research position
9. Other

In general, the ranking of placement quality is more closely linked conceptually to the generation (and publication) of knowledge than to dissemination (i.e., teaching) or application of knowledge. Other indicators of program quality include evidence of student research productivity, both at graduation and 5-6 years later. Like all quality-oriented organizations, the Ph.D. program is also committed to continuous renewal and improvement over time.

Strategically, there are two broad mechanisms by which output (i.e., placement) quality can be enhanced: input quality (i.e., student qualifications) and throughput quality (i.e., curriculum and other aspects of doctoral training).

Input Strategy—Historically, admissions decisions have been based largely on an assessment of the student's raw intellectual ability, as measured by GMAT/GRE scores (especially the quantitative score), undergraduate grades, and, in some instances, letters of recommendation. Typically, some indication of the "fit" between the student's interests and program emphasis is also sought.

In general, the admission decision attempts to forecast the probability of professional success. Typically, the major concern has been the ability of the student to conduct publishable research. Criteria related to probable teaching ability, knowledge of and experience in business, and, in general, the prospects for excellent placement upon graduation, have entered into the admission decision less systematically. These latter criteria are now being given more consideration at the admission stage. An MBA degree and/or significant managerial experience, though not a requirement, is becoming a more valuable indicator of eventual placement quality. Careful consideration is also being given to the "mix" of domestic and foreign students in the program, as well as the representation of women and minorities. Our primary "customers," i.e., those universities hiring our graduates, operate in an environment of increasing political (and central administration) pressure to have culturally diverse faculties. At the same time, business schools are under increasing scrutiny by, and are increasingly reliant on, the external business community. For businesses to support business schools, they need to be convinced that students (undergraduate and MBA) learn about business from knowledgeable faculty, and that faculty are conducting meaningful research on substantive problems of immediate or potential interest to the business community. The foregoing implies greater emphasis on attracting as students mature individuals with both significant experience and genuine interest in the world of business. This in no way suggests movement away from scholarly potential as the overriding criterion for admission; it does suggest, however, a somewhat broader construal of scholarly research and an adjustment in certain tradeoffs that are made (e.g., a 30 year old MBA with a 620 GMAT versus an undergraduate math major with a 700 GMAT).

Throughput Strategy—It is safe to say that the dominant—perhaps, sole—emphasis of the University of Florida Ph.D. program has been on research training. Though many students taught at some point in the program, there was little formal training involved and, in many cases, no direct faculty supervision or mentoring. That situation is changing.

Although classroom teaching experience is not a formal program requirement (because some students opt for non-teaching careers), it is the norm rather than the exception; all students are strongly encouraged to teach as an essential part of their education. More systematic training, supervision, and feedback have been instituted. The emphasis of the program has shifted from a near-exclusive focus on research to the concept of a "complete faculty professional" who is strong not only in research but also in teaching, and is sensitive to the other aspects (e.g., university service) of faculty life.

Feedback/Benchmarking—In support of this College-level philosophy for Ph.D. education, each of our six academic units (accounting, economics, finance, decision and information sciences, management, and marketing) produced a plan at the unit level. A fundamental aspect of the unit-level plan was the identification of peer institutions to be used for comparative assessment of performance.

The following universities are in the College peer set, and were listed as peers by at least 4 of the 6 academic units: Illinois, Indiana, Iowa, Michigan, Ohio State, North Carolina, and Texas.

These schools form the "core" peer group for the Ph.D. program; however, each academic unit obtains placement data from an additional three or four schools that comprise peer institutions at the departmental level. The information collected from peer institutions includes: placements; size of program; size of faculty; stipend amount and number of years; non-waived tuition (if any); number of applicants annually; and student qualifications (e.g., GMAT, work experience). Collection of the data are the joint responsibility of the College Director of Graduate Studies and the Graduate Coordinator in each academic unit. The single most important piece of information is placement of graduates annually. Obviously, this information is inclusive and not just their top graduates. The other data collected help to establish the degree to which programs are comparable in terms of size and support.

Finally, it is useful to obtain other sorts of data, not so much for comparative evaluation, but rather as a source of ideas about new approaches and philosophies, e.g., program brochures, student manuals, curricula, teaching training programs, etc.

In general, internal performance measures are used to supplement the key placement and student research productivity criteria. When the College began reforming the Ph.D. program, improved placement performance was not anticipated immediately. Nevertheless, a number of intermediate indicators were used to track progress toward the ultimate goals. The measures shown in Exhibit 1 are classified into three groups: *output*; *throughput*; and *input*. Within the latter two groups, the measures are further broken down into *process* and *outcome* measures.

Academic units are responsible for compiling this information on all graduates and maintaining a database. Each year, curriculum vitae of all students who are on the market are submitted to the Director of Graduate Studies for review.

Exhibit 1 Internal Performance Measures

OUTPUT
- Student Placement
    - First position accepted
    - Job offers
    - Campus visits
- Student Productivity (during first five years after graduation)
    - Top-tier publications
    - Other published research
    - Research awards
    - Teaching awards

- Student Productivity (at time of graduation)
    - Top-tier publications accepted
    - Papers under review
    - Other publications
    - Conference presentations
    - Teaching ratings
    - Teaching awards

INPUT
Process

    Recruiting activities
    - Unit brochure, materials sent to applicants
    - GMASS (GRE Locator) followup
    - Minority GMASS followup
    - Campus visits by candidates
    - Phone interviews with candidates
    - Evidence of proactive recruiting efforts, especially relative to women
      and minorities

Outcomes
    - Total applications
    - Total "quality" applications (defined subjectively as possessing
      potential to be among the top one-third of the students in the unit)
    - Total women and minority applications
    - Acceptance rate on admission offers

    - Competing schools
    - Composition of entering class
          GMAT/GRE
          UGPA and institution
          MBA
          Previous GGPA and institution
          Managerial experience
          Representation of women and minorities
          Domestic/international mix

THROUGHPUT

Process
    - Student orientation
    - Program description document
    - Annual feedback to students
    - Early "weedout" mechanism
    - Early research emphasis
    - Teaching opportunities and training
    - Mentoring
          Research
          Teaching
    - Preparation for placement

Outcomes
    - Compliance with Graduate School regulations
    - UF GPA
    - Student annual reports
    - Time-to-graduation
    - Students completing Office of Instructional Resources TA workshop
    - Student assessment of overall program, research mentoring, teaching mentoring
    - Practice interviews prior to job market
    - Research presentations
    - Papers co-authored with faculty

Exhibit 2 displays a short list of internal performance measures that could be used by a school desiring to incentivize globalization activities. All the activities in the Exhibit are reflective of initiatives already in place at one or more CIBERs; what the measures are intended to reflect is the degree to which academic units avail themselves of the opportunities afforded by the CIBER or other College-level resources. This list of measures easily could be expanded or contracted to fit the needs and sophistication of a given institution with respect to its globalization effort.

Exhibit 2 Possible Internal Performance Measures

- Number of dissertations with international content
- Number of faculty/Ph.D. workshops on international issues
- Participation in Ph.D. student exchange study program
- Participation in overseas study programs for Ph.D. students
- Incorporation of global perspective in discipline-based Ph.D. seminars
- International Ph.D. seminar at the departmental level
- Number of students completing international business minor field

CONCLUSIONS

In closing, let me strike an optimistic chord regarding the future of the globalization in Ph.D. education. Combining the international flavor of Ph.D. student cohorts with continued developments in international telecommunications (e.g., e-mail) suggests a more global network of academics in the future. Just as the information highway may elude some in our generation but is accepted as a "given" by our children, it is a virtual certainty that our academic offspring will reside in a much more globally-integrated future than we do. Thus, while it is important that we begin their education in this regard, in many ways it will happen naturally, regardless of what we attempt and how effective we are at accomplishing it. In the global world of the future, new and improved cats will actually herd themselves!

Internationalizing the Teaching/Curriculum Dimension of Doctoral Education: The Ivey Business School Experience

Paul W. Beamish

Introduction

The purpose of this chapter is to share the experiences of the Western Business School, Ontario, Canada, in its attempts to internationalize the teaching and curriculum dimension of doctoral education. It is not intended to be prescriptive because internationalization depends in great part on the institutional context. Nonetheless, some of what we have found useful (and not useful) may be applicable to other schools.

While we have found some of the initiatives to be effective, several major barriers still exist. First, not all doctorals want to be internationalized. As a consequence, they neither capitalize on available opportunities nor expend any more effort than is required in the I.B. course. A second barrier is incomplete buy-in to internationalization by certain individual faculty members. Without positive reinforcement from faculty colleagues in the respective area groups, all of the Ph.D. program internationalization efforts in the world will not be effective.

Notwithstanding these caveats, progress has been evidenced on several fronts. The two cornerstones of our approach have been the use of (a) field experiences and (b) a unique set of components within the International Business course which all our doctorals are required to take. Each of these areas will be considered in turn. Before doing so however, a brief historical overview of the Richard Ivey School of Business and its Ph.D. program will be provided in order to set the institutional context.

Historical Overview of the Ivey Business School

The Ivey Business School is a professional school within The University of Western Ontario. Western is an academic community of 17 faculties and pro-

201

fessional schools, serving more than 26,000 students and over 4,000 faculty and staff. Located in London, Ontario, a city of 330,000 people, it is halfway between Toronto and Detroit and 100 kilometres from the United States border at Port Huron.

Historically the School has been a leader in management development. A partial list of achievements follows. They illustrate the proactive nature of change at Ivey, and provide the context for the school's internationalization efforts.

- In 1922 the first undergraduate business department in Canada was established.
- In 1932 the school began to publish its own journal. Known as *Business Quarterly*, it reaches out to both academic and management audiences and in 1994 enjoyed a circulation of 10,000 in 25 countries.
- In 1948, Canada's first executive development program was established (from the beginning, faculty members were required, as part of their responsibilities, to produce case material for the new programs being designed).
- In 1948, the School of Business Administration and the first MBA program in Canada were established.
- In 1961 Canada's first Ph.D. program in business was introduced.
- In 1974, official designation by the Federal Government as Canada's first, of what are now eight, Centre(s) for International Business Studies (CIBS) (forerunner to the CIBERs in the United States). Financial support for this Centre continues to be provided by the Federal Department of Foreign Affairs.
- In 1975, opened its own case and publications office. This office holds an inventory of 2,500 Canadian cases and is the Canadian clearing house for 5,000 Harvard cases.
- In 1978, commencement of its first international student exchange program with the London Business School, England; over twenty such exchange programs are now in place.
- In 1984, the school took a leading role in establishing the National Centre for Management Research and Development with support from the Canadian Federal Government.
- In 1987, the case clearing house at Cranfield in the UK began to distribute Ivey cases in Europe. In 1991, Western cases were being distributed to over 100 teaching institutions and 100 corporations in over 20 countries. Ivey is

the second largest producer of management case studies in the world, with over 1,000,000 copies studied each year by people outside the university.

- In 1992, Ivey was selected to be the editorial home for the 1993-97 period for the *Journal of International Business Studies*.
- In 1993, Canadian Business magazine's survey rated Ivey as the top MBA School in Canada, according to all groups: CEOs, human resources executives, and placement consultants. This ranking was re-confirmed in 1994. In 1994 Asia, Inc. rated Ivey among the World's Top 25 Business Schools for Asians.

As of 1994, the school had 65 full-time faculty who annually taught 500 regular and executive MBA, 300 undergraduate, and 40 Ph.D. students, plus executives in a wide range of non-degree programs. Its broad objective is to be widely recognized as one of the top 10 business schools in the world on the basis of its outstanding teaching programs, with a creditable research record in selected areas.

Internationally, the school has been involved with major offshore projects for 30 years, and currently is involved in China and several republics in the former Soviet Union. These projects have typically involved the establishment of local management training capability.

THE PH.D. PROGRAM

Ivey has a small doctoral program. Forty doctoral candidates are currently studying full-time in one of the following fields: Business Policy; Finance-Economics; Management Science/Management Information Systems; Managerial Accounting and Control; Marketing; Organization Behavior; and Production/Operations Management. The largest number (about one third) of the 8 to 10 doctorals admitted each year now register in Business Policy and most do International Business dissertations. Their interest often stems in part from their origins and backgrounds. Recent Ph.D. students have come from over a dozen countries.

Although one field of study must be selected, candidates may undertake studies and do research spanning different fields. For example, international research may take place in any discipline.

Many of our nearly 140 Ph.D. graduates teach and perform research at universities in Canada. Increasingly, others are employed by universities in the U.S.A. and elsewhere in the world (i.e., England, Switzerland, Singapore,

Indonesia, Hong Kong, Mexico, West Indies, New Zealand). Others have chosen to go into public service or the private sector. The median time to completion is four years after completion of an MBA or other master's degree.

PROVIDING FIELD EXPERIENCES

The first of the two key approaches used at Ivey to internationalize doctoral education is to provide international field experiences. These international field experiences occur primarily through curriculum, teaching, and thesis related activities. These are in addition to the common practice of encouraging doctorals to attend international conferences (AIB sponsored or other) and participate in doctoral consortia (i.e., in 1994 with LBS and INSEAD in France).

CURRICULUM ACTIVITIES

All doctorals at Ivey spend the summer between first and second year working on supervised research and case writing. In many of the area groups, the case writing function takes primacy and entails the preparation of two comprehensive, decision-oriented case studies written under the supervision of a professor. As the attached Exhibit 1 suggests, increasingly these cases are not only international in terms of issue, but the student travels (usually with the supervising professor) to the country for the interviews and data collection.

The international cases that are prepared are typically for internationally-oriented electives. Yet efforts are being made to have international cases used in the required MBA/undergraduate courses in hopes of further internationalizing their content.

Doctoral students are paid a salary for their summer research/case writing efforts. There is clearly an incremental financial cost for airfares/hotels because these cases require international travel. This incremental cost is one which the school has been willing to bear because it is consistent with Ivey's strategy. Without this financial support, the number of international cases written would most certainly be lower.

Another curriculum-related initiative which several doctorals have been able to capitalize on is the international study tour. For each of the past two years, a small group of MBA and undergraduate students and faculty have visited Monterrey, Mexico, during Reading Week in February. For the MBA students this is an opportunity to have a short high-quality international experience. Most MBA students will use the insights gained during the plant and university visits and interviews as part of a course project for that term. Ph.D. students, although this is not part of their curriculum, have been able to piggy-back onto this existing program in order to gain some international exposure that would not otherwise be available. Such exposure has proved helpful in determining subsequent interest in working or doing research in that particular country.

TEACHING ACTIVITIES

Unlike the practice at many U.S. universities, it is not common practice at Ivey to use doctorals to teach entire undergraduate courses. Nonetheless, all doctorals at Ivey receive teaching training. In some area groups they participate in weekly teaching group meetings, and teach (with or without professor observation) a certain number of class sessions (4-10) throughout the second year. Almost always, they also teach the cases they have written. Since many of these cases are international, this provides a unique opportunity to apply their summer field experience.

In instances where Ivey faculty have been invited to teach short courses overseas, but are unable to go, several doctoral students have been able to take the faculty member's place. While this is only appropriate for doctorals at the later stages of the Ph.D. program, and even then only appropriate for those whom the faculty are confident will do a good job, it nonetheless has been a useful vehicle to internationalize doctorals. An example of this in practice is Patrick Woodcock and Kent Neupert teaching International Business for three weeks in New Zealand in the place of the professor who had originally been invited.

Another example of the international teaching opportunities available to doctorals is the LEADER project. Starting in 1991, 25 to 60 Ivey MBAs have travelled each year to one of five republics in the ex-USSR to teach three-week courses in Introductory Business. In the last few years, several doctorals have joined the teaching teams. As with some of the curriculum activities noted earlier, this is an opportunity for doctorals to piggy-back on to existing school programs.

THESIS RELATED ACTIVITIES

The final major locus for gaining field experience as a doctoral student at Ivey is through thesis-related travel. In part due to the school's practitioner-relevance emphasis and case writing experience, a significant number of the doctoral dissertations at Ivey include international field work. Exhibit 2 provides some recent examples of internationally oriented theses in the policy area, and where the candidate visited.

To financially facilitate the writing of international dissertations, the school's Centre for International Business Studies has often provided up to an additional $4,000 in expense money for international travel. This is on top of the $2,750 that is made available by the school to all candidates.

The existence of financial support for international dissertations cannot, by itself, guarantee that more international dissertations will be undertaken. The bigger issue continues to be functional area commitment. To assess this, we reviewed all of the business dissertations ever completed at Ivey for their international content.[1] "International" was very broadly operationalized, involving *any* of:

1. non-local (i.e., non-Canadian) research settings;
2. data collected from more than one country;
3. foreign companies doing business in Canada.

This evaluation (Exhibit 3) indicated that while the proportion of internationally-oriented dissertations had risen to 50 percent in the most recent time period, these were heavily concentrated in only four of the seven functional areas. Almost all of the management (business policy and organizational behaviour) dissertations at Ivey have been international for the past 5 years. The levels in Production/Operations Management and Finance/Economics have been moderate while those in other functional areas have remained low.

COMPONENTS OF OUR REQUIRED PH.D. LEVEL COURSE

As with most Business Ph.D. programs where there is a commitment to International Business, we offer a required course that examines the theoretical evolution and scope of international management theory and research—both as a distinct field of inquiry and as an interdisciplinary resource. The course builds upon concepts first presented in our seminars in Research

Methodology and Foundations of Management, and supplements the various functional level Special Fields offerings.

The course is organized into two overlapping areas. The first half of the course explores the various underlying theories used to understand international business—including their assumptions and limitations. The second half examines some of the unique research methodology issues present in international studies. This section involves a visitor's program. Major contributors to the international business literature (from different functional areas) will lead in-depth interactive analyses of their work (i.e., Masaaki Kotabe, Bernard Yeung, Stephen Young, Philip Rosson, Mary Ann Von Glinow, S. Tamer Cavusgil).

An innovation currently underway is to have the foreign faculty visitor join the class through video-conferencing. The Ivey Business School's newly-installed video conference facility will be used, in part, for Ph.D. program internationalization.

The assigned readings/literature in Ivey's Ph.D. level course in I.B. overlap with that offered in many other Ph.D. programs. In our view, however, reading the literature is not enough for true internationalization to occur. It must be applied, and placed in context, from one's functional perspective.

Recognizing that most of our graduates will not be hired directly for I.B. positions, our objective in this course is to ensure that they can better understand and capitalize on the international dimension in their function. To that end, both the course content (which includes sessions on how to do I.B. research) and in part, evaluation, have been geared to such a context.

To that end, in addition to being evaluated on the basis of in-class participation, students in 1993 and 1994 were required to complete any two of the following three assignments:

International Heritage: Functional Perspectives.

This 20-25 page paper details the existing/potential international contributions to a primary paradigm/theory in the student's functional area. Cross functional contributions are included. The paper is written in JIBS format. One class session is devoted to the presentation of selected papers. Some of these papers were eventually presented at conferences and published.

The Internationalization of the MBA/HBA program.

Do either (A) or (B). This portion of the student's grade is determined in consultation with the relevant area group faculty member.

(A) Each student is required to provide a teaching package (lecture and/or case material) to his/her area group for internationalizing at least two classes in an MBA/HBA elective or required course of their choosing. This package must identify the class sessions to be replaced, the new material to be used, the theory-based rationale for the new sessions and the fit with overall course design.

(B)[2] Many of the paradigms, metaphors, theories and constructs that students are introduced to during their HBA/MBA studies are arguably "culture bound." More significantly, this often goes unacknowledged by the professor. Those doctoral candidates choosing this option are required to (1) identify two classes of their own choosing in the MBA/HBA program that have culturally-bound lessons; and (2) prepare a position paper on each (maximum 3 pages each) for the professor which explains why the class/case is inappropriate as taught, and why it should be either replaced in its entirety or its teaching focus modified. The theory-based rationale for the new session must be clear.

PUBLISHING INTERNATIONAL BUSINESS RESEARCH: FUNCTIONAL PERSPECTIVES.

This paper entailed an analysis of the existing journal publishing opportunities for I.B. research in each student's functional area. This required students to classify journals in terms of type and size of audience, reputation, emphasis, acceptance rates, and other criteria they deemed appropriate. This individual paper became a massive 10-student project,[3] with positive results. Over 80 journal editors responded to a questionnaire. This has resulted in a journal article that deals with publishing strategies for I.B. research (JIBS, Volume 26, Number 1, 1995 pg 69-89.) as well as a comprehensive working paper (available from Ivey Business School) which details the raw responses.

While this third paper is not suitable as a topic again right away, the idea of having the students actually contact people in a variety of countries—as part of the course—can provide at least some insight with respect to what I.B. research entails. Other possibilities for future years might include having them work with doctorals in another country on a common project (or even to spend a term on an exchange basis in another institution's Ph.D. program), to have them replicate an existing research project in their countries-of-origin with a view of writing a comparative article, and so forth.

CONCLUSIONS

The range of methods for internationalizing the teaching/curriculum dimension of doctoral education is broad. While other approaches may be equally effective, Ivey's focus has been on field experiences and the I.B. course composition. These strategies for internationalization were chosen on the basis of institutional need, and an inherent faculty belief that such initiatives would be worthwhile. Certainly the student perception of these activities has been uniformly positive. We believe that it has also contributed to the placement of our doctoral graduates onto the faculties of internationally-oriented institutions such as Thunderbird, ITESM, and the Stockholm School of Economics.

Whatever method of internationalization is preferred, the key is to move forward now. All methods will be required if we are to effectively train the future trainers.

NOTES

1. This assessment follows on that of John Stopford at LBS.
2. This assignment was inspired by a comment in Brian Toyne's paper.
3. See Barbara Pierce's paper in this volume for a description of the process.

Exhibit 1. Ivey Business School

Current BP Area Doctoral Candidates, Location of Case Writing, and Case Examples

Candidate	Country Visited	Case Example
Doug Reid	Taiwan	P.T. Sekbang
Azimah Ainuddin	Malaysia	Pewter Industry
Carl Fey	Russia	Dialogue
Barb Pierce	Belgium	Sabena Airlines
Katy Paul-Chowdury	Mexico	Taco Bell
Honorio Todino	Russia	Pepsi in Russia
Shige Makino	Japan	Toppan-Moore

Exhibit 2. Ivey Business School

Recent Internationally Oriented Dissertations in Policy Area and Location of Field Work

Name	Thesis Title	Location of International Field Work
Jonathan Calof	"The Internationalization Process: Mode Change, Choice, Performance"	Canada, USA, UK
Andrew Inkpen	"Learning and Collaboration: An Examination of North American-Japanese Joint Ventures"	Canada, USA
Louis Hébert	"Division of Control, Relationship Dynamics,and Joint Venture Performance"	Canada, USA
Honorio Todino	"Country-of-Origin Effects on Price"	Philippines
Shige Makino	"Joint Venture Ownership Structure and Performance: Japanese Joint Ventures in Asia"	Japan

Julian Birkenshaw	"Entrepreneurship in Multinational Corporations:The Initiative Process in Foreign Subsidiaries"	Canada, USA, UK
Kent Neupert	"Implementing Strategic Buyer-Supplier Alliances for Product Development"	Canada, USA
Bob Blunden	"Financing Patterns, Resource Scarcity and New Venture Performance"	Canada, USA
Kerry McLellan	"Outsourcing Core Skills Into Non-Equity Alliance Networks"	Canada, USA, UK

Exhibit 3. *Historical Analysis of The International Content of Doctoral Dissertations at The Ivey Business School*

| | 1990s | | 1980s | | 1970s/60s | | All Years | |
	Total	Int'l	Total	Int'l	Total	Int'l	Total	Int'l
Business Policy	11	10	4	2	6	2	21	14
O. B.	6	6	9	1	5	0	20	7
Finance/Economics	7	2	5	3	6	1	18	6
Marketing	7	2	9	1	17	3	33	6
MS/IS	9	1	10	1	2	0	21	2
Accounting	2	0	5	1	4	0	11	1
Production/Operations Management	4	2	7	3	5	2	16	7
TOTAL	46	23	49	12	45	8	140	43
INT'L as % of Total		50%		24%		18%		31%

Source: Compiled in October 1994 by Andrew Delios, Nick Bontis, Tom Clift, Natasha Koziol, Karl Lewies, Chantell Nicholls, and Olga Volkoff-Richardson.

INTERNATIONALIZATION OF THE DOCTORAL PROGRAM CURRICULUM: A REVIEW OF SOME APPROACHES AT TORONTO

Daniel Ondrack

INTRODUCTION

The globalization of the economy has provided the major impetus for the internationalization of the MBA curriculum at Toronto. These same forces are now encouraging a review of the curriculum for the doctoral program. Many years of effort were devoted to changing the MBA curriculum and the process is by no means complete. Basically three changes were made to internationalize our MBA program: addition of international content in compulsory courses in first and second years; addition of international option courses in the second year to permit a major in International Business; and development of numerous exchange programs with international partner schools. These changes are consistent with those proposed by Jacob (1993) for the internationalization of management education. Since almost all members of our faculty have worked or studied outside Canada and many are active with international research projects, no special attempt was made to internationalize the professors.

The changes for the MBA curriculum provide a base for options for internationalization of the doctoral curriculum, but a number of other considerations became evident when we tried to implement some of these changes in the doctoral program. These issues will be discussed in more detail in this paper. While the need for internationalizing the doctoral program is recognized by many, there are also several opposing forces in our faculty with legitimate points of view (see Alutto 1993). The basic position of this paper is that our doctoral program must provide an international education to all students, regardless of their major, in order to provide them with an additional, but fundamental level of competency for their academic or other careers. In other words, "the only business is international business" and our

213

doctoral graduates will not be qualified for their careers in teaching and research if they are not educated in this area.

The Doctoral Program at Toronto

The doctoral program in management at Toronto was established in 1970; there have been 97 graduates to date, essentially in four areas: finance; marketing; organizational behavior/human resources; and operations management. Only a very few have graduated in Strategy or International Business due to limited teaching resources in these areas. The program operates at a steady state of about 40 students in residence and each year 10-12 new students come into the program after a master's degree. About 1/3 of the students are from outside Canada. The attrition rate is 45 percent and each year 4-5 students graduate, after approximately 5.6 years in the program (the university-wide average for time to completion after a master's degree is 5.7 years). Most of our students speak at least one other language in addition to English.

The School of Graduate Studies at Toronto regulates admissions and academic standards for graduate programs across all the faculties of the University. SGS conducted a major review of doctoral programs in 1993 which concluded that the time to completion for a Ph.D. is too long. New policies were announced to reduce the average completion time. All faculties with doctoral programs were directed to review and restructure their programs so that the average length of time to completion after a master's degree would be reduced to four years. Starting with admissions for September 1994, Ph.D. students' eligibility for university doctoral fellowships would cease after four years of enrollment and a cap of six years would be allowed for continuous enrollment.

Finally, the doctoral program at Toronto has also followed the pattern of numerous other schools of introducing new courses and workshops for teaching and communication skills for all students. After completing these courses, we want all students to have some experience both as a teaching assistant and as an instructor for a course. The purpose of these changes has been to make students more marketable in the job search (e.g., better presentations skills for job interviews), to strengthen their CV with a record of teaching experience, and to make their professional life of teaching somewhat easier when they start their careers. (Another possible benefit is improved consulting skills.)

THE POLITICAL AND POLICY CLIMATE FOR INTERNATIONALIZATION

Given the new directive from SGS to shorten doctoral programs, while at the same time adding courses on teaching and teaching duties to make students more marketable, it is clear that the possible addition of new curriculum content in the program will be a contentious matter. A further source of contention is that many of the doctoral program specialists in the faculty also want to add to the required courses in their particular areas. In this situation, we not only have a zero-sum game for the competing interests, the total sum of course time available is also being reduced.

In terms of receptivity to internationalization, members of the faculty fall into approximately three camps: indifferent; strongly in favor; and strongly opposed. Among the strongly opposed, there are some in favor in principle, but they are strongly opposed to reducing any of their parts of the curriculum. Even those who are indifferent are generally opposed to a reduction of their part of the curriculum. This sort of political environment is likely to be found at many schools (Jacob 1993; Daniels in this volume).

GOALS FOR INTERNATIONALIZATION OF DOCTORAL EDUCATION

A doctoral program that offers an internationalized curriculum should provide added value to students in at least three ways:

- An improved level of **knowledge** of the importance of international business;
- an **appreciation** of the impact of cultural differences in their fields; and
- enhanced **competence** to do relevant research for the contemporary and future business environment.

In terms of learning about international aspects of management, Brislin and Tomoko (1994) have identified four basic types of learning content for international training programs: awareness; knowledge; emotions; and skills.

- **Awareness** is simply a matter of becoming more conscious of the phenomenon of international business and the importance of international business to any aspect of doctoral studies.
- **Knowledge** is more specific to particular cultures, regions or aspects of international business.
- **Emotions** refers to the adaptation process people might go through in the actual process of international business or research (e.g., the experience of

trying to gather research data in another culture, or the experience of being an expatriate in another culture).

- **Skills** refers to the achievement of a higher level of competence in working with other cultures or doing any aspect of international business or research.

The Brislin and Tomoko framework will be used in discussing a number of approaches to modifying the doctoral curriculum. These options are not mutually exclusive and most schools would follow a variety of these options at the same time (Ivancevich and Duening 1993).

International Content in All Core Courses for Each Area—This option would require instructors for all doctoral seminars to add some consideration of international or cross-cultural aspects of their field to their current courses. The immediate sources of resistance for this option are the reduction of time from current content and the start-up required to add new dimensions of content. Since most of our faculty members have already gone through such a start-up with the MBA curriculum, resistance is not strong to this aspect of internationalization. A more subtle form of resistance can occur if professors have to rethink some of their fundamental assumptions about their field when they start to teach about some international aspects of their field (Miller in this volume).

In Organizational Behavior, for example, do all of our assumptions about motivation theory hold true for other cultures or is a large part of our OB knowledge an artifact of research in American and western European cultures (Hofstede, 1980)? Some of our people have found it to be difficult to teach some prescriptive material with the rider that "of course, this might not be true in other cultures." For example, try teaching the importance of goal-setting as a motivational technique to people who come from a culture of 'past-orientation' to time (Adler 1991).

In terms of Brislin and Tomoko's framework, international content in core courses would contribute mostly to "awareness," although some "emotion" may be involved for those who have to rethink some of their assumptions after awareness exposure. With individual professors teaching some international content as part of their regular courses, this option lacks any standardization of coverage of international content across the doctoral program (e.g., different instructors will give different amounts of coverage to international material).

Since all of the major areas of the program at Toronto are under pressure to reduce the amount of course work to complete a major, no one is receptive to any proposals for new courses. Similarly, there will be resistance in some areas to "watering down" some of their current content to add international content. The only way to succeed with some degree of internationalization across core courses is to convince instructors that their core material will not be current if international material is overlooked. The outlook for this option at Toronto is: initial reluctance to cooperate by some areas; uneven international coverage across areas; but better coverage in all areas in the long term as international content becomes more "mainstream" for all areas. A similar pattern for the doctoral program at Indiana is reported by Daniels (in this volume).

An International Core Course Added to the Curriculum—This option is similar to common core courses in research methods or teaching skills that exist in many programs. All students would be required to take the International Business seminar regardless of their major area. The theory behind this option is that all students in management should receive systematic exposure to International Business to provide a context for any of their future studies/research in any area. This option provides a common education for "awareness" to all doctoral students that satisfies a desire for standardization of this aspect of international education. Such a core course is offered in the doctoral program at the Western Business School (Beamish, in this volume) and is planned for the program at Indiana (Daniels, in this volume). More specialized international knowledge would have to come from other areas of the program. We have a strong preference for the addition of a new International Business seminar as part of the common core of our program, but of course, there is a problem with adding courses to an already heavy course load. The option of adding a new core international course is not viable given the University directive to reduce the total length of the program to four years.

Cross-Cultural Content in Courses for Teaching Methods—For those programs that offer teaching and communication skills courses, this option requires the addition of cross-cultural content, exercises, etc., in such a course. This would be a very useful addition to the curriculum as many potential teachers can expect to have students from a variety of cultures in their classrooms or may expect to work with international colleagues in the future. For those programs that offer, or plan to offer, courses in teaching and communications skills, the addition of cross-cultural content could achieve a greater level of "awareness," "knowledge" and "skills" (Brislin and Tomoko 1994).

Those schools that have a high proportion of international students can also use their knowledge and experience to achieve considerable enrichment of the skills aspect of the curriculum. Working in cross-cultural groups with international students can also provide some degree of "emotion" learning for international content (Ondrack and Leiba 1994).

The addition of cross-cultural content to our new course on teaching and communication skills will be fairly straightforward now that we have managed to add a new course on teaching methods and communications to the common core of our program. This addition has been achieved despite the other pressures for reducing course work in the program. By adding international content into the new course for teaching and communications skills, the outlook for successful implementation of this option is good.

International Dimensions in Thesis Research—A logical extension to offering international content in core courses would be to require doctoral theses on any topic to have some consideration of international aspects of the topic. This could range from reviews of relevant international literature to discussion of international aspects of any research study (e.g., even if a particular study is completely domestic in focus, the discussion section could review some international aspects of the results). This type of discussion would be similar to the section of a thesis that discusses "practical applications" of the results. The option of some international content in a thesis requires students to maintain awareness of international issues, but the option can only succeed with support from the thesis supervisor. A significant number of doctoral dissertations with international content are reported for the programs at Western (Beamish in this volume). Stopford (in this volume) reports that "it is rare for a thesis to be exclusively on domestic matters at the London Business School."

We will not be able to mandate this sort of change in our thesis requirements at Toronto. This option, therefore, will be entirely dependent upon the wishes of thesis supervisors. However, the more that faculty members pursue international research themselves, the more that this option will start to appear within thesis research. The outlook is highly variable in the short run with more use of this option expected in the long run.

Visiting Scholars from International Sources—It is obvious that international scholars can offer a high potential for international aspects of teaching and research, but some domestic professors may be reluctant to give up their own doctoral teaching time in favor of lectures by a visitor. Some programs may be reluctant to trust parts of doctoral education to relative strangers, unless the visitor has a strong reputation in a relevant area. Another difficulty may be the temporary nature of a visiting scholar's relationship to doctoral students. A much less problematic approach is to make extensive use of visiting scholars for guest lectures and seminars and to encourage the use of international scholars as members of thesis committees or research teams. Certainly, it is very valuable for doctoral students to begin to obtain exposure to the international network of scholars, particularly if the student hopes to pursue international research in his/her career.

To implement this option effectively, a doctoral program should have access to fairly substantial funding (such as a CIBER) to support visits by international scholars for joint research projects and doctoral workshops, as well as to support student travel to international sites for research (e.g., see Beamish in this volume) and doctoral workshops. This option is highly desirable for our program, but due to our limited resources, we will be unable to have a systematic implementation of this option. Instead we will have to continue with our present ad hoc arrangements, dependent upon visits from international scholars and contacts by individual faculty members.

For example, we recently hosted a delegation of visiting OB professors and doctoral students from Austria and organized ad hoc workshops for presentations of doctoral research from both schools. Our students had an opportunity to have their ideas discussed from a European perspective and to see how the Austrians approached their research projects. The outlook for this option is highly variable for the long run, dependent on travel budgets for ourselves and visitors.

From Awareness to Involvement—The options discussed so far have mainly involved tinkering with existing courses or adding a few new courses to the curriculum. Even this degree of "tinkering" can be quite contentious if the changes threaten academic territorial rights, impose new work loads or cause individuals or departments to perceive the addition of international content as a loss in a zero-sum game. In terms of the Brislin and Tomoko framework, the main effect of any of the changes discussed so far would be increased "awareness" among doctoral students. Knowledge of a specific culture or area of international business might be enhanced through the focus of a particular research project or exposure to particular individuals. Otherwise, these options would have minimal effects on emotional experience or behavioral skills.

The next few options require a different magnitude of commitment and involvement both by a school and students, but these options can offer a different and broader type of learning experience (Ivancevich and Duening 1993). Each option also involves more risk in terms of diminished faculty control over the content of education in the program.

International Exchanges for Doctoral Workshops/Seminars—It is already fairly common for students to participate in doctoral student consortia at North American academic societies (such as the Academy of Management). This activity can provide students with valuable exposure and experience. An international dimension can be added (unfortunately at great expense) by student participation in international workshops or doctoral consortia. For example, students could be encouraged and possibly supported financially to participate in the bi-annual off-shore meetings of the Eastern Academy of Management (Singapore in July 1995) in addition to the annual North American meetings of the Academy.

In Europe, for example, doctoral students in management from across Europe regularly participate in workshops organized by the European Institute for Advanced Studies in Management (EIASM) in Brussels, or those funded by the European Commission (Stopford in this volume). One of the goals of EIASM is the fostering of a European network of academics in management. Many European doctoral students begin entering the network through participation in the various EIASM workshops. (Incidentally, I am a co-chair of the annual EIASM doctoral workshop in Human Resource Management.) In recent years, we have been encouraging some of our students at Toronto to present papers and participate in such international workshops, but we can only offer very limited financial support for this activity.

Participation in international workshops provides students with a high level of awareness, informal knowledge and some degree of emotional experience from meeting and socializing with professors and students from a variety of cultures. The experience does not always have to be positive in order to be useful for a better appreciation of the complexities of international business. The major limitations of international workshops are cost and the short duration of a somewhat artificial foreign experience (e.g., the experience of going to a 2-3 day conference in a foreign location is not the same as living in the same location). However, students can gain a lot from the experience of even a week at an international workshop and this only takes students away from their studies at "home" for a short time. In the absence of any regular financial support for student travel to international workshops, the use of this option at Toronto will remain ad hoc.

Student Exchanges for Doctoral Study at Other Schools—MBA student exchanges for a term or more of study abroad are quite common in most schools of management. A fundamental assumption for these exchanges is that the quality of education is equivalent between each of the partner schools. As a result, academic integrity is maintained in students' education regardless of where they study. A second major assumption is reciprocity in numbers between partners. Each school does not want to receive a greater number of incoming students than it sends out to others. (The ERASMUS program of travelling scholars in Europe depends upon both these assumption for 100+ universities).

Student exchanges in doctoral programs are not nearly so common and most arrangements for visiting students are probably ad hoc for individuals and not based on a system of reciprocity. Individual students might spend one term abroad as a visitor to work with a specialist in some area, but there is no expectation that the host school will send a reciprocal visitor to the other school. For example, in my own doctoral studies at Michigan, I worked with Milton Rokeach as a visiting student at Michigan State University, but there was no reciprocal visit by a student from MSU to Michigan. (One term at MSU doesn't qualify as a foreign experience, but it was very valuable to my studies.)

Another pattern is that one school might routinely send doctoral students to another school that is perceived to be stronger in some area of studies. The sending school may pay a fee for this privilege, may accept MBA students in lieu of doctoral students, or may offer visiting professorships to those who agree to work with the incoming doctoral students. We have such an arrangement with three of our international partner schools. We receive two or three visiting doctoral students each year, but so far none of our doctoral students has chosen to participate in such an exchange. Both Western and London Business Schools have reported some attempts to establish doctoral student exchanges with partner schools such as INSEAD.

One or two terms abroad would provide students a high level of all four dimensions of international education, but there are at least four reasons for doctoral student reluctance to participate in such exchanges:

- lack of support (or worse) from their supervisors;
- lack of perceived strength at the doctoral level in the partner school;
- lack of financial resources for one or two terms abroad; and
- family mobility difficulties (e.g., working spouse, children in school, etc.).

Many of our students express interest in principle for study abroad, but the perceived difficulties for students are too high. Many supervisors in our program would discourage study abroad as being a distraction or providing too little value-added for students in terms of mastery of their major subject or completion of their thesis. The only exceptions to this pattern would be those students whose thesis research requires gathering of original data from a foreign location.

It is interesting to note from the description of the doctoral program at Western (Beamish in this volume) that doctoral students are frequently employed to do case study research in international locations, both to develop new case teaching material for Western and to provide some international experience for the students. This practice can be very expensive for a school, but Western is willing to bear the cost because it is consistent with their strategy. This option would be extremely effective for international business education, but the outlook for this option at Toronto will be extremely limited in the future.

Major Faculty Research Programs on International Topics—It is quite common in doctoral programs for students to be employed as research assistants in faculty projects. In many such cases, a student's choice of thesis topic is strongly influenced by exposure to and participation in a large, ongoing program of research. For many students, an expedient choice of topic is to do some piece of work associated with the larger research program. Therefore, the more that faculty members have large, multi-faceted, long term research agendas that involve international business, the more doctoral students will receive exposure, education, support and socialization for involvement in international aspects of their subject area.

A strong research and teaching role in international business by faculty members active in doctoral programs will act as a powerful role-modelling force for internationalization in doctoral programs. Such leadership by faculty members is essential to provide legitimacy and consistency to any of the other mechanisms for internationalization that have been discussed in this paper. Schools with CIBER programs obviously have a great advantage for this option (Miller in this volume).

In terms of Brislin and Tomoko's framework, student participation in international research programs can be powerful for learning in "awareness," "knowledge" (at least for one specific area), "emotional" experience and "behavior" skills. The strong effect from apprenticeship learning in international research does not mean that the whole doctoral program or everyone's research has to be devoted to international topics. Instead, the degree of internationalization of a doctoral program will be greatly enhanced by the existence of a number of on-going major research programs that either focus on international business issues, or at least consider international aspects of a topic.

The outlook for this option is quite good at Toronto because a number of faculty members who are active in doctoral teaching and supervision are also active in major research projects with an international focus. The faculty also have some research centers with an international focus to their programs and with major funding available to "encourage" faculty members to shift their research interests in these directions. It is highly likely that many of our doctoral students will be employed as research assistants in these projects, be involved in various conferences sponsored by the research centers, and will do thesis projects that fit in with the research agendas of the centers. In effect, the powerful influence of research funding will cause a greater shift in emphasis to our doctoral program than any well-intentioned philosophies and policies.

CONCLUSIONS

We would like to utilize many of the options discussed in this paper, but this is not possible given our situation and resources. A combination of organizational and individual inertia, scarce resources in the system, and pressure from the central administration to reduce program requirements limits our degrees of freedom for internationalization of the program. Therefore we have to make trade-offs between options and settle for partial implementation of some objectives for the time being.

The three most viable options in the short run are: the introduction of cross-cultural and international content in the new core course for teaching and communication skills; the encouragement of international students to raise awareness of international issues for research topics; and the growing power of international research agendas and funding in our research centers. We will continue to make ad hoc use of visiting scholars and international workshops as circumstances permit and over time, more and more individuals will likely add international dimensions to their regular doctoral seminars. What is highly unlikely to be implemented will be the addition of any new common core courses with an international focus, any systematic addition of international content to existing core courses, or regular sponsorships for international travel or research by doctoral students. Despite these compromises in our efforts for internationalization of doctoral education, we are confident that our program will continue to promote international awareness and learning among our students.

REFERENCES

Adler, N. 1991. *International Dimensions of Organizational Behavior*. PWS Kent Publications, 30-32.

Alutto, J. 1993. "Whither Doctoral Education? An Exploration of Program Models." *Selections*. 9(3) (Spring): 37-43.

Beamish, P., "Internationalizing the Teaching/Curriculum Dimension of Doctoral Education: the Western Business School Experience." in this volume.

Brislin, R. and Tomoko, Y. 1994. *Intercultural Communication Training: An Introduction*. Beverly Hills, CA: Sage Publications.

Daniels, J. "Internationalizing Doctoral Programs in Business: The Indiana Experience." in this volume.

Hofstede, G. 1980. "Motivation, Leadership and Organizations: Do American Theories Apply Abroad?" *Organizational Dynamics*. (Summer): 42-63.

Ivancevich, J. and Duening, T. 1993. "Internationalizing a Business School: A Partnership Development Strategy." *Selections*. 10(1) (Autumn): 23-36.

Jacob, N. 1993. "The Internationalization of Management Education." *Selections*. 10(1) (Autumn): 18-22.

Miller, E. "Helpful Institutional Arrangements for Internationalizing Doctoral Education in Business." in this volume.

Ondrack, D. and Leiba, S. 1994. "Assessment of a Multi-Cultural Education Program for MBA Students." EIASM Workshop on Cross-Cultural Perspectives in Management, Henley Management College, England, November 10-12.

Stopford, J. "International Business as a Context, Not a Discipline." in this volume.

Dimensions of Internationalizing Doctoral Education in Business in Europe: A Discussion of the Concept, Dynamics, and Policy

Reijo Luostarinen

Internationalization of education has become a widely debated topic globally, especially in Europe, during the last few years. This is due to several factors: (1) the globally more enabling environment; (2) the increasing internationalization of business and cultural life in general; (3) the advancing integration in Europe; and (4) the transition of the Eastern and Central European countries to market economies.

These developments have led to an uninterrupted flow of U.S.-based studies on international business education conducted under the umbrella of the Academy of International Business (AIB) (Terpstra 1969, Daniels & Radebaugh 1974, Grosse & Perrit 1980, Thanopoulos & Leonard 1986; and Arpan et al. 1993). The first European study was completed within the European International Business Academy (EIBA) in 1990 (Luostarinen & Pulkkinen 1991). Several studies have also been conducted on the internationalization of education in general and on the internationalization of business education in particular (see Cavusgil 1993). However, very little research focusing on the internationalization of doctoral studies in business administration has taken place (for two examples, see Kuhne 1990; and Rose's follow-up survey of Kuhne in this volume). In Europe this topic has been included only as a part of the study mentioned above (Luostarinen & Pulkkinen 1991:55-56, 69, 73, 119; see also Van den Bulcke 1993).

The purpose of this chapter is to discuss internationalization of doctoral education on the basis of the European study and experience, focusing on three issues: (1) concept and contents of the internationalization of doctoral education; (2) dynamics of internationalization; and (3) policy recommendations.

The survey on International Business Education in European universities was implemented in three stages using mailed questionnaires and interviews. The questions were divided into structural information on the type and level

Exhibit 1 Components and Characteristics of the Internationalization Stages of Business Education

DIMENSION	START UP	DEVELOPMENT	GROWTH	MATURITY
1. Substance of IB Teaching or Curriculum	IB as an extension	Separate IB courses	IB Program	Fully inter-nationalized
2. IB Research	Nonexistent or only a few separate efforts by faculty	Separate efforts by faculty, short term research projects	Doctoral Program in IB, long-standing research, separate research projects in IB	Doctoral Program in IB and fully internation alized research
3. Organization	No specific organization	No specific organization separate IB faculty	IB Department	IB School
4. Faculty	• Exchange is nonexistent or very limited, •International faculty is nonexistent or very limited	• Exchange is limited, •International faculty size is limited	• Extensive exchange, •International faculty size about 5-25 %	• Extensive exchange, •International faculty size about 25-80%
5. Student Body	• Exchange is nonexistent or very limited, •International student body is nonexistent or very limited	• Exchange is limited, •International student body size is limited	• Extensive exchange, •International student body size about 5-25 %	• Extensive exchange, •International student body size is about 25-80%
6. Language Studies	Nonexistent or very limited	A foreign language is recommended or compulsory	Compulsory	Language studies are extensive and compulsory
7. Language of Instruction	Native language	Native language, only visitors use foreign language	50% native and 50% foreign language	Instruction provided in a foreign language
8. Orientation -Research -Teaching	Domestic	Mainly Domestic but some international aspects identifiable	International but not fully	Almost global, domestic trade considered special
9. Attitudes of -Administrators -Other Staff	Ethnocentric	Mostly ethno-centric, partly polycentric	50% ethno-centric, 50% polycentric	Mostly poly-centric or geocentric
10. Culture of the School	Negligible cultural sensitivity	Cultural sensitivity is recognized	Cultural sensitivity is highly recognized	Cultural sensitivity essential

of international business education at the target institutions and into information on international business research and its administration. A total of 231 institutions in 20 countries participated in the first stage (a 60 percent response rate was achieved—an excellent return for the first international survey in the field).

In the second, more comprehensive stage, questionnaires were mailed to the institutions that responded to the first survey. The questionnaire posed questions in undergraduate, graduate, and doctoral international business education. Surveys were mailed to 152 institutions; 59 responded to the undergraduate/ graduate/doctoral questionnaire, giving rise to 65 cases. For MBA programs, 20 questionnaires were returned. Seven institutions responded both to the undergraduate/graduate/doctoral and MBA questionnaires. Hence, altogether 72 institutions participated in the second stage for a response rate of 47 percent.

In addition to the two questionnaires, 18 European professors and experts in intarnational business were interviewed at the 15th Annual EIBA Conference held in Helsinki on December 17-19, 1989. The focus of these in-depth interviews was the different approaches utilized to internationalize traditional business education and the current status of international business education at each respective institution. During the conference a panel session on the "Dynamics of International Business Education" was held. The findings of that session are integrated in the present discussion.

CONCEPT AND CONTENTS OF INTERNATIONALIZATION

What do we mean by the internationalization of doctoral education? On the basis of earlier studies and accumulated experience, internationalization seems to be a multidimensional phenomenon and a stagewise process where a mainstream pattern can be identified. A number of dimensions may be developed and emerge in a different order thus yielding varying patterns. The four dimensions of internationalization that emerged from our study include: curriculum; faculty; student body; and the language of instruction (Exhibit 1).

Curriculum

Four major alternatives have been developed by different institutions:

- include the international business dimension in existing courses (infusion strategy);

- start special international business courses (specialization strategy);
- develop particular international business programs (specialization strategy);
- internationalize the whole curriculum (holistic strategy).

Among 184 European institutions, only 14 offered educational inputs in international business at the doctoral level in 1990. Out of these, 4 offered some international business courses, 9 had organized international business programs, and one was fully internationalized (Luostarinen & Pulkkinen 1991:123). In the U.S., 28 universities offered a Ph.D. in international business in 1987. Out of these, 8 offered it as a major subject, 7 as a minor subject, and 13 offered both alternatives (Kuhne 1990). The figures for 1994 show that only 21 universities still offered a Ph.D. in international business. Out of these, 6 offered it as a major subject, 4 as a minor subject, and 11 offered both alternatives (Rose, in this volume). Since the number of European Ph.D. programs has been steadily increasing, it can be argued that European business schools regard international business as a separate and growing field requiring a separate curriculum. On the other hand, U.S. business schools regard international business either as an inherent component of each traditional business discipline or believe that the market for international business Ph.D.s is too limited or declining (Rose, in this volume). An increasing emphasis on doctoral education in international business in Europe and a simultaneous decline of international business doctoral programs in the U.S. may be one of the major reasons for the relative paucity (5 percent) of European students enrolled in leading U.S. business schools observed by Kuhne (1990) and Rose (in this volume).

The basic question whether international business is a separate discipline or just a dimension or context of studies has persisted as long as the field has existed (Stopford in this volume). I am inclined to believe in the pressure theory that posits that the larger the country in question, the lower the pressure to internationalize and vice versa; i.e., the smaller and more open the country, the higher the pressure to internationalize (Luostarinen 1979). The size of the domestic market in the U.S. means there is less pressure for firms or universities to internationalize. In Britain, Germany, and France, where domestic markets are smaller (and where history, geographic proximity, and trading traditions have evolved over centuries), firms and universities must respond to a greater pressure to internationalize. For SMOPECs (Small and Open Economies) internationalization is a must—it is the major development, growth, and survival strategy for firms and universities. The main concern of SMOPECs is how firms and universities can become *more* internationalized.

If internationalization of the whole curriculum and becoming an international school are the ultimate objectives in a SMOPEC, then the university has two major options: (a) to have international business as a separate discipline first and then, step-by-step, fully internationalizing all disciplines; or (b) skip over the stages and incorporate the international dimension simultaneously in different disciplines, gradually internationalizing them fully. The choice between these two major options depends on the human and financial resources available. If resources are limited and if there is considerable resistance to internationalizing rapidly in the different functional areas, creating a separate international business faculty with visiting scholars may be the right way to start.

The Helsinki School of Economics (HSE), located in a SMOPEC, is one of the schools that started a full-fledged doctoral program in international business (in autumn 1988). The program targeted mainly those students who had graduated from the school's international business programs at the M.Sc. or MBA levels. The school has proceeded through the first three alternatives and is striving towards the fourth one, that is, towards the internationalization of the entire curriculum. This seems to be typical for all leading Nordic business schools. In this effort, however, a new alternative is emerging: while international business is developing as a separate discipline, traditional functional areas are adding more and more international business dimensions to existing courses. This means that both infusion and specialization strategies are being implemented simultaneously resulting in a holistic strategy. Even if the school has been able to fully internationalize the existing functional areas, it may still regard it necessary to have the central core elements of international business as a separate international business course.

The Faculty—One of the major challenges in internationalizing doctoral studies is the lack of qualified, specialized teachers. In a U.S. study, 55 percent of business schools indicated that the faculties teaching doctoral courses lack the international expertise to prepare students (Myers & Omura, in this volume). This is why the internationalization of the business faculty is often a requirement, especially in SMOPECs where the international business share of the GNP is between 30 and 60 percent.

To facilitate faculty internationalization, international business scholars in Europeean SMOPECs have begun a cooperative group—under the working name of "SMOPEC-group." The first official meeting of 20 scholars from 12

SMOPEC countries took place in Vienna August 26-28, 1994; the second meeting was held in conjunction with the EIBA conference in Warsaw 11-13 December, 1994.

Within doctoral education, the internationalization of the faculty seems to include the following main strategies: (1) internationalization of the domestic faculty (short- and long-term visits abroad for teaching, research or training; domestic scholars who have earned their Ph.D. abroad); (2) foreign members on doctoral committees, doctoral tutorial groups and/or evaluation committees; (3) foreign, short-term visiting faculty (less than one year); (4) foreign, long-term visiting faculty (more than one year); and (5) foreign, permanent faculty. It could be argued that the real, long-term success in the internationalization of business studies occurs through the internationalization of the permanent faculty. This means the hiring of permanent foreign scholars and the internationalization of the domestic faculty members. Foreign doctoral tutors and short- or long-term visitors are naturally of great assistance but, due to the temporary, non-administrative nature of their stay, permanent, long-term development does not follow.

Exchanges can play a vital role in internationalization. The number of exchange agreements within 231 European institutions offering international business education in 1990 was 164 for the teaching faculty and 92 for the research faculty. The major problems in developing faculty exchanges in many SMOPECs are the language of instruction and financing.

The Student Body—Internationalization of doctoral students can bring considerable benefits to the school: the international atmosphere is enhanced; individuals are personally internationalized; an interest in comparative and cross-cultural studies is generated, etc. The strategies employed include: (1) sending domestic doctoral students abroad to complete a part of their studies there (special student status or joint degree); (2) accepting visiting foreign, non-degree or joint degree students; and (3) accepting foreign degree students. The problems in internationalizing the student body are financing, language, and tutoring requirements.

The number of student exchange agreements in European institutions was 183. However, no data on the specific number of foreign doctoral students and on the domestic doctoral students studying abroad is available. According to a recent U.S. study, 94% of the schools did not require an international business Ph.D. student to travel or study abroad as a part of the program (Rose, in this volume).

The Language of Instruction—According to Finnish national legislation, every Finnish student has the right to study domestically in his/her native language. The "constitution" of international business, however, states that if only the Finnish language is used, there is no international business! This is why international business programs at all levels (B.Sc., M.Sc. and D.Sc.) at HSE are in English. Of the 11 U.S. business schools offering an IB-doctoral major, only 3 (Indiana University, the University of Miami, and the University of South Carolina) require a foreign language (and only the University of South Carolina requires a stay abroad as a part of the curriculum) (Arpan et al. 1993:242-245).

Using a foreign language (in this case English) as the language of instruction, teaching, and publishing is a challenge for faculty and students. One of the most common complaints heard at HSE is that if all in the class are home country nationals, it is artificial to use a foreign language for instruction. This complaint notwithstanding, introducing English as the official language of the program was the only reasonable way to get the process started and to get the foreign student and faculty exchanges to work.

Increasing integration, cooperation, and interaction between universities require that future faculty members develop their language capacity further during their doctoral studies. The same is true for those doctoral graduates who enter the global business world after completing their studies.

Language studies and the use of a foreign language (English) as a language of instruction seem to offer many advantages: (1) enable studying abroad as a visiting or a permanent doctoral student; (2) facilitate the receipt of tutorial help for doctoral dissertations from foreign experts; (3) enhance the attraction of foreign degree students; (4) facilitate the recruitment of faculty and the signing of exchange agreements with foreign institutions; (5) facilitate the participation in and the presentation of papers at international conferences (tutorials, seminars, symposia, study tours); (6) facilitate participation in international research projects and programs; (7) facilitate the conduct of research in other countries;) (8) facilitate publishing in international journals (working papers, research reports); (9) facilitate organizing joint doctoral courses with foreign universities and contributing as a visitor at foreign universities; (10) correlate with greater understanding of the impact of culture and other environmental factors on international business; and (11) help to establish area study programs and intercultural negotiation courses in the internationalization of the curriculum.

INTERNATIONALIZATION OF ADMINISTRATION AND FINANCE

Under this heading, the institutional structure for internationalization, i.e., the university organization, finance, attitudes, and culture are analyzed. The organizational schema for international business include: the presence of international business faculty within existing departments; establishing an international business coordinating unit (or department); establishing an international business department; and/or establishing an international business school. There are also several variants on these four major organizational schema. This is especially so for those who started to internationalize in the 1960s or 1970s. Newcomers tend to skip over the intermediate stages. Institutions that do not have adequate resources to internationalize create cooperative arrangements or joint ventures with other schools to share costs and make programs available to students from participating institutions.

According to the European study, organizational arrangements where international business has an acknowledged (explicit, formal) status are more typical in Europe than in the U.S. (Luostarinen & Pulkkinen 1991:120-121). In addition to the language problem, the financing of doctoral student and faculty exchanges was found to be one of the major barriers in Europe.

The attitudes of administrators are critical to internationalization. Creating a global culture within the university is the primary responsibility. of administrators. It is true that every foreign student and faculty member generates more administrative and tutorial work than domestic students, but if central and departmental administrators are properly informed, they are usually willing to accept the additional inconvenience caused by internationalization. Arranging seminars/conferences on the advantages, objectives, and financing of the internationalization process for the administrators and faculty may help reduce resistance.

DYNAMICS OF THE INTERNATIONALIZATION OF DOCTORAL EDUCATION

The internationalization of business studies can take place in a more orderly—rather than ad hoc process. For example, internationalization of the curriculum may start by adding an international dimension to existing courses, develop through the establishment of specific international business courses, and mature towards a totally internationalized curriculum through the build-up of international business programs (see Exhibit 1). Similarly, on an organizational level, internationalization seems to start with functional area faculty adding international dimensions to their courses, moves through professional development undertaken with international business scholars under existing department(s) (with some acting as international business coordinators), and to maturity through establishing a separate international business faculty, separate international business departments, or eliminating the artificial distinction between domestic and international business by internationalizing the entire school. In this sense, the organizational development may parallel that of companies (see Exhibit 2). Only three institutions in Europe—INSEAD in France, IMD in Switzerland, and the London Business School in England—have reached the "mature" stage of thoroughly internationalized education (Luostarinen & Pulkkinen 1991; Stopford in this volume).

The curriculum and the organization are just two out of the many different dimensions of internationalization. In which order are these different dimensions of doctoral studies internationalized? Is it the organization or the faculty that is internationalized first? When is the student body or the curriculum internationalized? Is the language used in teaching/ research internationalized last? I would argue that there is no single best answer to any of these questions that would be universally valid. Instead, there are many alternatives that can be used as best practice depending on the internal and external limitations of the school.

The European experience suggests two important factors about internationalization. First, the evolution of internationalization is a situation- and school-specific phenomenon. Schools that have a high demand for its international business graduates and have adequate human and financial resources are more willing to internationalize than those who ascertain a low demand and who have limited resources. Second, internationalization has developed differently in different times. Those who started to internationalize in the 1960s began with the curriculum, followed by the internationalization of the organization. In the 1970s, this trend continued, with the addition of the internationalization of the faculty and the student body. Institutions that started in the 1970s followed the same path, but in a few cases the internationalization of the first two dimensions took place simultaneously and the development of all four components was implemented within a shorter time period.

Institutions that commenced internationalization of business education in the 1980s have been able to utilize the experience and lessons of the pioneers. Due to the changing global nature of business, the demand to initiate international business education has increased. Thus, the pace of internationalization has accelerated and the process has been shortened. A consistent order of internationalization could no longer be identified. Some institutions started by internationalizing the faculty and/or the student body, others by internationalizing the organization and the curriculum at the same time, while a few skipped over some stages in the development of the four components (Luostarinen & Pulkkinen 1991:131-148).

These results do not reveal the internationalization process of the doctoral studies in specific but rather the internationalization process of business education in general. However, in light of the case study presented below, it is clear that internationalization has begun at the bachelor's and/or master's level(s), after which institutions have extended the process to the doctoral level. The stages followed at the lower levels of education have had a great impact on the process at the doctoral level. If, for example, teaching and research at the bachelor's and/or master's level(s) have taken place through separate programs, or programs organizationally have been taken care by a separate faculty, it is very likely that the internationalization of doctoral studies will follow the same scheme, i.e., by utilizing the existing structure and the dimensions of research and teaching that have already been internationalized. If international business is treated as a separate subject it is worthwhile to remember the warning set forth by John Daniels (in this volume): international business faculty may sometimes be an obstacle to international activities that might occur outside what they see as their domain.

CASE: EVOLUTION OF INTERNATIONAL BUSINESS EDUCATION AT HSE

At the outset of the development of international business education, HSE concentrated on strengthening the curriculum, which was followed by the internationalization of the faculty. Since then, business education has been internationalized through the student body and, since 1988, through doctoral studies. In the following analysis, this gradual development has been divided into four major stages: (1) Start-up; (2) Development; (3) Growth Phase A; and (4) Growth Phase B.

1. Start-up Stage: Internationalization of the Curriculum and Research

1956   First book in foreign trade
1964   First course in international business (Export Marketing)
1968   Launching of PRODEC, the international business program for developing countries

1974   Establishment of FIBO (Finland's International Business Operations-Research Program)

1976   Establishment of large data banks within the FIBO Research Program on international business operations, the foreign subsidiary operations of Finnish firms, and the subsidiaries of foreign and multinational companies in Finland

2. Development Stage: Internationalization of the Programs and Faculty for Basic Studies

1977   M.Sc. (Econ.) International Marketing Program begun as a specialization within the Marketing Program
First visiting foreign faculty member in International Marketing (there have been visitors continuously ever since)

1979   First doctoral dissertation in international business defended and published within the department of Marketing

1983   First Finnish full professor in international business (International Marketing)
The International Center established
International student and faculty exchange started and first agreements signed

3. Growth Phase A: Internationalization of the Programs, Faculty and Students for BBA- and MBA-studies; Organization for M.Sc. and Doctoral Studies

1984   The two-year International MBA Program in English launched

1987   Separate International Marketing faculty established
Separate International Business program organized
M.Sc. (Econ.) International Business Program for Forest Industries established jointly with the Helsinki University of Technology and the University of Helsinki.

1988   Doctoral Program in International Business in English commenced
The International Executive Program started in Lahti

1989   The International BBA-Program started in Mikkeli

4. Growth Phase B: Internationalization of Teaching Methods and Further Internationalization of Doctoral Studies and Research

1990   The M.Sc. Program in International Business implemented completely in English

M.Sc. program held almost completely on an intensive basis
First Nordic course in international business theory building
offered jointly in Copenhagen, Helsinki, Oslo, and Stockholm
First foreign tutors contributed to the international business
doctoral program.

1991   Center for International Business Research (CIBR) established for
        doctoral students within all business subjects

1992   12 international business teaching videos prepared on the
        internationalization of Finnish firms—a gift from industry.

1993   First foreign student completed his licentiate degree as an
        international business doctoral candidate.
        The first large multinational research projects in international
        business started under the umbrella of the World Bank and the OECD.
        Two doctoral and six licentiate degrees in IB received (a record year)

1994   International B.Sc. program in English commenced
        Area Studies Program launched (coordinated by international
        business faculty and the Departments of Economic Geography,
        Economic History, Law, Languages, and Entrepreneurship)
        The International Design Management Program plans to develop a
        doctoral degree as a joint program between the Helsinki University
        of Technology, the University of Arts and Design, and the Helsinki
        School of Economics-coordinated by the HSE

1995   The International Business faculty at the HSE was granted the top
        teaching unit of the year award in Finland by the Ministry of
        Education
        The first exchange of doctoral students occurs between Indiana
        University and the HSE.

International student exchanges have increased significantly. In 1983, when the International Center began the exchange schemes, six students were sent abroad; in 1994, 165 HSE students participated (120 basic degree students and 45 MBA students). The number of foreign students has also increased; there was one in 1985, and in 1994 there were 60 (in various international programs).

While the above time line sets forward HSE's internationalization process in general, the following discussion addresses four specific levels of internationalization: international business subject; school; national; and international.

IB Subject Level—The international business doctoral program has been operating in English since 1988. The program currently has 25 active doctoral students (200 in the whole school) and next year will increase its licentiates with 4 (20 for the whole school) and its doctoral degrees with 2 (8 for the whole school). An international business doctoral research seminar is held weekly in which doctoral students and faculty continue the close relationships established during special reception hours. FIBO international business data banks are available to both students and faculty for their research. Every doctoral student belongs to an international business research project that is based on accumulated experience, areas of excellence and/or demand, and information in the data banks. Every doctoral student also participates in tutorial groups with foreign scholars and in at least one international IB-conference/tutorial workshop annually. Every student must publish one paper or case annually, many as a result of participating in international business faculty research. Studies in foreign universities are strongly recommended, and 10 percent of IB doctoral students are from abroad.

School Level—The CIBR was established in 1991 as a coordinating and locational body for international business projects of the doctoral program. International Center takes care of foreign exchange programs and exchanges for faculty and students. Between 1991 and 1994, 58 publications were produced by the research fellows from the CIBR. In 1994, 7 projects employing 23 students were in operation. The Basic Research Institute, another unit within the business school, includes some international business doctoral students. The school has been financing doctoral students (who are also faculty members) to attend international business teacher education programs since 1994. The research register is a part of national data base. The Research Council takes care of entry requirements, exit regulations, policy and strategic planning for doctoral studies. If the Ph.D. applicant does not possess the required basic knowledge in business administration or in international business he/she might be able to supplement his/her program with M.Sc. courses and, subsequently, reapply for the doctoral program. Eight international programs serve as the basis for the international doctoral studies program. The school has established a follow-up system for the evaluation of the performance of doctoral students (exit criteria). The business school has also requested that every discipline within the school offer at least one course in English (international student and faculty exchange). To allow a Finn or a foreign student to earn any degree (B.Sc., M.Sc. and Ph.D.), English was established as the language of studies in 1994.

National Level—Under the coordination of HSE, the Finnish Graduate School of International Business (FIGSIB) was established in 1994 between four full-member schools and four associate schools to pool the resources for joint financing and studies. The national doctoral training program, KATAJA, organizes international tutorials, workshops, and courses on a joint basis for the doctoral studies in Finnish business schools. Because of these joint arrangements, cooperative agreements for doctoral studies were established among Finnish universities. The Ministry of Education sets output targets for doctoral programs in Finnish universities (all are public) and The Finnish Academy of Sciences finances many doctoral research projects.

International Level—An international Nordic business theory building course is offered jointly by the Helsinki School of Economics, the Stockholm School of Economics, the Bedriftsekonomiske Institutt, and the Copenhagen Business School. Doctoral students participate regularly at the AIB, EIBA, EMAC, and EIASM doctoral tutorials and workshops. HSE is a founding member of the SMOPEC-group. Doctoral students have received funding for research through projects sponsored by The World Bank and OECD. Doctoral students are active participants in EDAMBA, the European Association of Doctoral Programs in Management and Business Administration. They are divided into two groups -part-time and full-time, with resources largely allocated to the latter.

SUMMARY, IMPLICATIONS AND POLICY RECOMMENDATIONS

In light of increasing globalization and market integration in Europe, all levels of international business education, i.e., BBA, MBA, Ph.D., will continue to be one of the major growth areas of business schools in Europe. This means there will be a continuously increasing demand for international business Ph.D.s both in academic and business life, contrary to the U.S. where there has been a decline in demand for international business Ph.D.s.

It is apparent that the internationalization of business education is a multidimensional concept, not only at the bachelor's and master's levels, but also at the doctoral level. The dimension to be given the highest priority at the doctoral level depends on the way business studies at the bachelor's and master's levels have been internationalized (and vice versa!). In the 1960s and 1970s, the order of stages and steps of internationalization were quite similar in European universities and business schools but, today, such a consistent pattern of internationalization does not exist. Instead, newcomers are leapfrogging the stages, internationalizing several dimensions simultaneously, and proceeding through the stages much faster. This has given rise to the emergence of very different patterns, depending on the internal and external limitations of the schools. European business schools are internationalizing their programs more rapidly at all levels (B.Sc., M.Sc., Ph.D.) than the U.S. business schools; they are also striving for a higher degree of internationalization.

As Lyman Porter argues (in this volume), it is quite natural that not all schools offering doctoral education should internationalize their programs fully. Not all faculty instructing doctoral students must be internationalized, not all doctoral students within the school should be required to meet the same level of international business competence, and not every doctoral program should offer instruction in a foreign language or language studies. Business schools vary in their international visions, missions, business ideas, objectives, and strategies. They also vary in their developmental endowments, i.e., resources, location, image, stage of development, to become more internationalized. There is a need for almost every institution to consider the internationalization challenge.

POLICY RECOMMENDATIONS FOR ACADEMIC INSTITUTIONS

Academic institutions should carefully consider whether the demand, supply, and competitive situation, on one hand, and the financial and human resources available on the other hand, justify the establishment and development of doctoral studies in international business. If so, a mission statement, objectives, and strategies to reach the objectives of internationalization should be developed after discerning what the role of international business studies, in general, and doctoral studies, in particular, will be for the school.

With particular reference to SMOPECs, the institutions should start to cooperate nationally and internationally when offering international business doctoral courses on theory and methodology and when considering tutoring and larger research efforts.

Financial resources should be allocated for international business doctoral students to study abroad, to participate in international conferences and research tutorials, and for foreign faculty and/or permanent students to visit from abroad. Special incentives should be used for foreign language studies and for using an international language for instruction. Special efforts should be made to recruit doctoral students to participate in international research projects and teaching programs and to secure financing from international sources (e.g. Erasmus, Comett, Nordic Council, the World Bank). Internationalization strategies should address not only the student body and the faculty, but also the administrators, the board, the scientific council, and the advisory council. "Internationalize or die" may not be a valid slogan only for business, but also for the academic world, especially in SMOPECs.

RECOMMENDATIONS FOR PUBLIC POLICYMAKERS

Public policymakers should encourage institutions to internationalize their doctoral studies by offering different types of incentives. Umbrella agreements should be crafted linking international academic and scientific organizations to forge multilateral cooperation and exchange agreements between universities. Funding should be made accessible through these agreements to internationalize the faculty and students. To ensure a flow of well-educated graduates, government could identify the skills needed for different foreign service positions (for example, there is a need for 500 Finns within the European Union).

If the program outputs—Ph.D.s—are able to find positions within academia, within the business world, and international agencies (UN, World Bank etc.), it will strengthen the university's image and reputation as a unit of international excellence. This image, in turn, will attract more and more internationally-oriented students, faculty members, administrators and external advisors. The trend will be visible, not only on a national, but also on a global basis. Earlier, business schools and universities selected the best students available. In the future, the best students will select the best schools worldwide. This will be especially so as Europe continues to open and integrate. That is why a strategic plan for internationalization must be conducted in academic institutions and in government so that each can reinforce the other. All in all, it may be concluded that "Internationalize or die" may be a valid slogan not only for business, but also for academia, especially in the small and open economies (SMOPECs).

Exhibit 2. Stages of Internationalization and Organizational Development.

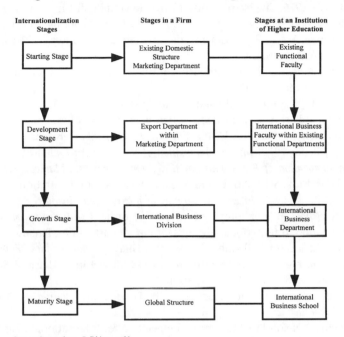

Source : Luostarinen - Pulkkinen, p. 30.

REFERENCES

Arpan, Jeffrey S., William R. Folks, Jr., Chuck C.Y. Kwok. 1993. *International Business Education in the 1990s: A Global Survey*. University of South Carolina.

Beamish, Paul W. "Internationalizing the Teaching/Curriculum Dimension of Doctoral Education: The Western Business School Experience." in this volume.

Bulcke, Daniel van Den. 1993. Doctoral Studies and Research Activities in European Business Schools and Universities in S. Tamer Cavusgil (ed.). *Internationalizing Business Education: Meeting the Challenge*. East Lansing, MI: Michigan State University Press.

Cavalle, Carlos. 1987. *Managing Successfully in a Multicultural Environment: What Does It Mean to Management Development*. EFMD. 13, 19.

Cavusgil, S. Tamer (ed.). 1993. *Internationalizing Business Education: Meeting the Challenge*. East Lansing, MI: Michigan State University Press.

Daniels, John D. "Internationalizing Doctoral Programs in Business: The Indiana University Experience." in this volume.

Daniels, John D. and Radebaugh, Lee. H. (eds.). 1974. *International Business Curriculum Survey*. Academy of International Business.

Ghertman, Michel and Leontiades, James (eds.). 1978. *European Research in*

International Business. Papers selected from four conferences held during the period 1973-1976. The Netherlands: North-Holland Publishing Company.

Grosse, Robert and Perrit, Gerald W. (Eds.). 1980. *International Business Curricula A Global Survey*. Waco, TX: Academy of International Business, Advertising and Marketing Associates, Inc.

Kedia, Ben. "A Pyramidical Approach to the Internationalization of Doctoral Business Education." in this volume.

Kuhne, Robert J. 1990. "Comparative Analysis of U.S. Doctoral Programs in International Business." *Journal of Teaching in International Business*. 1(3-4): 85-99.

Luostarinen, Reijo. 1990. *EIBA-Membership Study*. EIBA/HSE, Helsinki.

Luostarinen, Reijo. 1979. *Internationalization of the Firm: An Empirical Study of the Internationalization of Firms with Small and Open Domestic Markets*. Series A:30. Helsinki: Helsinki School of Economics and Business Administration.

Luostarinen, Reijo. 1975. *Integrated Planning of International Business Education in a Business School*. Paper prepared for the Nordic Conference of Business Administration, International Business Group, August, Turku, Finland.

Luostarinen, Reijo and Pulkkinen, Tuija. 1991. *International Business Education in European Universities in 1990*. EIBA. Series D-138. Helsinki: Helsinki School of Economics and Business Administration.

Madura, Jeff. 1991. "Internationalizing the Ph.D. Program." *Journal of Teaching in International Business*. 3(1): 21, 26.

Miller, Edwin L. "Helpful Institutional Arrangements for Internationalizing Doctoral Education in Business Administration." in this volume.

Myers, Matthew B. and Omura, Glenn S. "The Internationalization of Doctoral Programs: A Survey of Program Directors." in this volume.

Porter, Lyman W. "Internationalizing Doctoral Education in Business: Cost-Benefit Trade-Offs." in this volume.

Rada, Juan F. 1989. *The Challenge of Management Education*. The AIESEC Lind Newsletter. February. AIESEC-International.

Rose, Peter S. "A Dual Approach to Internationalizing Business Ph.D. Programs." in this vol.

Stopford, John M. "International Business as a Context, Not a Discipline." in this vol.

Terpstra, Vern. 1969. *University Education for International Business. A Survey of American Business Schools*. Benton Harbor, MI: Association for Education in International Business.

Thanopoulos, John and Leonard, Joseph (eds.). 1986. *International Business Curricula. A Global Survey*. Mentor, Ohio: Academy of International Business, Dwight Publishing Co.

Toyne, Brian. "Internationalizing Business Scholarship: the Essentials." in this vol.

Welch, Lawrence and Luostarinen, Reijo. 1988. "Internationalization: Evolution of a Concept." *Journal of General Management*. 14(2) (Winter): 34-55.

PART V: SPECIFIC INTERNATIONALIZATION STRATEGIES

INTRODUCTION

S. Tamer Cavusgil

Each internationalization strategy developed for a business school doctoral program must be translated into concrete activities. In this section, authors present several specific internationalization activities they have implemented within their specific functional area.

David Tse describes five related aspects of conducting an effective doctoral seminar in international marketing research he implemented when in British Columbia. He introduced students to various aspects of the field that established its international identity, explored research traditions, critical theories, methodological issues, and provided hands-on research experience.

Barbara Pierce reports on a research project undertaken in a first-year doctoral seminar on Theory and Research in International Business at Western Business School, Ontario, Canada. The assignment was to identify publishing outlets for international business research. In forming a group composed of Canadian and international students to accomplish this task, she learned how cross-cultural miscommunications occur. Her reflective essay points out a number of ways students of one nationality can learn from their international colleagues. Most importantly, she identifies a number of areas where intercultural understanding is critical to conducting business across international boundaries.

William Folks, Sharon O'Donnell and Jeffrey Arpan report on a survey they implemented at the University of South Carolina on the usefulness of knowing a foreign language and engaging in foreign experiences in the course of doctoral studies. They outline the current requirements of the doctoral concentration in International Business in order that the reader understand the context in which these two facets of the program are required. Fourteen graduates of the program were asked for their perception of how valuable language and experience components of the degree have been to their careers. After presenting their findings, the authors discuss some of the costs and benefits of these requirements.

Those who read this section will find very specific assistance in how to translate the vision of internationalization into praxis on several different dimensions. Many other specific suggestions are made in the papers appearing in the previous section.

Developing and Teaching a Doctoral International Marketing Research Seminar: Issues, Experiences, and Rewards

David K. Tse

Introduction

The difficulties one encounters when designing and conducting a doctoral seminar in international marketing (IM) include the complexities generated by the lack of literature in IM as well as the need to develop a coherent approach to IM research that will assist students in their research. While there is no single solution to these challenges, this case study of my course is presented in the hope that ideas will be stimulated on how to conduct an effective doctoral seminar in IM and point a direction on how to internationalize doctoral research programs.

An International Marketing Research Seminar

Purpose

My experience both as a student and later as an instructor suggests that there are five related aspects instrumental to a doctoral seminar's success: (1) defining the seminar topics (fields); (2) exploring research traditions and approaches; (3) examining critical theories; (4) understanding methodological issues; and (5) providing hands-on research experience. Conventional doctoral seminars in marketing are usually comprised of marketing theory, marketing research methods, quantitative models, and consumer/behavioral research.

Conscientious students taking a doctoral seminar in IM for the first time are likely to ask the following questions: (a) What is the definition of international marketing research? (b) Why do we need to conduct international marketing research? and (c) What are the essential differences between international and domestic marketing research (aside from more than one data set)? These questions are indicative of the ethnocentric approach taken in the teaching of marketing by faculty who are unaware of the diversity of approaches inherent in IM research.

Responses to these questions are varied. One obvious response is that we need IM research because firms need to market their products internationally. I am currently working in Hong Kong. The most often asked question in and out of the classroom is "Do you really think what you tell us applies to Hong Kong?" I have to reply honestly—"I don't know. You have to try it out first." We can also respond by analyzing the "tradition" of IM research to illustrate how marketing practices differ from country to country, relying on the arguments in Clark (1990), i.e., different national characteristics justify research in IM.

In meeting the challenge of designing and conducting a course in IM, I explored how social scientists approach their international research. I was most enlightened by psychologists who, at a conference in 1980, sought to evaluate objectively what they uniquely contribute to the field of psychology through studying psychological processes across cultures. They identified the specific insights gained from expanding research into the cross-cultural domain. Drawing from their success, IM research can:

1. test the universality of marketing theories;
2. extend marketing knowledge beyond the North American context;
3. remove confounding variables that otherwise cannot be controlled in a homogenous cultural setting;
4. better define national uniqueness; and
5. contribute to marketing theories through knowing how marketing phenomena function in other nations/cultures.

In consulting with Michael Bond, Kwok Leung, and Geert Hofstede, I was not only convinced of the need for and the benefits of international research, but I was also able to clarify the purpose of the seminar, respond to participants' questions, and to be motivated to continue my work in IM. In subsequent studies, I asked myself—in the spirit of the cross-cultural psychology approach—what contribution can an international study make beyond merely extending the findings from one culture (often the North American culture) to another. Too often we forget to search for the unique contribution that an IM study will bring to the field. In my seminar, students were presented with a justification of IM research as a field and its contribution to marketing theory. I insisted that the participants develop a study that would make the same contribution.

RESEARCH TRADITIONS AND APPROACHES IN INTERNATIONAL MARKETING

When beginning research in any academic field, it is useful to understand the historical context of the field by tracing its research traditions. Exposure to historical perspectives creates a sense of confidence in and respect for the field. In IM research, the tradition is limited. Early IM studies did not detail how the authors resolved many current methodological issues. The failure of earlier studies to clarify these issues and their contributions to IM knowledge tend to create a misperception of the quality of IM research. To compensate for this lack of understanding, I classify IM studies into five approaches:

The Inductive-Comparative Approach—Using this approach researchers observe and compare (through equivalence measures) selected market phenomena that researchers regard as important. At times, the researchers may not have very precise or clear notions as to why a certain phenomenon would differ among the multinational/multi-cultural samples. Typically, one may label such an approach as an inductive approach, i.e., from observation to theory building. Some past studies that followed this approach did not specify their purpose and they did not provide significant insights for future research. These studies resembled fishing expeditions and at times came to incorrect conclusions (see discussion in Adler and Graham 1989).

The "National Characteristic" Approach (as described by Clark 1990)— Following this approach, researchers derive propositions from the characteristics of the nations/cultures under investigation and then verify these propositions in their studies. This approach is deductive and has resulted in a number of key IM papers (e.g., Capon, Christodoulou, Farley and Hulbert 1987).

The "Extension" Approach—Researchers aim to test whether some models or causal relationships proven in one country or culture apply elsewhere. The study by Lee and Green (1991), which tested whether the Fishbein model applied in Korea, is a good example. A similar approach was taken by Takada and Jain (1991) who extended the diffusion model to Pacific Rim countries.

The "Cultural Dimension" Approach—In using this approach, researchers decompose culture into dimensions (e.g., individualism—collectivism) and propose how other independent variables would be affected by differences in culture. Researchers often go beyond superficial differences and explore philosophical aspects of the culture in question. Based on this work, researchers then derive meaningful hypotheses and design their studies accordingly. These studies are more theory driven and demand much more work. Recent papers in IM are moving in this direction, e.g., Stayman and Despande (1989), Tse, Lee, Vertinsky and Wehrung (1989), and Tse, Francis and Walls (1994).

The "Etic" Approach—This approach argues that a theory should not be culturally or nationally bound. It suggests that if researchers formulate their theories at an appropriate level of conceptualizaton, the theories can apply to all cultures. This approach differs from the work by Levitt (1983), who argued that there are megatrends that show different markets in the world are becoming similar. Although this etic approach is popular in other basic disciplines (e.g., psychology, sociology), few IM researchers have adopted it.

While some researchers and journal reviewers prefer a particular approach, it is important to realize that the above-described approaches complement each other and can be tailored to meet individual researcher's needs and study purposes.

Once the students in my class understood these approaches, they held IM research in greater regard. My own approach, as I explained to them, most closely resembled the deductive cultural dimension approach. Consequently, I included more papers on the definition of culture and examples on unbundling culture on my reading list.

CRITICAL THEORY AND THEORETICAL FOUNDATIONS OF KEY TOPICS

The third prerequisite of a successful doctoral seminar is the exposure of participants to both the critical theories of the field (theoretical orientations fundamental to the field's development) and the theoretical explanations of selected topics within the field.

In IM research, there is no clear definition of critical theories. In the seminar, I introduced the "firm's orientation" by Cavusgil (1989), "national character orientation" by Clark (1990), "cultural dimension orientation" by Triandis (1964), and "borrowed orientation," that is, borrowing theories from other fields including international business (Buckley 1990; Daniels 1991), and other behavioral sciences (e.g., Swidler 1986).

In addition to critical theories, a successful doctoral seminar needs to cover the breadth and depth of the theoretical foundation of the key topics in the field. The breadth of the literature may help to improve the participants' critical thinking skills, while the depth provides insights into the wealth of the topic. Such exposure helps to acquaint the participants with the literature so that they can develop a solid research orientation.

Some instructors argue that the best combination of reading materials on each research topic contains four papers: a classic work; two reasonably new top journal articles that disagree on key theoretical orientations; and a recent working paper or conference paper that describes future research opportunities. Recent research in IM allowing for the utilization of this approach includes:

- Country-of-Origin Effects: Johansson, Douglas and Nonaka 1985; Johansson 1990; Han 1989; Darling and Wood 1990; and Tse and Lee 1993;
- Export Behavior and Market Entry: Ryan 1988; Kogut and Singh 1988; Chao 1989; and Anderson and Coughlan 1987;
- International Comparison of Advertising Contents: Belk and Pollay 1985; Pollay 1986; and Gily 1988;
- Joint Ventures and Cross-Cultural Negotiations: Campbell, Graham, Jolibert and Meissner 1988; Graham, Kim, Lin and Robinson 1988; Geringer 1991.

In addition, I highlighted the issues of globalization (Levitt 1983; Jain 1989; Tse and Wong 1993; and Tse, Lee, Vertinsky and Wehrung 1988).

METHODOLOGICAL ISSUES

In general, to meet the standards for publication in respected journals, researchers must be able to conduct research using both quantitative and behavioral methodologies. IM research is not restricted to either one or the other. Hence, an IM research methodology course should follow on other courses that equip students with the range of skills necessary to conduct research using a variety of methodologies.

Compared to other marketing fields, IM incorporates a unique set of issues. Many questions that journal reviewers would not ask in conventional market research emerge when they review IM papers. For example, reviewers seldom ask whether a sample population of undergraduate students from a West Coast public university is representative of the population of North America. Yet, such a question is posed when IM papers are reviewed. I am not arguing that these questions should not be asked; I am positing that IM researchers need to be trained to resolve the underlying issues in designing IM research and to justify their samples accordingly.

I found it most helpful to show students how authors of IM papers handled and resolved reviewers' questions. To illustrate, I had students read several chapters from the Craig and Douglas (1984) volume on IM research. I also found that research methodologies in cross-cultural psychology and sociology useful in introducing new methods to resolve some age-old problems.

In the seminar, the issues of validity, reliability, causality, and measurement as they relate to multicultural contexts were discussed. The classic works I included on the reading list were: Bagozzi 1981; Cook 1979; Churchill 1978; Craig and Douglas 1984.

RESEARCH EXPERIENCE

In teaching seminars, I have learned that hands-on research experience by students is an effective research training tool—especially in exploring consumer behavior. By providing a field experience, students acquire more in-depth critical thinking skills. Additionally, students learn how to design their own studies (a skill that cannot be acquired solely by critiquing the research designs of colleagues).

In IM studies more than one data set is usually required. As a result, hands-on experience cannot normally be provided within the time frame of the seminar. As a substitute, I asked the participants to design a study to be implemented in the future. The results of this assignment were commendable. An extension of one participant's paper assisted me in developing a database that has assisted us in writing a conference paper, a book chapter, and a paper currently being reviewed by a top journal. Another participant further developed her paper for presentation at a conference. Another obtained some important insights and changed her dissertation design substantially.

REWARDS

When first approached to conduct the doctoral seminar in IM research, I was quite reluctant. I doubted my ability and questioned whether the literature was sufficient to deliver an effective seminar. Throughout the seminar, I was continuously anticipating participants' questions. I was forced to venture into areas I would not normally have explored. Some of these issues challenged me to reevaluate the work I have done and what needs to be done in future.

I also benefited in another way. I included three published papers and six working papers on which my colleagues and I were working. To date, except for the two that are still in the review process, all working papers have been accepted for publication. The seminar helped me to redefine my work, respond to reviewers, and generate new research ideas. Students also changed. After a lengthy discussion on an IM paper, one student said, "I had a lot of questions about this paper in the beginning, but now all the questions I had were shredded, and I guess I am too—shredded."

CONCLUSIONS

No longer can we afford to ignore the pressing need to internationalize courses in doctoral programs. In meeting this need, we change the paradigms of research, especially in international marketing.

I am hopeful that the insights I have shared in this chapter on developing and conducting a seminar on international marketing research will benefit others in developing their own seminars. When we do our job well as instructors and as model researchers, young scholars will be attracted to building a career in international marketing where new issues of globalization present challenges on a daily basis.

REFERENCES

Adler, Nancy J and John L. Graham. 1989. "Cross-Cultural Interaction: The International Comparison Fallacy?" *Journal of International Business Studies.* 20(3): 515-38.

Anderson, Erin and Anne. T. Coughlan. 1987. "Interactional Market Entry and Expansion via Independent or Integrated Channels of Distribution." *Journal of Marketing.* 51(1): 71-82.

Bagozzi, Richard. 1980. *Causal Models in Marketing*. New York, NY: John Wiley & Sons.

Belk, Russell W. and Richard Pollay. 1985. "Images of Ourselves: The Good Life in Twentieth Century Advertising." *Journal of Consumer Research*. 11 (March): 887-97.

Buckley, Peter J. 1990. "Problems and Developments in the Core Theory of International Business." *Journal of International Business Studies*. 21(4): 657-66.

Campbell, Nigel, John L. Graham, Alain Jolibert and Hans Gunther Meissner. 1988. "Marketing Negotiations in France, Germany, the United Kingdom, and the United States." *Journal of Marketing*. 52(2): 49-62.

Capon, Noel, Chris Christodoulou, John U. Farley, and James M. Hulbert. 1987. "A Comparative Analysis of the Strategy and Structure of United States and Australian Corporations." *Journal of International Business Studies*. 18(1): 51-74.

Cavusgil, S. Tamer. 1989. "International Marketing Research: Insights in Company Practices." *Research in Marketing*. 7: 261-88.

Chao, Paul. 1989. "Export and Reverse Investment: Strategic Implications for Newly Industrialized Countries." *Journal of International Business Studies*. 20(1): 75-92.

Churchill, Gilbert. 1979. "A Paradigm for Developing Better Measures of Marketing Constructs." *Journal of Marketing Research*. (February): 64-73.

Clark, Terry. 1990. "International Marketing and National Character: A Review and Proposal for an Integrative Theory." *Journal of Marketing*. 54(4): 66-79.

Cook, Thomas D. 1979. *Quasi Experimentation: Design & Analysis Issues for Field Settings*. Boston: Houghton Mifflin.

Craig, Samuel and Susan Douglas. 1982. *International Marketing Research*. American Marketing Association.

Daniels, John D. 1991. "Relevance in International Business Research: A Need for Core Linkages." *Journal of International Business Studies*. 22(2): 177-86.

Darling, John and Van R. Wood. 1990. "A Longitudinal Study Comparing Perceptions of U.S. and Japanese Consumer Products in a Third/Neutral Country: Finland 1975 to 1985." *Journal of International Business Studies*. 21(3): 451-68.

Davidson, Andrew R. and Elizabeth Thompson. 1980. "Cross-Cultural Studies of Attitudes and Beliefs," in Triandis, Harry C. and Walter Lonner (eds.). *Handbook of Cross-Cultural Psychology*. 3: 25-70.

Geringer, Michael J. 1991. "Strategic Determinants of Partner Selection in International Joint Ventures." *Journal of International Business Studies*. 22(1): 23-40.

Gilly, Mary C. 1988. "Sex Roles in Advertising: A Comparison of Television Advertisements in Australia, Mexico, and the United States." *Journal of Marketing.* 52(2): 75-85.

Graham, John L., Dong Ki Kim, Chi-Yuan Lin and Michael Robinson. 1988. "Buyer-Seller Negotiations Around the Pacific Rim: Differences in Fundamental Exchange Processes." *Journal of Consumer Research.* 15(1): 48-54.

Han, C. Man. 1989. "Country Image: Halo or Summary Construct?" *Journal of Marketing Research.* 26(2): 222-29.

Hofstede, Gert H., Bram Neuijen, Denis aval Ohayy and Geert Sanders. 1990. "Measuring Organizational Cultures: A Qualitative and Quantitative Study across Twenty Cases." *Administrative Science Quarterly.* 35: 286-316.

Jain, Subhash C. 1989. "Standardization of International Marketing Strategy: Some Research Hypotheses." *Journal of Marketing.* 53(1): 70-79.

Johansson, Johnny K. 1990. "Determinants and Effects of the Use of 'Made-in' Labels." *International Marketing Review.* 6(1): 47-58.

Johansson, Johnny K., Susan P. Douglas, and Ikujiro Nonaka. 1985. "Assessing the Impact of Country-of-Origin on Product Evaluations: A New Methodological Perspective." *Journal of Marketing Research.* 22 (November): 388-96.

Kimura, Yui. 1989. "Firm-Specific Advantages and Foreign Direct Investment Behavior of Firms: The Case of Japanese Semiconductor Firms." *Journal of International Business Studies.* 20(2): 296-314.

Kogut, Bruce and Harbir Singh. 1988. "The Effect of National Culture on the Choice of Entry Mode." *Journal of International Business Studies.* 19(3): 411-32.

Lee, Choi and Robert T. Green. 1991. "Cross-cultural Examination of the Fishbein Behavioral Intentions Model." *Journal of International Business Studies.* 22(2): 289-306.

Lee, Wei-na and David K. Tse. 1993. "When Cultures Interact: Towards a Model of Consumption Acculturation by Ethnic Consumers." Working Paper, University of British Columbia.

Levitt, Theodore. 1983. "The Globalization of Markets." *Harvard Business Review.* 61 (May-June): 92-102.

Parameswaran, Ravi and Attila Yaprak. 1987. "A Cross-National Comparison of Consumer Research Measures." *Journal of International Business Studies.* 18(1): 35-50.

Pick, Anne D. 1980. "Cognition: Psychological Perspectives." in Triandis, Harry C. and Walter Lonner (eds.). *Handbook of Cross-Cultural Psychology.* 3: 117-53.

Pollay, Richard W. 1986. "The Distorted Mirror: Reflections on the Unintended Consequences of Advertising." *Journal of Marketing.* 50 (April): 18-36.

Ryan, Adrian B. 1988. "Strategic Market Entry Factors and Market Share Achievement in Japan." *Journal of International Business Studies.* 19(3): 389-410.

Stayman, Douglas M. and Rohit Deshpande. 1989. "Situational Ethnicity and Consumer Behavior." *Journal of Consumer Research.* 16(3): 361-71.

Swidler, A. 1986. "Culture in Action: Symbols and Strategies." *American Sociological Review.* 51 (April): 273-86.

Takada, Hirozaku and Dipak Jain. 1991. "Cross-National Analysis of Diffusion of Consumer Durable Goods in Pacific Rim Countries." *Journal of Marketing.* 55(2): 48-52.

Triandis, Harry. 1964. "Cultural Influences Upon Cognitive Processes." *Advances in Experimental Social Psychology.* 1: 1-48.

Tse, David K. and John K. Wong. 1993. "Are We There Yet? Testing and Extending Levitt's Market Globalization Paradigm." Working Paper, University of British Columbia.

Tse, David K., Kam-hon Lee, Ilan Vertinsky, and Donald A. Wehrung. 1988. "Does Culture Matter? A Cross-cultural Study of Executive's Choice, Decisiveness and Risk Adjustment in International Marketing." *Journal of Marketing.* (October): 81-95.

Tse, David K. and Wei-na Lee. 1993. "Removing Negative Country Images: Effects of Decomposition, Branding and Product Experience." *Journal of International Marketing.* 1(4):25-48.

Tse, David K., June Francis, and Jan Walls. 1994. "Cultural Differences in Conducting Intra- and Inter-Cultural Negotiations: A Sino-Canadian Comparison." *Journal of International Business Studies.* 25(3): 537-55.

Wallendorf, Melanie and Eric J. Arnould. 1988. "My Favorite Things: A Cross-Cultural Inquiry into Object Attachment, Possessiveness, and Social Linkage." *Journal of Consumer Research.* 14(4): 531-47.

Multicultural Research: A Lesson in Cultural Diversity

Barbara Pierce

Experience is not what happens to a man;
but what a man does with what happens to him.

Aldous Huxley

Introduction

This paper presents a mini-case study based on my experience as a member of a group of students at the Western Business School. The group was formed to conduct a research project as a requirement of the first year doctoral seminar called Theory and Research in International Business. Conducting an actual research project increased participants' practical knowledge about research design and implementation in ways that were not possible by either reading books or completed research reports. The experience also provided valuable lessons about the management of large group research projects. The focus of this case study, however, is not on the process of the research or the results of the project, but rather on what I learned about the dynamics of working with researchers from other cultures. The project did have a specific "deliverable," but in my case, the full value of the activity was not derived from the destination but rather from reflecting on what happened along the way.

Over the three months of the project I had many experiences that were interesting, some that were aggravating and others that were extremely meaningful. Now that the project is over, taking time to reflect on what happened and why is providing me with an opportunity to derive benefit from what seemed at the time to be a flurry of unconnected events. It is important to be clear from the start that the interpretation I am constructing for this paper is based on my personal observations and interpretations. I am speaking for myself only and what is reported here is a very personal and admittedly anecdotal account. It is my map of the territory which may or may not reflect the experience or understandings of any other member of the group.

There are many perspectives that I could take to reflect on what I learned from participating in this project. The one I selected was to interpret this experience as a cross-cultural encounter. When the project began I would not have considered the multicultural nature of the project team as a dimension of the project worth considering. It was well along in the process before I realized the possibility of interpreting the experience in this way. The multicultural nature of the team was one of the many things that we failed to take into account when we undertook the project. As a result, we missed an opportunity to gain benefit from cultural diversity and to learn the skills of cross-cultural collaboration. I hope that by preparing this paper I can learn from these missed opportunities.

THE EXPERIENCE (THE MINI-CASE)

The events described in this case study began with a fairly straightforward assignment. Students were asked to conduct a review of publishing outlets for International Business (IB) research. The professor assigned the project believing it would familiarize students with the variety of IB research journals, increase their understanding of the research publishing process and demonstrate the importance of establishing a publishing strategy early in an academic career. Although the project was originally designed as an individual task, someone proposed that we work together and complete the project as a group. By doing so, we could increase the number of journals reviewed and the amount of information collected. Our professor said he would agree to change the format to accommodate a group project with the condition that the students who did not want to participate could select an alternate assignment and those who did would accept a group grade as their individual grade.

When the idea was suggested, the seminar had been in session for six weeks. Most of the students were in the first term of their first year and felt they knew each other well enough to be comfortable with the prospect of working together on a joint project. There was some apprehension about the potential size of the group and, as expected, the problem of "free riders" was raised, but there did not seem to be an equitable way to restrict either the size or the composition of the group. It was agreed that the "Journal Project

Team" would include everyone who wanted to participate. On that basis, ten of the twelve students in the seminar opted in. Six of the students were from Canada and the others were from the United States, Japan, Malaysia and Saudi Arabia. It should also be noted that each of the foreign students had come directly from their home countries to attend the doctoral program at Western.

When the group formed, it would be fair to say that none of us understood the full significance of the seemingly simple change from individual to group project. If we had thought about it longer we might have realized that not only had we created a significant research project to manage, but the success of the endeavor would be tied to our ability to control a potentially complex group process.

The Journal Project Team began holding meetings in October 1994 to develop a research design. Our first task was to identify a sample of appropriate journals to include in the review. Through a number of processes, an initial list of over 250 journals was reduced to a final sample comprised of 63, representing the functional areas of Business Policy, Finance, Management Information Systems (MIS), Accounting, Marketing, Management Science and Organizational Behavior, and a further 20 journals considered to be multi-disciplinary. The group then determined what information would be collected about each journal and how the data collection would take place. It was decided that part of the information would be gathered by reviewing past issues of the journals and the rest would be collected by sending a survey questionnaire to journal editors. During October the team spent a considerable amount of time in meetings selecting appropriate journals, identifying relevant information, and designing the data collection instruments. To coordinate the workload, each member of the team was assigned responsibility for a group of journals within one of the functional areas.

During November and early December, questionnaires were sent to journal editors. While waiting for editors to reply, team members conducted reviews of past issues of journals and contributed the information they gathered to a joint data base. To increase the return rate of FAXed questionnaires, team members were assigned follow-up responsibility for their list of journals. Editors that did not reply to the initial questionnaire were contacted by a team member and encouraged to complete the questions. For a small number of journals, past issues were not available in the University's library system. In this case the entire data collection was attempted through telephone contact with the editor. Results were compiled in mid-December and a report prepared for submission on the 29th of December 1994. Each team member was required to summarize the results of all the information gathered about their group of assigned journals and these summaries were included in the results section of the report. Individual members of the team also volunteered to write the other sections of the text, to edit the final document and to prepare the paper for submission to the professor.

The preceding description of what the team went through appears reasonably straightforward and activities similar to these would be documented in the methodology section of any research report. However, a listing of the activities and accomplishments of the team provides nothing of the rich fabric of processes that lay behind the achievement of these tasks. The group faced a number of difficulties during the three months of the project. To begin with, group leadership was never clearly established nor agreed upon by the members of the team. As could have been predicted, the workload was unevenly distributed. This caused problems of resentment on the part of those overburdened, and guilt on the part of those unable to carry their "fair" share of the load. Toward the end of the project, as the submission deadline loomed and completion appeared uncertain, another member of the group and myself "took charge" to ensure that the job got done. Naturally, taking over in this manner led to further resentment and misunderstanding among team members. In addition, problems arose with the research design, inconsistencies occurred in carrying out the research methodology, and the quality of individual contribution varied.

Although there were problems, the team did manage to produce a completed research document of reasonable quality and in the process most of the team members learned something about publishing international business research. However, it would be fair to say that lack of clear leadership, varied levels of commitment, and significant group diversity contributed to a rocky, and for many participants, somewhat unsatisfying experience.

AN INTERPRETATION: ANALYSIS OF THE MINI-CASE

What I intend to do at this point is reflect on both the behaviors I observed and the behaviors I exhibited to try and understand, from a cultural perspective, why these particular behaviors might have occurred. Such an understanding could help me develop a better appreciation of how cultural influences affect task accomplishment and working relationships in multicultural research teams. My analysis will draw on the work of a number of authors, including Edward T. Hall and Geert Hofstede, who have developed theoretical frameworks to describe important dimensions of cultural variation and have applied these frameworks to classify various cultures. However, before doing so, it is important to acknowledge that this type of analysis runs the risk of what has been referred to as "ecological fallacy" (Lane and DiStefano 1992). They point out that culture is a concept that has meaning at the group level and must be applied with caution when individual behavior is the focus of attention. Because an individual has a certain nationality or belongs to a particular cultural group it does not necessarily follow that his or her behavior will be the result of the influence of that particular affiliation. To make such claims would border on stereotyping in its worst application. Individual differences exist within cultures as well as between cultures, and behavior is a complex blending of both dispositional and situational factors. However, as Lane and DiStefano (1992:46) point out, "the ultimate usefulness of the framework depends on the learning subsequent to the initial analysis of a situation with the concepts as a guide."

The first set of observations addresses forms of participation within the team. There appeared to be a lack of active participation on the part of the three non-North American foreign students. They did not volunteer to take on work assignments without being asked, and did neither more nor less than what was required of them. The North American students, on the other hand, focused entirely on task completion. In an attempt to move the project along, they took the initiative and made most of the decisions seeking little or no contribution from the foreign students. The foreign students did not take responsibility for the leadership of the team. The North Americans assumed leadership and, although rocky at times, led the process to its completion.

The second set of observations concerns communication patterns. Although the foreign students attended most of the meetings, they contributed little to group discussions, for the most part remaining silent and uncommunicative unless directly spoken to. They willingly agreed to complete the tasks assigned to them, but if at all uncertain as to how to proceed, they sought clarification or more detailed instructions by contacting one of the North American students outside the team meetings.

Finally, the foreign students stayed removed from the sometimes frayed relationships that developed among the North American members of the team. While one could say that the foreign students were included "in" the team, they were clearly not "of" the team.

FORMS OF PARTICIPATION

One of the interesting dynamics of the team was that although multicultural in nature, it could be divided into two groupings of students on the basis of Hofstede's individual/ collectivistic dimension (see Table 1). The North American students belonged to cultures that rank high on the individualism dimension; the other three students belonged to cultures that rank relatively low making them collectivistic in nature. "Individualism implies a loosely knit social framework in which people are supposed to look after themselves and of their immediate families only, while collectivism is characterized by a tight social framework in which people distinguish between in-groups and out-groups; they expect their in-group (relatives, clan, organizations) to look after them, and in exchange for that they feel they owe absolute loyalty to it" (Hofstede 1980:46).

Table 1. Positioning of Countries according to Frameworks of Hofstede and Hall[1]

	Individualism	Power Distance	Uncertainty Avoidance	Masculinity	Hall's Context
Canada	80	39	48	52	low
United States	91	40	46	62	low
Japan	46	54	92	95	high
Malaysia	38	80	68	53	high
Saudi Arabia	26	104	36	50	high

1. Gudykunst, William B., Stella Ting-Toomey and Elizabeth Chua. (1988). Culture and interpersonal communication. Newbury Park: Sage Publications.

Individualistic cultures encourage independent actions and in these cultures value is placed on personal initiative and achievement (Gudykunst, Ting-Toomey & Chua, 1988). In collectivistic cultures, a high degree of conformity is expected, extending to paternalistic care in some situations (Argyle 1982). Members are compliant to the wishes of their leaders, often behaving in such a way as to harmoniously fit in with the group (Adler 1991). In collectivistic cultures value is placed on belonging to the group and smoothing group process to ensure its survival.

Stewart (1985) describes how this behavior manifests itself in Japanese culture:

The individual Japanese is subjugated to the group and when faced with a decision leading to action, he or she shrinks and may go to what seem fantastic lengths to avoid making a decision. He lacks a sense of personal responsibility; he feels only a sense of group responsibility. If at all possible, he will try to throw the onus of decision responsibility on a group or at least on some other person (p. 191-192).

Passive participation on the part of the foreign students can possibly be explained by understanding the perspective of people raised in collectivistic cultures. Since the idea for the joint project was suggested by North American students, the foreign students saw themselves as group participants not leaders. When they agreed to participate, they agreed to function as members, not leaders. As members they understood that their role was to follow directions, complete assigned tasks and remain loyal to the project, which they did. The North Americans, on the other hand, believed that task completion would result from individual effort and participation. There were few attempts to purposefully bring the foreign students into discussions by direct questioning or asking for opinions. The North Americans did not see this as necessary since their understanding of group process assumed that when members of a group have something to contribute, they take the initiative to do so.

Due to lack of participation on the part of the foreign students, there was a feeling that they were not taking their fair share of the responsibility for the project. This was troublesome for the North Americans since the grading system awarded the same mark to each person of the group regardless of participation. Gudykunst, Ting-Toomey and Chua (1988) suggest that individualistic cultures ascribe to the norm of equity in group activities whereas collectivistic cultures believe in equality.

Cultures that value the equity norm foster the importance of individual contributions, individual ideas and individual rights and needs. Cultures that value the equality norm foster the importance of group harmony, group consensus and group rights and obligations (p. 63).

North Americans expect that a person will be rewarded based on the level of individual effort contributed to a group project. If the outcome is to be equally distributed, as was the case in the journal project, then each person should have contributed equally to the work of the project. Because of their collectivist orientation, fairness had a different meaning to the foreign students. To them, membership in the group entitled each person to equal reward, regardless of actual contribution to the outcome.

COMMUNICATION PATTERNS

Hall (1978) approaches cultural diversity from the perspective of communication patterns. His research differentiates cultures on the basis of whether they communicate through high-context or low-context messages. *In high-context* communication cultures "most of the information is either in the physical context or internalized within the person, while very little is in the coded, explicit, transmitted part of the message" (p. 79), whereas in *low-context* communication cultures "the mass of information is vested in the explicit code" (p. 79). Table 1 categorizes the context of the cultures represented in the journal project team. On this dimension, the group falls into the same two groupings as before. The North American students come from low-context cultures and the foreign students from high-context. Ting-Toomey's (1985) description of the communication behaviors common in these two contexts very accurately describes what was experienced in the Journal Project Team:

> Whereas meanings and interpretations of the message are vested mainly in the explicit communication codes in the low-context cultures, meanings and interpretations of a message are vested primarily in the implicit shared social and cultural knowledge of the context in the high-context system ... in the high-context system, what is not said is sometimes more important than what is said. In contrast in the low-context systems words represent truth and power (pp. 76-77).

The North Americans did not understand the meaning or interpretation of the implicit behaviors of the foreign students and because of this lack of awareness they interpreted the behaviors as uncommunicative. Behavior considered uncommunicative by the North American students may have included a great deal of information but because they expected information in verbal, explicitly stated form, and had limited experience with high-context communication patterns, they made no attempt to derive meaning from what did occur.

Silence on the part of the foreign students was interpreted by the North Americans to mean agreement. If the foreign students did not contribute in the group meetings it was assumed they had no objections or concerns. Given that the foreign students belonged to collectivistic cultures, however, silence may have been used for "face" saving purposes and may have actually masked disagreement or alternative views on their part. As Gudykunst et al. (1988) point out:

> Members of high uncertainty avoidance, high context cultures have a high apprehension level of unpredictable situations. The more novel the situation, the more likely they will use understatements and silence to manage the situation. Understatement and silence are good ways to preserve the face of oneself and at the same time, not to offend someone else's face in public. The purpose of face negotiation for them is to maintain group harmony (p. 108).

The fact that the foreign students would approach the North American students on a one-to-one basis outside the group meetings supported this interpretation. They did not want to raise questions or challenge others' opinions during the group sessions. The project was under stringent time constraints and the task oriented North American students did not feel they had the time to invest in group dynamics or activities that were not directly related to the accomplishment of their goals. In some ways the lack of involvement on the part of the foreign students made things easier for the North Americans. The North American students, however, did not make any adjustment to the group process to accommodate this difference in approach. If anything, they tended to assign the foreign students simple or straightforward tasks, partly to reduce the amount of after-meeting discussion and clarification required, and partly because silence was interpreted to mean lack of understanding. It was easier and more expedient to ask the foreign students to do simple tasks than take the time to discuss more complicated assignments.

GROUP STRUCTURE

The group had instrumental value to the North Americans and we did not value the group beyond its role in accomplishing the task. There was no attention paid to establishing group norms, processes or objectives beyond completing the task. Although in this paper I have referred to the group as the Journal Project Team, the group did not refer to itself in that way. The North Americans saw the group meetings as a forum for coordination, an opportunity to determine what needed to be accomplished and to bring together independent work for contribution to an end product. It was assumed that the foreign students felt the same way, since they made no attempt to suggest an alternate approach.

Although it would be difficult to call the Journal Project Team a group, there was clearly a differentiation between members. From the perspective of the North American students, the other North Americans may not have been an "us" but the foreign students were clearly a "them." It would be inaccurate to suggest that the foreign students were discriminated against on the basis of their being considered part of an out group, but it would be correct to say that they were perceived to be sojourners. Gudykunst (1985) describes a sojourner as a person interested in visiting and leaving but not belonging to an in-group. The in-group in turn is ambivalent or indifferent toward the sojourner. This would be an accurate description of the attitude of the North Americans toward the foreign students in the Journal Project Team. They were not looked at as individuals but considered as "the foreign students" and for the most part, since they appeared uninvolved, they were ignored. Because the foreign students did not participate on North American terms, no attempt was make to include them. There was also no attempt to individuate them (Bochner 1982) that is, to consider each an individual with distinct skills. This tendency not to consider each an individual, further reinforced their lack of participation.

This leads to a consideration of attribution, the tendency to make judgements of people's behavior based on perceived personality traits or cultural characteristics. In a review of attribution theory in psychology, Brislin (1981) notes that there is a tendency to attribute undesirable behavior to personality traits in others and to attribute the same undesirable behavior to situational factors when applied to ourselves. "He did not participate because he is shy; I did not participate because the group was hostile toward my involvement." Lack of participation on the part of the foreign students was attributed to personal characteristics rather than situational factors. It was assumed that they did not participate because they were shy, did not understand English well enough, or were free riders. However, if the North American students had considered the way they ignored and discounted the involvement of the foreign students, they might have acknowledged that the situation did not encourage their participation either.

LESSONS LEARNED

From my participation in the Journal Project I would suggest the following as lessons learned:

(1) Any work or task involving people from different cultural backgrounds should be viewed as a cross-cultural or multicultural experience and the implications of this fully understood. There should be an initial acknowledgement that differences will arise and agreement that everyone involved will be respectful of these.

(2) Before getting involved in such a project it would be helpful to prepare ahead of time by learning about potential cultural differences and consciously adjusting group processes to allow for and benefit from these differences. Highlighting ethnocentricity and its potential for damage is a useful facet of working interculturally.

(3) Leaders of multicultural groups need to be aware of the additional responsibility to manage the intercultural dynamics of group processes.

Brislin (1981) makes a meaningful contribution to our understanding of multicultural interaction when he suggests that task groups can improve their cross cultural collaborative efforts by:

(1) carefully selecting individuals to participate;
(2) building a knowledge base about cross-cultural relations;
(3) exploring and arranging fully the nature of the collaborative relationship before the task begins;
(4) establishing prior agreements regarding acceptable interpersonal behaviors (trust, respect, tolerance);
(5) specifying plans and objectives before the task begins;
(6) establishing a pattern of regular, frequent and open communication; and
(7) paying greater attention to the role of leader.

CONCLUSIONS

The above analysis is by no means exhaustive, but pausing to reflect on the experience and attempting to understand it from the perspective of a multicultural experience has been helpful to me. It is very likely that in the future, management researchers will have increasing opportunities to work collaboratively with colleagues from cultures very different from their own.

Becoming more sensitive to the cultural dimension of interpersonal relationships will hopefully enhance these encounters and improve the products of our collaboration.

Although it was not originally designed for such purposes, experiences like the one described in the mini-case can be a valuable addition to the curriculum of a doctoral program. Much of what we do in preparation for a Ph.D. degree is independent work. An opportunity to participate in a multicultural collaborative project not only introduces students to a different way of doing research, but if properly prepared, allows them to experience a different way of working with colleagues from other countries.

Despite the fact that the Journal Project had its problems and tribulations, I could not have asked for a more timely or valuable experience. I learned how important it is to do more than sit at the same table with students/researchers from other cultures. It is clear from my experience that learning to work with others requires preparation and attention to process. It is a natural tendency to ignore or discount the contributions of others who do not share the same cultural orientation but by doing so, doctoral students lose the opportunity to benefit from the diversity of opinion and outlook. It is not just managers in training who need to be prepared to function effectively in a global environment. Students in all academic programs can benefit from an introduction to and experience with multicultural work environments.

REFERENCES

Adler, Nancy. 1991. *International Dimensions of Organizational Behaviour.* 2nd ed. Boston: PWS-Kent Publishing Company.

Argyle, Michael. 1982. "Inter-Cultural Communication." Bochner, Stephen (eds.). *Cultures in Contact: Studies in Cross-Cultural Interaction.* Oxford: Pergamon Press.

Bochner, Stephen. 1982. "Cross-Cultural Interaction: Theory and Definition of the Field." In Stephen Bochner(eds.), *Cultures in Contact: Studies in Cross-Cultural Interaction.* Oxford: Pergamon Press.

Brislin, Richard W. 1981. *Cross-Cultural Encounters: Face-to-face Interaction.* New York: Pergamon Press.

Gudykunst, William B. 1985. "Normative Power and Conflict Potential in Intergroup Relationships." Gudykunst, William B., Lea P. Stewart and Stella Ting-Toomey (eds.). *Communication, Culture and Organizational Processes.* Beverly Hills: Sage Publications.

Gudykunst, William B., Stella Ting-Toomey and Elizabeth Chua. 1988. *Culture and Interpersonal Communication*. Newbury Park: Sage Publications.

Hall, E.T. 1976. *Beyond Culture*. New York: Doubleday.

Hofstede, Geert. 1980. "Motivation, Leadership, and Organizations: Do American Theories Apply Abroad?" *Organizational Dynamics*. 9(1): 42-63.

Lane, Henry W. and Joseph J. DiStefano. 1992. *International Management Behavior: From Policy to Practice* 2nd ed. Boston: PWS-Kent Publishing Company.

Stewart, Lea P. 1985. "Culture and Decision Making." Gudykunst, William B., Lea P. Stewart and Stella Ting-Toomey (eds.). *Communication, Culture and Organizational Processes*. Beverly Hills: Sage Publications.

Ting-Toomey, Stella. 1985. "Toward a Theory of Conflict and Culture." Gudykunst, William B., Lea P. Stewart and Stella Ting-Toomey (eds.). *Communication, Culture and Organizational Processes*. Beverly Hills: Sage Publications.

Foreign Language and Foreign Experience Requirements: Are They a Valuable Component of a Doctoral Program?

William R. Folks, Jr., Sharon O'Donnell, and Jeffrey S. Arpan

Introduction

The well-documented absence of an international dimension in the preparation of the next generation of scholars in business administration is arguably the weakest link in the U.S. business educational system. As reported in Arpan, Folks and Kwok (1993), the average percentage of doctoral students receiving an advanced level of international business education is 6 percent at U.S. business schools, with an average of 70 percent receiving minimal or no international business education.[1] When asked to rank the importance of sources of faculty knowledge in international business, U.S. business schools rated "Academic Education" as one of the three *least* important sources (3.2 on a 5 point scale), tied with "Other Educational Training" and only more important than "Consulting."[2] Yet, the primary method cited by which the internationalization of the business school was enhanced was through the hiring of new faculty with international expertise,[3] and the effectiveness of "Academic Education" ranked highly (3.7 on a 5 point scale), behind only "Teaching/Living Abroad" and "International Research."[4] Clearly, enhanced internationalization of doctoral programs would result in more valuable and more marketable faculty.

In addition to international course work in the curriculum, it is frequently argued that a key component of the internationalization of business school programs is the inclusion of a foreign language requirement (Cavusgil 1993). Furthermore the proliferation of internship programs makes it increasingly evident that an international work or study experience is also desirable. In fact, it is becoming common in undergraduate and masters level business programs, as over 50 percent of U.S. business schools offer an "international" experience to their undergraduate students, and 36 percent to their masters

271

students.[5] The benefits of foreign language and international experience to masters level graduates are clear. Such skills enable them to compete more effectively for jobs and to perform more competently in an international business atmosphere. Several academic programs at this level, including the Masters of International Business Studies (MIBS) program at the University of South Carolina, require all students to acquire proficiency in a foreign language and spend time working or studying overseas.

The benefits of foreign language and international experience for doctoral students are less clear. Up until the 1970s virtually all Ph.D. programs required students to develop at least a reading proficiency in one or more foreign languages. The primary rationale was that true and meaningful scholarship required knowledge of work done outside one's native language country. The underlying assumption was that scholars needed foreign language skills to be able to read each other's writings.

While the same rationale and assumptions exist today, U.S. business schools have essentially eliminated foreign language requirements from their doctoral programs. One major reason is that English has become the dominant "second language" in the world, and especially in business, the primary subject of teaching and research in business schools. A second reason is the widespread use of computers in business research, and more recently in communication with colleagues throughout the world (via internet, e-mail).

As a result, in most cases "computer language" proficiency replaced foreign language proficiency in terms of "language" requirements in U.S. business schools. Thus today's American Ph.D. students in business are more apt to "speak" Cobol and Fortran than Spanish or French, and business faculty around the world are more likely to communicate with each other in English.

The recent USC study cited above provides ample evidence. Only 8 percent of doctoral programs at reporting schools had a foreign language requirement for all their students in business. None required a foreign experience of all their business students.[6] Based on such data one might indeed question the relevance of a foreign language and overseas experience for an academic career. And in fact, it has been argued that requirements for foreign language competence and international experience are a distraction and misuse of time for Ph.D. students.

However, students in doctoral programs who major or minor in international business will be teaching courses with significant international content to future graduate and undergraduate students, who, themselves, will be required to have language competency and international experience. Arguably, the pedagogical capability of these doctoral students would be enhanced by developing competence in at least one foreign language and having experience working or studying overseas. Further, it is questionable that a researcher can effectively address pertinent questions in international business without having lived and worked internationally. Yet, of the twenty-two U.S. business schools participating in the USC curriculum survey which reported offering an International Business doctoral major, only three (Indiana University, the University of Miami, and the University of South Carolina) required a foreign language, and only the University of South Carolina required a foreign experience as part of the curriculum.[7] This compares with nine of twenty-one respondent schools in Europe who reported having a foreign language requirement in their doctoral programs.

Because the University of South Carolina was the only U.S. doctoral program that reported requiring both foreign language competence and an international experience of all of its international business majors students, those connected with the program seek to determine on an ongoing basis the value of these requirements. In this paper, an attempt is made to provide an assessment of the value of these requirements by reviewing the impact they have had on the careers of the doctoral graduates of the International Business program at the University of South Carolina. Later in the paper, the potential benefits of such requirements to doctoral students *in general,* are addressed, regardless of a student's major area of specialization.

BACKGROUND

A concentration in international business (IB) was introduced into USC's Ph.D. program in 1980. Its development was significantly influenced by the success of the college's Masters of International Business Studies (MIBS) degree program, which requires advanced foreign language competency and a six month internship outside the United States for all citizens. In developing the doctoral concentration in IB, the IB faculty unanimously agreed that graduating a doctoral student with a major in IB without foreign language skills or any meaningful experience outside the U.S. would simply not be credible to an increasingly globalized business community. In addition, the IB faculty believed that foreign language competency and international living experience would enhance opportunities for USC's Ph.D. in IB program graduates to consult, teach, and conduct research internationally, and also would improve their teaching of international business in any location, as well as give them greater credibility with students and colleagues. In addition, it was believed that these skills would fit the increased needs of business schools to internationalize their education and research programs.

USC's international business faculty recognized the necessity for the development of foreign language skills beyond the classical reading knowledge requirement which was a feature of many Ph.D. programs up to the 1970s. USC's original IB doctoral program required competency in a language equivalent to that achieved in the MIBS program's intensive summer language course. While the language competency developed in this program varies with the degree of difficulty of the given language, the criteria developed for the German course is representative:

> In a ten-week program the students were to be exposed to the material normally covered in seven courses: two courses each in Elementary German and Intermediate German, and one course each in conversation, composition, and culture. The projected final profile of MIBS-German track students, was that they be able (a) to comprehend 90 percent of *any* written German, (b) to express themselves in simple German on *any* conversational topic and be understood, and (c) to write what they can say.[8]

The current Ph.D. requirement is as follows:

> The candidate majoring in International Business must demonstrate both oral/aural as well as written competency. This effectiveness can be demonstrated by means of a competency examination or the successful completion of BADM 700 or its equivalent. Selection of the language must be approved by the candidate's committee and the Director of Graduate Studies. It is recommended that students take this intensive language training prior to their overseas research activities.[9]

In the original doctoral program design, it was envisioned that the doctoral student would satisfy the overseas experience requirement by conducting research for a six month period in an overseas location. That concept proved ineffective, as the early students in the program selected research topics that were global rather than region-specific and were dependent upon close interaction with the USC faculty and close proximity to the library resources of the university. In the summer of 1986, the period of time required to be spent overseas was reduced to three months and the scope of permissible activities was broadened. The current policy is as follows:

International Business majors from the United States must spend at least three months overseas researching, teaching, working and/or studying. The exact nature of this overseas experience must be approved in advance by the candidate's Ph.D. Advisory Committee and the Director of Graduate Studies. An "Independent Study or Internship Contract" form (AS-6) must be submitted by the student.[10]

The offshore residency requirement applies only to U.S. citizens in the doctoral program. It is assumed that foreign nationals in the program satisfy the intent and purposes of this requirement by their study at USC. Further, foreign nationals satisfy the "foreign" language requirement by demonstrating their command of English in the classroom and their studies at USC.

The inclusion of extensive foreign language and foreign experience requirements in a doctoral program does not come without some costs. The intensive language programs at South Carolina are offered in a ten week period during the summer, eliminating one summer of potential course work. If the overseas experience is scheduled too early in the program, the doctoral candidate is not as adequately prepared to conduct research and must again sacrifice some academic course work. Further, delays conflict with preparation for comprehensive examinations and with the development of a dissertation topic and selection of a committee. In a few cases doctoral students lost up to a year of progress toward their degree by an inopportune choice of timing for their overseas experience. Hence, there does not appear to be an optimal time for the overseas experience, except for combining it with the dissertation research. Yet USC's experience has shown that this optimal combination typically does not occur.

Consequently, the research project reported below was undertaken. Its objective was to assess the value of these two requirements and to generate conclusions about the impact they have had on the career path of USC graduates.

METHOD

To assess the value of the foreign language and international experience requirements, in 1994 a questionnaire was developed and administered to the fourteen native English-speaking graduates of the IB doctoral program at USC who were required to meet *both* the foreign language and overseas experience components of the program. From 1986 to 1994, a total of twenty students graduated with an IB major from USC's Ph.D. program. Of these, ten had already met both the language and international experience require-ments *prior* to entry; six of these ten students were foreign nationals and were thus exempt from the requirements; while the other four were U.S. citizens with considerable experience abroad and knowledge of at least one foreign language. Twelve of the fourteen surveyed provided usable responses.

Graduates were asked for their perception of how valuable the language and experience components of the degree have been to their careers. The questionnaire consisted of three parts: (1) questions regarding the respon-dent's career path; (2) questions regarding the language requirement; and (3) questions regarding the foreign experience requirement. The question-naire included items designed to assess the benefits of each of the two requirements to the respondent's overall career, as well as items to measure the value of the language and experience to specific aspects of an academic career, such as research, teaching, consulting, and administrative responsi-bilities. Likert items using a one to five scale were used to assess how *benefi-cial* these skills have been to the careers of the respondents and how *often* they used these skills. Similar items were used in each of two sections addressing the foreign language requirement and the foreign experience requirement. The Likert scales used one as low and five as high. For items assessing benefit, 1 = Not Very Beneficial, 5 = Extremely Beneficial. For items assessing frequency, 1 = Very Rarely, 5 = Very Often. Open-ended questions were asked at the end of each of the two sections on foreign language and foreign experience to assess *how* these skills have benefited the respondent's career. The questionnaire also asked respondents to list any perceived draw-backs of the two requirements.

RESEARCH FINDINGS

The first finding was that a foreign experience was perceived to be more valuable and more frequently used in an academic career than a foreign lan-guage. The mean and median of the variables measured with the Likert items are shown in Table 1. For nearly every item in the two sections, the mean and median score in the experience section was higher than the corresponding score in the language section. In the primary academic endeavors of research and teaching, the foreign experience clearly provided greater perceived ben-efit than the learning of a foreign language, even though the foreign lan-guage requirement was set at a level well above the traditional reading knowledge requirement.

Table 1. Variable Means and Medians

Foreign Language

Benefit To:	Mean	Median
Overall Career	3.00	3.0
Research	1.75	1.5
Teaching	2.75	2.5
Consulting	2.64	2.0
Administrative	1.78	1.0
Other Career Activities	3.18	4.0

Frequent of Use In:		
Overall Career	2.67	3.0
Research	1.92	1.5
Teaching	2.25	2.0
Consulting	2.55	2.0
Administrative	1.90	1.5
Other Career Activities	2.91	3.0

Foreign Experience

Benefit To:	Mean	Median
Overall Career	3.82	4.0
Research	3.09	3.0
Teaching	3.82	4.0
Consulting	2.90	3.0
Administrative	2.22	2.0
Other Career Activities	3.40	2.5
Overall Career	4.00	4.5
Research	3.00	3.0
Teaching	4.25	4.5
Consulting	2.73	3.0
Administrative	2.30	2.0
Other Career Activities	3.09	3.0

Only one of the items in the language section had a mean or median that exceeded three, the midpoint of the scale. The highest scores in the language section were for the items assessing its value to the respondent's "overall career" and "other career activities," as opposed to those evaluating the contribution to specific components of an academic career. This finding suggests the respondents perceived that the language ability was useful, but not directly applicable to their research, teaching, or consulting. Foreign language skills seem to have more of an *indirect* value. The most common open-ended responses in the language section cited the benefits of "increased credibility," "cultural awareness" and "the ability to function in a foreign culture." All of these are benefits of language skills not directly associated with specific elements of an academic career (such as teaching or research) but are indirectly valuable to a professor of international business. Some of the open-ended responses that mentioned a more direct benefit to an academic career included "rapport and communication with foreign students and/or clients" and "the ability to use or understand foreign source materials."

In sum, the foreign language skills gained in the doctoral program appeared to be more contextual rather than functional in an academic career. Faculty were not required to teach directly in the foreign language, nor did their research involve a foreign language. However, indirect benefits applicable particularly in teaching were present.

On the other hand, a foreign experience appeared to have more direct value for both teaching and research, as well as for respondents' overall careers. Nearly all of these items had a mean and median equal to or higher than the midpoint of the scale. Open-ended responses frequently cited "class examples" as a benefit of the foreign experience to teaching, and "a better cultural understanding" and "a source of ideas" as benefits to research. These responses suggested a more direct benefit to an academic career from the foreign experience than from the foreign language. This conclusion regarding the value of the foreign experience is supported by Arpan, Folks and Kwok (1993), who found that "Teaching/Living Abroad" was rated as the most effective method for internationalizing faculty overall and in U.S. business schools.[11]

A second major finding was that both requirements appeared to benefit and be more frequently used in the teaching component of the respondents' careers, compared to the research component. As indicated in Table 1, both the benefit and frequency of use means were higher for teaching than for research for both the foreign language and the foreign experience requirements. Given the variety of career paths taken by the graduates, an attempt was made to determine whether the variability of research productivity in graduates would have an impact on the conclusion just reached, i.e., some respondents had been in a research/publishing career track since they received their degree, while others had emphasized teaching and administrative pursuits.

The number of refereed publications per year of experience in academia was utilized as a measure of research emphasis in the graduates' careers. The number of publications was determined by a search of the respondent's name in the author index of the UMI Proquest database, Global Edition. This database includes publications in business periodicals from 1987 to present. The earliest graduates of the IB doctoral program at South Carolina received their degrees in 1986, so this database included the vast majority of the research output of Carolina graduates.

Respondents were classified into two categories based on the number of publications per year. Those respondents with 0.5 publications per year or greater were classified as being in a research oriented career path (Group 1) and those with fewer than 0.5 were classified as being in a non-research, or teaching, career path (Group 2). Significant differences were found between these two groups on several variables, as shown in Table 2. In the foreign language section, scores were averaged across the items assessing the benefit of the language to the respondent's career to obtain an "average benefit" score. The same was done for the items assessing the frequency of use of the language. Scores were also averaged across "benefit" and "frequency of use" for each component of an academic career (e.g. research, teaching, consulting, etc.) to obtain a score for the average utility of the language for each component. The same calculations were performed for the foreign experience section of the questionnaire.

Although not all variables yielded significant differences between the high and low publishing graduates, the overall results for the two groups did show some differences. In terms of the foreign language requirement, the research oriented group had lower means and medians on six of the seven variables measured. Open-ended responses from some members of the research group stated that there were no benefits of a foreign language to a career in academic research and teaching. Overall, graduates pursuing a research career path seemed to feel that their foreign language skills were less valuable to their career than did graduates who have been more engaged in academic pursuits other than research.

The results of the group comparisons were less clear for the foreign experience requirement. The tests of group differences yielded no significant differences, with the research group scoring higher than the non-research group on some items in the foreign experience section and lower on others. It appeared that the foreign experience was equally valuable across the groups, regardless of their orientation toward research or teaching.

Table 2. Results of Parametric and Nonparametice Tests of Group Differences

	Mean			Median		
			One-tailed			One-tailed
Variable	Group 1	Group 2	Signif-icance	Group 1	Group 2	Signif-icance
Foreign Language						
Average 'Benefit to Career'	1.75	2.95	**	1.58	2.75	**
Average 'Frequency of Use	1.67	2.68	*	1.42	2.50	*
Average 'Benefit' and "Fequency'						
OverallCareer	2.25	3.13		2.25	2.75	
Research	1.63	1.94		1.50	1.75	
Teaching	1.75	2.88	*	1.25	2.50	*
Consulting	1.50	3.21	**	1.50	2.50	**
Administrative	1.25	2.08	*	1.00	2.00	
Other Career Act.	1.87	3.71	**	1.50	4.00	**
Foreign Experience						
Average 'Benefit to Career'	3.67	3.10		3.83	3.00	
Average 'Frequency of Use	3.25	3.33		3.25	2.92	
Average 'Benefit' and "Fequency'						
OverallCareer	2.88	3.31		2.75	3.255	
Research	2.63	2.38		2.75	2.00	
Teaching	2.62	3.19		2.75	3.50	
Consulting	2.13	2.93		2.25	3.00	
Administrative	1.50	2.33		1.25	2.00	*
Other Career Act.	2.50	3.36		2.50	3.50	

* = Significant at 0.10   Group 1 = Research Group
** = Significant at 0.05   Group 2 = Non-Research Group

The open-ended questions regarding the drawbacks of the foreign language and foreign experience requirements yielded three common responses: (1) additional time necessary to complete the degree; (2) additional financial burden (especially for the foreign experience); and (3) a lack of integration of the two components into the overall doctoral program, particularly with regard to research. Nonetheless, 86 percent of the respondents indicated that despite program completion drawbacks, the skills that they gained from the language and international experience requirements were worth the additional time and money.

DISCUSSION

The results of this survey bring up several important points, although all conclusions must be viewed in light of the limitations of the study. The data were collected from a small sample (twelve out of fourteen) and all respondents attended the same university. Despite these limitations, the data suggested that having some international experience, whether it be related to work or study, was more valuable in an academic career than was knowledge of a foreign language. The respondents indicated that their foreign experience had more direct benefits and applications to their jobs as international business professors than did their language skills. The benefits of knowing a foreign language seemed to be more intangible and less quantifiable; respondents felt that their language skills were important, but not in a direct fashion. One response that appeared many times, in both the language and experience sections of the questionnaire, was *credibility*. A majority of the respondents felt that having these skills afforded them greater respect as international business professors (with students and colleagues).

Another factor that should be considered when evaluating the results of this study is the difference between the responses to the Likert items and the open-ended items. While many respondents indicated in the open-ended questions that they felt the two requirements were important and that they should not be dropped from the curriculum, few of the scores on the Likert items exceeded the midpoint of the scale. It appeared that the responding graduates valued the skills that they gained while fulfilling these requirements, but that the skills had not been directly useful to their academic careers thus far. However, it is conceivable that these skills may become more important to the graduates in later stages of their careers. Overseas teaching and international consulting opportunities are more likely to increase as younger faculty mature, and are more likely to be pursued after tenure has been obtained. Arguably, foreign language competency and international experience should facilitate the undertaking of these kinds of opportunities, and increase the competitiveness of the faculty who possess such skills for such opportunities.

In addition, research conducted later in one's career tends to involve greater collaboration and multiple authorship. Put in the vernacular of the global economy, it involves more "international alliances." Such alliances should be facilitated and enhanced by having foreign language competency and international experience.

The differences in the results of the more and less research oriented groups may have some implications for the design of doctoral programs. In evaluating the utility of foreign language and international experience requirements in a doctoral program, the goals of the program should be taken into consideration. The drawbacks to the language and experience requirements cited by the respondents should also be considered. Such requirements put an added financial burden on the student because of the extra time and expense involved. If language and international experience are important enough to be a required part of the curriculum, the university, as well as the student, must make a commitment to integrating them into the doctoral program, both in terms of administrative support and curriculum design. The requirements should be designed so that they have direct benefits to the doctoral program and to the student's future career as a professor of international business.

Finally, some comments are in order about the desirability of foreign language skills and international experience for *all* doctoral students in business—not just those majoring in international business. Going a step further, some comments are in order about the broader issue of the *internationalization* of *all* doctoral students, be it by course work, international experiences, foreign language training or other methods.

To some degree, the broader issue of internationalization depends on whether one regards "international" as a context, a discipline, or specialization of business. If viewed more narrowly as a "specialization," then it follows that internationalization of Ph.D. programs is most appropriate for those seeking to develop such a specialization, but less so, if at all, for all other Ph.D. students. If viewed as a "context" of business (i.e., that business takes place in a global context, and hence to understand business properly one must understand the context in which it takes place), then internationalization should be achieved for *all* Ph.D. students in business. Otherwise, they might not know that what they have learned applies only in a national context.

The authors of this paper believe that international business is a context, a discipline, *and* a specialization—a viewpoint shared by most participants at a recent symposium on internationalization of doctoral programs in business.[12] In this respect, participants in one of the sessions examining the redesign of doctoral programs in business agreed unanimously that *all* students should be *required* to have at least one out-of-country experience before graduating (duration not specified), and be encouraged (although not required) to have a minimal level of *conversational* foreign language ability, such as that which can be obtained from a high quality intensive summer language program. Some went further, arguing that foreign language competency and international experience should become an *admission requirement* for all doctoral students.

In the final analysis, the professional career benefits resulting from foreign language abilities and international experience, while not demonstrably significant, are evident and measurable. The personal benefits to the individual may be even more significant in terms of one's personal development, self assessment, and awareness and understanding of the global village. Therefore, if academia is to be concerned with the development and enhancement of both the professional and personal dimensions of its students, appropriate internationalization of these students is necessary. What remains arguable are the extent of and best methods for their internationalization.

NOTES

1. Arpan, Jeffrey S., William R. Folks, Jr., and Chuck C. Y. Kwok (1993), *International Business Education in the 1990s: A Global Survey*, Academy of International Business, American Assembly of Collegiate Schools of Business, and the Center for International Business Education and Research, University of South Carolina, Exhibit 8, Table B.11, 63.
2. Ibid., Exhibit 8, Table B.16, 65.
3. Ibid., Exhibit 8, Table B.26, 69.
4. Ibid., Exhibit 8, Table B.17, 65.
5. Ibid., Exhibit 8, Table B.1, 59.
6. Ibid., Exhibit 8, Table B.2, 59.
7. Ibid., Exhibit 15, 242-45.
8. Beazley, Garnett F., William R. Folks, Jr., and Gerda P. Jordan, "Development and Initiation of a Master in International Business Studies," *Journal of International Business Studies*, 6/1 (Spring 1975), 101.
9. "Policy Statement for the Ph. D. Program in Business Administration", University of South Carolina, Spring 1992, 3.
10. Ibid.
11. Arpan, Folks and Kwok, op. cit., Exhibit 7, Table B.17, 43, and Exhibit 8, Table B.17, 65.
12. Internationalizing Ph.D. programs. A symposium sponsored by the Center for International Business Education and Research at Indiana University, University of South Carolina, Texas A&M University and Michigan State University; September 1994, East Lansing, Michigan.

REFERENCES

Arpan, Jeffrey S., William R. Folks, Jr., and Chuck C. Y. Kwok. *International Business Education in the 1990s: A Global Survey.* Academy of International Business, American Assembly of Collegiate Schools of Business, and the Center for International Business Education and Research, University of South Carolina, 1993.

Beazley, Garnett F., William R. Folks, Jr., and Gerda P. Jordan. "Development and Initiation of a Master in International Business Studies." *Journal of International Business Studies.* 6(1) (Spring 1975): 99-106.

Cavusgil, S. Tamer. "Internationalization of Business Education: Defining the Challenge." In S. Tamer Cavusgil (Ed.). *International Business Education: Meeting the Challenge.* Michigan State University Press: East Lansing, MI, 1993.

University of South Carolina (USC). "Policy Statements for the Ph.D. Program in Business Administration." Spring 1992.

PART VI: CONCLUSION

INTRODUCTION

S. Tamer Cavusgil

I n this final section of the book, the reader is presented with a number of challenges to internationalize doctoral programs in business.

James Schmotter illustrates how business itself had to internationalize in order to remain competitive. He challenges us to look at business for models in internationalizing doctoral business programs.

Charles Hickman summarizes the main points made at the Roundtable emphasizing the need for administrators and faculty to develop an internationalization vision for their schools to meet the learning needs of future generations of faculty.

S. Tamer Cavusgil presents us with the final set of challenges. If we do not meet these challenges, business schools are facing a perilous future.

Lessons for Doctoral Education from Successful International Companies

James W. Schmotter

Introduction

Georges Santayana's famous dictum that "those who cannot remember the past are condemned to repeat it" resonates deeply today for faculty and administrators concerned with American doctoral education in business. While the often threatening winds of change buffet business schools everywhere, many doctoral programs go on about their work much as they have since their reinvention in the wake of the Gordon-Howell and Pierson reports of the late 1950s. They remain producer-based and largely self-referent, narrowly focused on the preparation of graduates for discipline-based research careers. In a world defined by the editors of the academic journals of the disciplines, by an academic job market that has grown exponentially since the 1960s, and by university governance structures that provide autonomy, they seek to ignore the turmoil affecting so much of undergraduate and MBA education today. In this, they resemble those American companies that refused to confront dramatic changes in the global economy over the past two decades, an attitude whose results are painfully evident today in places such as Detroit, Michigan, Armonk, New York, and Bethlehem, Pennsylvania.

The fact is that the economic and environmental pressures that are affecting all of American higher education will soon reach doctoral programs in business everywhere, if they have not done so already. Severe financial cutbacks in large public university systems and a constricting job market for doctoral graduates are placing new limits on the expansion of Ph.D. programs in business. Public criticism from external constituents about the supposed irrelevance of academic research is gaining wider acceptance than ever before, often among university trustees and potential financial contributors. And increasingly all of higher education is becoming a global endeavor, with advances in telecommunications and travel, creating genuine global markets for both knowledge and human resources.

It is this trend toward globalization that presents the greatest challenges—but may also offer the greatest opportunities—for American doctoral education in business. While the growth of business education has slowed in the United States, it continues unabated elsewhere. The great 1980s surge in the establishment of new business schools in Western Europe has peaked, but the popularity of business as a field of study continues. Growth is even stronger in Asia, with major new universities under construction in Singapore and Hong Kong and with a huge demand for business education still unsatiated in countries such as Malaysia, Indonesia and China. The end of the Cold War presents an even more dramatic potential demand for schooling in capitalism from the transforming economies of the former Soviet Bloc. If the American job market for Ph.D.s in business has peaked, opportunities for appropriately prepared graduates overseas would seem virtually unlimited.

The globalization of demand for business education is paralleled by an internationalization of its intellectual content. Years of exhortation by corporate constituents, students, and enlightened faculty have convinced most on our campuses that business today is indeed a global endeavor and must be addressed as such. This recognition is perhaps best exemplified by the Harvard Business School's massive efforts to produce new case materials that are more international. With enthusiasm on some campuses and grudging resistance elsewhere, this understanding is working its way into the consciousness of the professoriate of most business schools.

The demographics of today's doctoral students—and tomorrow's faculty members—also reflect the trends toward the globalization of business and business education. More than ever before, doctoral students in American business schools come from abroad. And while some hope to remain and pursue academic careers in the United States, increasing numbers are returning to their home countries to take advantage of burgeoning academic career opportunities there.

The trend toward the globalization of business education's markets, intellectual content and human resources seem unlikely to reverse themselves in the foreseeable future. For doctoral students and faculty alike, an understanding of the international dimensions of their particular academic fields promises increasingly to be the competitive edge in the tight North American academic hiring environment as well as in the expanding job markets overseas. Likewise, the worldwide marketplace for the intellectual products of business school research will be increasingly amenable to—and will reward—research on international business phenomena.

Those who direct doctoral programs in today's business schools cannot ignore this increasing globalization of their environment. In confronting this reality they face a set of strategic decisions about their programs' futures. Further, they do so in the context of a climate of financial constraints and competing demands from elsewhere on campus; mistakes or inaction promise to be damaging. Yet the decisions about globalization that these doctoral program directors and interested faculty face are not without precedent. As a matter of fact, they appear to be remarkably similar to those faced by American companies struggling to globalize themselves during the last two decades. In this growing body of experience— some successful and some not; some chronicled carefully in business school cases and some the stuff of legend—lie a variety of strategies, tactics and insights that could prove valuable to doctoral programs wrestling with the challenges of globalization. The follow paragraphs suggest what some of these might be.

INTERNATIONALIZING BUSINESS/INTERNATIONALIZING DOCTORAL PROGRAMS IN BUSINESS

STRATEGIC INTENT TO VALUE THE INTERNATIONAL DIMENSION OF DOCTORAL EDUCATION IS ESSENTIAL

Companies successful in cracking international markets have learned that true commitment to a global focus must go beyond lip service. It must include the internalization of the importance of a global outlook in the development of institutional goals and in the rewarding of activities that advance that outlook. For such companies, this means allocating to international markets the same strategic importance and resources as to domestic ones.

For doctoral programs, such a commitment means the active support of international research as well as the development of curricular requirements that ensure international competence. This competence can be demonstrated through the encouragement of the development of language proficiency or through comprehensive examination requirements that include the mastery of international material. Other possible means to develop such competence might include required courses on international topics relevant to one's discipline, required research projects utilizing non-U.S. data (increasingly available thanks to the Internet and other technlogical advances), or even a return to the stodgy old foreign language requirements that most doctoral programs in business and the social sciences abandoned long ago. Few doctoral programs permit graduation without certifying their students' competence in research methodology. Those serious about participating in the global marketplace for business education can scarcely do less with regard to their students' competence in understanding the international dimensions of business.

ORGANIZATIONS SERIOUS ABOUT GLOBALIZATION PLACE REAL VALUE ON THE INTERNATIONAL COMPETENCE OF THE PEOPLE INVITED TO JOIN THE ORGANIZATION

For companies successful in global markets, international competencies—for instance, cultural and language skills—have become hiring criteria of equal importance with technical skills. Increasingly, the applicant with fluency in a second language or a multicultural background has an edge over those possessing only the traditional tools of functional or technical expertise. Companies such as Citicorp and Sony are choosing to internationalize their operations through the characteristics of the people they hire. Given the continuing worldwide appeal of American doctoral education and the rich mix of national origins in their applicant pools and student bodies, this strategy seems an obvious one for doctoral programs to pursue in an effort to internationalize their activities.

Yet remarkably few programs have elected to leverage this demographic reality to their advantage. Experiences in other cultures and language skills are formally valued in few doctoral admissions processes. Likewise, the cultural and national backgrounds of new faculty hires are often ignored or deemed irrelevant when compared with research potential or technical facility. Indeed, much of American doctoral education for business today seems overtly to devalue such cultural and linguistic expertise and seeks instead to homogenize aspiring academics from Budapest and Bangkok into discipline-based specialists no different from their peers from Boston and Biloxi. Clearly this approach has brought academic rigor and intellectual respectability to the academic disciplines of business. Whether it is the appropriate route to follow to meet the challenges of the global marketplace and take full advantage of the international experience many of today's doctoral students bring to campus is another matter.

In today's business environment, the American-educated marketing manager born and reared in Taiwan or the trilingual Belgian with a degree from

INSEAD are valued for both their technical skills <u>and</u> their cross-cultural expertise. In disregarding the latter in most of its career rituals and requirements and focusing instead on producing "cutting edge research," doctoral programs in business emulate the values and priorities of the more established academic disciplines of the arts and sciences, not those of the world of practice they profess to study. As that world of practice changes faster and faster, this intellectual posture may become, as some critics now claim, increasingly irrelevant.

PROACTIVE RECRUITMENT PRACTICES SERVE TO INTERNATIONALIZE ORGANIZATIONS

Successful transnational companies today implement the above-mentioned strategies of internationalization through people by focused, proactive recruitment activities. These include worldwide sourcing of managerial talent, the use of specialized executive search firms, and carefully conceived on-campus recruiting. Companies such as Citicorp and Hewlett Packard, for example, send some recruiters to American business schools to interview *only* foreign nationals.

Such focused, proactive practices stand in sharp contrast to the admissions processes that bring students to American doctoral programs. Most such programs engage in only minimal informal marketing of their offerings. Sometimes personal networks are established by individual faculty members, but generally a central graduate school office serves as an order taker, responding to requests for information from prospective applicants. Because of historical traditions that view academic life as a calling and the strong demand for doctoral education in recent years, the aggressive marketing now prevalent in undergraduate and MBA admissions is viewed by most associated with doctoral education as unnecessary and even somewhat unseemly. Yet in the coming years, progress in globalizing doctoral programs— and perhaps their very survival— may require more focused approaches to both doctoral admissions and faculty hiring, approaches that take into account the importance of personal characteristics beyond technical abilities and standardized test scores. Heretofore in selecting future generations of the professoriate, we in doctoral education have tended to define merit very narrowly. Today's global markets would seem to argue for a broadening of that definition.

GLOBAL INITIATIVES AND COMPETENCE MUST BE RECOGNIZED AND REWARDED

It goes without saying that either within a transnational company or within a doctoral program, rhetoric about the importance of globalization will remain empty without concrete steps to recognize and reward international expertise. As the road to senior management these days in many companies includes stops at offshore business units, so might the journey through doctoral study and on to tenure and promotion more explicitly require the development of international competence. All too often today the activities necessary to develop such competence—overseas leaves, language study, interdisciplinary research—are undervalued in both doctoral education and the promotion and tenure process.

Deans can facilitate such development by making available resources such as leaves and research funding; faculty can enforce it through the priorities they establish in personnel policies. The American Assembly of Collegiate Schools of Business can also provide support for such development through the accreditation process. Such rewards and recognition must be real, concrete and capable of assessment if they are to be meaningful.

INTERNATIONAL ALLIANCES ARE INCREASINGLY NECESSARY IN TODAY'S GLOBAL ECONOMY

In the messy reality of today's global environment, individual firms often do not possess all of the requisite competencies or information necessary to take advantage of business opportunities. Hence cross-border corporate alliances have become a standard strategy for success. Such alliances, often struck for specific projects with limited lifespans, permit the comparative advantages of allies—or even competitors—to be brought to bear for purposes of mutual benefit. These experiences provide models that might serve doctoral education as well.

Recent demands for the development of global perspectives have only intensified the explosion of knowledge that has transpired within the academic disciplines of business during the past two decades. Fewer and fewer institutions, if they are honest, will attest that their faculties possess the intellectual breadth and depth sufficient to prepare doctoral students for all of the various challenges of academic life in the twenty-first century. While some may respond to this fact by limiting the scope and size of doctoral education on their campuses, a more promising future might be possible in more formal alliances with other institutions, especially with those overseas.

Such educational alliances, which have characterized European business education for years in schemes such as the TEMPO and ERASMUS programs, are appearing in North America at the undergraduate and MBA levels. The Ohio State Legislature considered recently funding the Ohio School of International Business, a consortium that brings together the expertise of faculty from Kent State University, the University of Akron, Cleveland State University, and Youngstown State University. The University of Michigan, New York University, and the University of California at Berkeley have joined with eight European universities to establish a certificate program in European Management Studies for MBA students. And four Canadian universities in the Montreal area have formed a collaboration to offer a Ph.D. degree in administration.

Such partnerships would seem especially appropriate means to address the needs of doctoral programs everywhere to enhance their international dimensions. While issues of governance and transfer academic credit may arise in the development of formal alliances, precedent for such collaboration exists in the common practice of service by colleagues from other universities on individual doctoral dissertation committees. Modern telecommunications technologies also promise to make such alliances more effective and rewarding for students. A recent doctoral dissertation defense at Lehigh University's College of Education that employed interactive video to include a colleague in Arizona is a modest example of how technology can facilitate partnerships across continents and time zones.

PREPARATION FOR OVERSEAS ASSIGNMENTS INCREASES THEIR EFFECTIVENESS

A significant literature exists to demonstrate that successful international companies are creative and diligent in preparing managers bound for overseas experiences. Many have developed organized programs to prepare employees for expatriate assignments or for the more routine travel required when one accepts responsibility for a business unit overseas. The lessons of the experiences of firms that have not engaged in such practices are all too evident in the frustrating, unhappy, unproductive assignments their expatriate managers often endure.

Such formal preparation for overseas experiences has similarly been missing for faculty and doctoral students. Long-standing traditions of faculty independence and individualism mean that the scholar bound for an overseas experience usually operates on his or her own. International networking among those in one's own discipline is common, but often little attention is paid to the particular cultural context in which this networking takes place. The potential richness of the intercultural contacts—and learning—that such overseas experience can provide are thus limited.

Ironically, the typical American campus provides valuable, but often untapped, sources of information and insights that can prepare scholars to take full advantage of overseas experiences. Colleagues in languages and linguistics and in area studies often possess expertise that they are more than willing to share, if asked. Further, their services usually come at a far smaller cost than those of the consultants that corporations sometimes hire to prepare expatriates.

Such preparation already happens on an *ad hoc* basis on many campuses. Some faculty members ask colleagues they happen to know from relevant fields for advice; others rely upon their international students for information; a few even take the time for formal language study. Yet every year hundreds of faculty members and doctoral students from the academic disciplines of business board jumbo jets for destinations abroad with little more preparation than acquiring a passport and packing their belongings. The experiences of many of these travelers is diminished because of this lack of preparation, an especially unfortunate result because of the easily available resources that might have helped them. Business schools have a comparative advantage in preparing scholars for international activities. In exploiting this advantage, they should follow the lead of successful international companies that have developed formal programs for employees involved in international business.

CONCLUSIONS

If considered seriously, changes like those suggested above represent significant redirections in emphasis for most doctoral programs. Some of these changes will require a reconceptualization of the nature of doctoral education as we have come to know it during the past twenty years. While these and other changes are already underway in some programs, no doubt some observers will discern in such suggested reforms challenges to academic freedom and intellectual rigor.

Yet, not considering such alternatives may well mean reduced competitiveness for individual doctoral programs in the increasingly global market for business education. In these days of restructuring of American higher education, an imprecise, often politicized process that sometimes fails to appreciate the value of doctoral education, such reduced competitiveness can be dangerous. The parallel with American companies facing stiff international competition and internal restructuring driven by economic forces is ominously obvious. Ultimately, self-defined academic rigor and campus-based rules of faculty governance will provide no better shelter from the winds of change than did self-promotional advertising and union work rules in industries such as steel, autos and consumer electronics in the 1970s and 1980s. This lesson is eloquently taught in business school classrooms from coast to coast. It is time that the message be heard in our own doctoral programs as well.

IMPERATIVES FOR THE FUTURE

Charles W. Hickman

A MONUMENT TO IRRELEVANCE

The papers and discussion groups that highlighted the 1994 Roundtable on Internationalizing Doctoral Programs in Business had a familiar ring to anyone who has been on the front lines of curriculum reform efforts in U.S. business schools over the last two decades. International business belongs high on a list of emerging topics that includes the management of technology, ethics, quality management, activity-based cost accounting, environmental responsibility, and the management of work force diversity in which business practice has led the teaching, research, and outreach initiatives of most schools. Papers and presentations at the Michigan State Roundtable profiled an internal culture that has been carefully constructed by business schools over the past 30 years. And while this culture has arguably contributed to prior success, as measured in terms of rising student enrollment, expanded funding, and enhanced academic prestige, it is clear to an increasing range of knowledgeable observers, both in and outside the academy, that "more of the same" is a formula for irrelevance or worse in the 1990s.

In recent years, an entire body of literature has been produced on the topic of why historically successful organizations fail. Narrow vision by leaders, complex infrastructures that inhibit response to environmental changes, performance evaluation systems that reward activity with no external value, a focus on disciplinary silos, an inability (or unwillingness) to form product development and production alliances, the failure to adopt new technology, new competitors, and unexpected events are typically among the signs of decline. Papers and presentations at the Roundtable offered a checklist of nearly all of these symptoms within U.S. business schools and reflect a cul-

299

ture that too often has encouraged faculty to think of academic colleagues as the ultimate customer. Most business school faculty are well aware of global economic trends and practices. Many are interested and willing to extend their teaching and research activity into these areas. But, in too many instances, the tyranny created by past business school success provides few resources and no rewards for initiatives of this nature.

PREREQUISITES FOR CHANGE

The Michigan State Roundtable highlighted numerous effective strategies for internationalizing business doctoral programs. However, the most critical question is whether those in academic leadership positions have the vision—and the will—to use the tools available to them. During the past decade, demands by prospective students and employers have caused remarkably rapid change in the content and structure of MBA and undergraduate programs at many business schools. Absent a shift in the product specifications made by the primary employers of business doctoral graduates (deans and faculty at hiring institutions), it is not realistic to expect a similar transformation.

Several Roundtable discussants, noting the recent impact of magazine rankings on MBA program reform, proposed the creating of a similar system for business Ph.D. programs. Others suggested that the AACSB apply more demanding accreditation criteria to test the "internationalization" of the doctoral experience at each institution. These requests for new, externally-created "hammers" to be used by school leadership in fashioning internal change may have a certain surface appeal. However, other Roundtable papers point out the reality that there is "no clear image or criteria of what constitutes excellence in international doctoral programs." As a result, specific ranking criteria imposed by magazines, accrediting agencies, or other professional groups are most likely to invite a certain conformity among schools at the precise moment when innovation and experimentation with many different program structures and methods is needed. MBA rankings have caused change because they can shift market demand for degree programs that generate significant profit at most institutions. Given the entirely different nature of the prospect identification and doctoral admission process, let alone the negative contribution of Ph.D. programs to the business school bottom line, it is unlikely that the change-causing features of magazine rankings could be duplicated at this degree level. Further, what dean or doctoral program director could justify the investment of scarce time and money in the kinds of public relations activities and debates over survey methodology that characterize the MBA rankings scene?

Perhaps the single most damning, yet realistic, declaration concerning the current state of business doctoral education was provided by Roundtable participate Robert May (in this volume), now acting dean at the University of Texas at Austin. He observed that "major intervention will be required to change doctoral education within 20 years or less." The contemporary world of business moves quickly. In this context, it is difficult to identify another institution that views itself as "best in class" on a world scale that would settle for a 20-year cycle time to improve its product. New methods of delivering management education are being tested every day, increasingly by business "schools" that are not based within a university. If successful internationalization of business doctoral programs takes 20 years, will anyone notice? Will anyone care?

STRATEGIES

Ballplayer/philosopher Yogi Berra once described the left field shadows at Yankee Stadium during late season games by noting that "it gets late out there, early." Visionary schools and management education associations should see the shadows cast by the realities of modern business practice and sense the urgency created by the changing economics of higher education. The Roundtable points to several initiatives that may help short cut the 20-year time cycle anticipated by Dean May. They include:

- Creating a context for change by making faculty more aware of: the shifting economics of higher education; the increasing dissatisfaction of corporations, government bodies, students, and other stakeholders whose funding supports the academic enterprise; and the emergence of new competitors fully able to compete for student market share. In the course of visiting numerous campuses and speaking to hundreds of business faculty each year, I continue to be struck by how few know what the tuition rate is at their institution, how it has changed over the past decade, or of the movement by corporate-sponsored "universities" to offer education and training to students not employed by the firm. Through workshops, teleconferences and research reports, the AACSB and other professional associations can do much to challenge institutional complacency and help faculty understand that their university employers no longer are in a monopoly position.

- Changing school employment practices by not hiring, or providing tenure, to faculty without international competence. In contrast to the 1970s and 1980s, the buyer calls the tune in the current business faculty labor market. Deans and department chairs who apply this philosophy to personnel decisions will send an unmistakable signal to doctoral programs.

- To compensate for any near term shortage of internationally competent faculty, schools should consider strategies proposed by Roundtable presenters, such as: hiring contract faculty; exploiting new distance learning technologies to benefit from skilled faculty at other institutions; and hosting visiting faculty from business schools in other world regions.

- To speed the process of "globalizing" existing faculty, business school administrators should target research and curriculum development funds for internationally-related issues. Schools should provide funding for faculty to: participate in professional meetings overseas, international study tours, and domestic conferences with global themes; and for the acquisition of international data bases and academic journals. Schools also should provide release time for faculty willing to take sabbaticals overseas.

- Borrowing from successful industry practice, U.S. business schools should selectively establish "strategic alliances" with overseas universities and with corporations engaged in international operations. Well-managed university alliances can provide a platform for "teamed" research and teaching that crosses national boundaries and provides important professional development opportunities. AACSB and allied business school associations in other regions could facilitate the institutional "matching" process by providing more complete information on the characteristics of business schools in different nations, and by creating new forums that bring together management educators from around the world. Real corporate "partnerships" (in contrast to donor/donee relationships) offer the potential for framing research issues that include an international dimension and provide field study experiences for faculty and students.

- Strategic alliances can be formed within universities. Most business doctoral programs exist within institutions that have active international relations or area studies programs. Economics departments often have experts on international trade. These partially hidden resources of excellence can contribute to joint taught courses, seminars, and doctoral committees. Universities do not, as Clark Kerr feared, have to be departments connected only by steampipes.

- To globalize the next generation of faculty members, business doctoral programs can adopt a variety of integrated or focused curriculum structures described at the Michigan State Roundtable. While each reflects a particular educational philosophy and requires varying levels of financial and faculty resources, all provide students with at least a measure of exposure to key international issues. These steps could be complemented by many of the same strategies proposed above for helping existing faculty adapt to new global realities, including internationally-targeted dissertation awards, international research consortia, opportunities for international field study and participate in professional meetings with global themes. Several Roundtable participants viewed admission of more non-U.S. citizen students as another globalizing strategy. However, Ph.D. programs too often encourage monolithic approaches to teaching and research. A Roundtable paper submitted by a doctoral student at the University of Western Ontario describing the learning process that occurred when a multi-cultural team was assigned a joint research project illustrates the unconventional methodologies needed to effectively utilize the diversity of students.

- Business doctoral programs are, in reality, an accumulation of programs specific to individual disciplines. Concerned deans, faculty, and other key groups should take the initiative within disciplinary associations representing functional areas such as management, finance, marketing, and accounting. Legitimizing international issues in journals, at conferences, through doctoral consortia, and at other events sponsored by these groups can have the same gradual impact on faculty that similar AACSB activities over the last 20 years have had on deans and other senior business school administrators.

The constituents of university-based management education have high and changing expectations. The price business schools will pay for not meeting these needs will be severe. The Roundtable raised the question of whether the administrators and faculty who comprise our institutions have the vision, and are willing to take the necessary risk, to respond to this environment.

THE GLOBAL CHALLENGE

S. Tamer Cavusgil

The challenge doctoral programs in business must accept is that of relevance. Can business schools, including both administration and faculty, continue educating future faculty, MBAs and BAs with anachronistic methods and content? The decline in demand for Ph.D.s in business shouts a deafening "NO!" Where does this dissatisfaction come from? What is the role of business schools in creating a declining demand for its products? The changing economic climate has led the corporate world into a phase of re-engineering—reorganizing to enhance efficiency. Obtaining efficiency, however, is not only a matter of identifying one's corporate peers and "one-upping" them in internal development strategies. Rather, corporate development now concerns itself with the global web of business—domestic business has become global business. To achieve efficiency and value for customers, businesses must now consult their global competitors to determine what niche they can create for themselves and how they can maintain that niche over the long term.

Are business schools educating students to these realities? Many of the papers presented in the Roundtable attest to the lack of preparation students receive in the global realities of business. Faculty are ill-equipped to teach courses on international business or to infuse international perspectives into their specific curricula. While many doctoral program administrators have asserted that their programs are internationalized, the lack of clear definition as to what this means leaves this assertion without full substantiation. Doctoral students themselves may assert their ability to teach their subjects from a global perspective. Can they?

From a number of papers presented on the internationalization of specific institutions, we can say that some schools have accepted the challenge and are forging a path through a drastically and ever-changing landscape of business as it is practiced globally. At Western Business School in Ontario, Canada, students are required to have an international field experience. In the Faculty of Management at the University of Toronto and at the Helsinki School of Economics and Business, a large number of courses have been infused with international perspectives. Students in international marketing address a range of topics from theory, research, methodology and content from an international perspective at the University of British Columbia. At the University of South Carolina, students must know a foreign language and participate in an overseas experience. Each doctoral program in business is struggling to define what internationalization means at their respective institutions, and each is creating a definition that "fits" with the particular culture and constraints of their institutions.

Is this the direction we need to take—to create distinct definitions of internationalization that "fit" each institution, or are there base standards that all business schools should ascribe to—and then augment in light of the particular emphases the school already has or wishes to develop? Here is the second challenge—how to define internationalization that will ensure standards but will allow for innovation at each institution.

At Michigan State, an International Task Force was convened in Fall 1994 for the purpose of developing recommendations that would strengthen the international capabilities of The Eli Broad College of Business. The Task Force was charged with the task of conducting a self-study and identifying new international initiatives for implementation by the faculty and administration. It is the underlying belief of the Task Force members that the long-term goal of the College is to create a total, global culture that promotes international experience, teaching, research, and business linkages. The international dimensions of business are to be nurtured as a core competence of the faculty, and that programs that build on this core competence will benefit the students, faculty, employers of our graduates, and the College as a whole. This belief serves as a core tenet of culture on the Michigan State University campus, not only because the president and deans will it so, but because of its 50-year tradition of international involvement. The culture of our business school may not have to be changed radically because our larger institutional culture provides us with the expertise and resources needed to commit ourselves deeper to internationalizing our operations. Hence, the way MSU defines internationalization, and the goals, objectives and strategies that we adopt to operationalize that definition might be very different from those developed at other institutions.

The International Task Force at the Eli Broad College of Business defines internationalization as:

A deliberate, programmatic, and ongoing effort to incorporate the international, comparative, and cross-cultural dimensions of business into our professional agenda (i.e., teaching, research, outreach), to reflect the realities of global competition and to meet student and business expectations.

This definition views internationalization as professional enrichment on the part of the faculty, and recognizes its importance in creating a responsive and competitive business school. To illustrate my assertions about varying definitions, Peter Rose defines internationalizing as:

. . . exposing doctoral students and graduate faculty (and through them the students they teach) to the similarities and differences across nations and across broad regions of the globe in: a) business institutions, practices, and methods; b) legal and regulatory policies affecting the business sector; and c) the variety of cultures that surround the business sector. Ph.D. students must be encouraged and stimulated to investigate how business decisions, business institutions, and cultural and regulatory environments differ from one nation, region, and continent to another, how they are similar to one another, and how and why those differences and similarities affect the performance and the welfare of themselves and of business customers (Rose, in this volume.)

The MSU definition stresses a conceptual, institutional approach, while the Texas A & M definition stresses student outcomes. Both seek the same philosophical goals, yet each will operationalize their definitions in a way that fits the culture, traditions, resources and budgetary and other constraints prevailing at their respective institutions. It may be that the internationalizing program at each institution will look very similar. And this will be good because each institution will struggle with the overarching issues and will develop a plan that might include similar components—e.g., overseas experience, language, cross-cultural understanding—but the "package" will be different. Each institution will decide the requirements for admission, i.e., whether to have had an overseas experience or language prior to acceptance, and the requirements for graduation, i.e., dissertation research abroad, as well as the international content of each discipline.

From these definitions and decisions, models of internationalization will emerge. As is the case with all doctoral programs, some institutions will assume leadership positions because they will become known for the quality of their graduates—their employability in other programs seeking to internationalize and in the international marketplace. These models will not appear overnight; it will take time to design, experiment, implement, evaluate, and redesign. And models developed in one institution are not easily transplanted to others, for all the reasons I discussed above.

As experimentation is occurring, the caution of transferability of ideas notwithstanding, success stories must be shared. This is my third challenge to you. It is the imperative to learn from each other, not in the spirit of surreptitious competition, but of collaboration toward the end of creating the best program possible for students. At annual meetings of discipline-based professional and related organizations, case studies must be presented that outline the process and content of internationalization efforts. How these efforts target teaching, research and outreach must be detailed as well as how the changing content of each of these courses meets the challenge of global business. Oral presentations must be augmented by publications appearing in renowned journals. Editorial policies must also change to reflect a broader paradigm of business education and research.

Many alternative visions of international doctoral business education will emerge. What will be of overarching concern is how current faculty will change their own behaviors to accept the challenge of global business. This is my fourth challenge—to consider how an institution can provide the supportive environment for faculty to develop their own internationalization plans and to experiment while at the same time meeting the needs of tenure and promotion committees. What incentives will a business school be able to offer to faculty to change the way they do business? It should be clear to all of us that learning takes time—to read, research, and reflect, and then to create a new course syllabus that includes an emphasis different from that currently being taught. Faculty also need access to resources—either at the home institution or elsewhere. They need to see for themselves how business has been affected by the globalization of the marketplace. This will entail time in the international field, in overseas workshops where they can interact with colleagues, and in international professional meetings where faculty can learn from each other how to translate international business praxis into a teaching curriculum.

Cultural change takes time, for that is what internationalization is asking of the professorate—changing the norms, values, beliefs and relationships in a field of activity. Changing these requires a multi-level approach like that advocated by Ben Kedia, taking into account the cognitive, affective and behavioral domains of learning. As Jim Schmotter has outlined, changes in business schools must take place in a time and manner that globalization took place in business. Internationalization begins with a strategic intent to value the international dimension and proceeds through initiatives and alliances, and overseas assignments to gain respect for and an understanding of the earth-shaking (no pun intended) implications of our globalized economy. A great deal of professional soul-searching is needed in order for faculty to reorient their thinking about theory, research design and methodology, and content in order to infuse the international dimension in their work.

Internationalization can proceed utilizing a cross-cultural focus, i.e., one that accepts basic norms and theories as universals in business that are applied in different cultural/national contexts. Is this enough? Or is there an underlying paradigm shift that must take place that challenges universals in light of cross-cultural realities? This is the fifth challenge—how deep should internationalization go? At what level do institutions, administrators and faculty wish to accept the challenge? At the level of an international business seminar, at the level of infusion, at the level of paradigm shift and program reorganization, or at some intermediary level? This question must be answered at each institution, because each will require a different strategy as well as a different set of resources in order for implementation to be successful.

The final challenge I pose to you is based in one thing we never seem to have enough of—time. When will we get started? When will we acknowledge that business has become international business, that teaching and research is not even near the cutting edge but is lagging behind the international realities of business, and that we are doing a disservice to our students because we have become blind and divorced from what is going on outside the institution?

It is time now. The imperative with which I charge you, the readers, is an urgency to act—to convene meetings at your respective institutions to define the terms, goals, objectives and strategies to internationalize, to identify strengths and constraints, and to begin experimenting in developing new syllabi, new research methodologies, new teaching strategies, and new relationships and alliances overseas. This is the ultimate imperative—to begin work now! To fail to heed this imperative imperils not only our own professional status, but also that of many generations to come.

About the Contributors

Jeffrey S. Arpan, Chairman and Kane Professor of International Business, International Business Department, College of Business Administration, University of South Carolina, USA; past Vice President, Academy of International Business.

Paul W. Beamish, Royal Bank Professor in International Business, Richard Ivey School of Business, University of Western Ontario, London, Ontario, Canada.

William Broesamle, President, Graduate Management Admission Council, Santa Monica, California, USA.

S. Tamer Cavusgil, Executive Director, Center for International Business Education and Research, and the John W. Byington Endowed Chair in Global Marketing, Michigan State University, East Lansing, Michigan, USA; past Vice President for Global Marketing, American Marketing Association.

Kerry Cooper, Cullen Professor of Business Administration, Executive Director, Center for International Business Education and Research, Texas A & M University, College Station, Texas, USA.

John D. Daniels, Co-Director, Center for International Business Education and Research, School of Business, Indiana University, Bloomington, Indiana, USA; past president, Academy of International Business.

Dale F. Duhan, College of Business Administration, Texas Tech University, Lubbock, Texas, USA.

311

William R. Folks, Jr., Director, Center for International Business Education and Research, College of Business Administration, University of South Carolina, Columbia, South Carolina, USA.

Charles W. Hickman, Director, Projects and Services, American Assembly of Collegiate Schools of Business, St. Louis, Missouri, USA.

Ben L. Kedia, Director, Center for International Business Education and Research, and Wang Professor of Management, The University of Memphis, Memphis, Tennessee, USA.

Reijo Luostarinen, Professor and Director of International Business Studies, and Director of the Center for International Business Research, Helsinki School of Economics and Business Administration, Helsinki, Finland.

Richard J. Lutz, Director of Graduate Studies, College of Business Administration, University of Florida, Gainesville, Florida, USA.

Robert G. May, KPMG Peat Marwick Professor of Accounting and Dean, Graduate School of Business and College of Business Administration, The University of Texas at Austin, Austin, Texas, USA.

Edwin L. Miller, Director of International Development, The Michigan Business School, University of Michigan, Ann Arbor, Michigan, USA.

Matthew B. Myers, Doctoral Candidate, Marketing, The Eli Broad College of Management, Michigan State University, East Lansing, Michigan, USA.

Sharon O'Donnell, Doctoral Candidate, College of Business Administration, University of South Carolina, Columbia, South Carolina, USA.

Glenn S. Omura, Department of Marketing and Logistics, Michigan State University, East Lansing, Michigan, USA.

Daniel Ondrack, Associate Dean, Ph.D. Program, Faculty of Management, University of Toronto, Toronto, Ontario, Canada.

Barbara Pierce, Richard Ivey School of Business, University of Western Ontario, London, Ontario, Canada.

Lyman W. Porter, Graduate School of Management, University of California at Irvine, Irvine, California, USA.

Peter S. Rose, Jeanne and John R. Blocker Professor of Business Administration, Finance Department, Texas A & M University, College Station, Texas, USA.

James W. Schmotter, Dean and Professor of Management, College of Business and Economics, Lehigh University, Bethlehem, Pennsylvania, USA.

John M. Stopford, Professor of International Business, London Business School, London, England.

Brian Toyne, Emil C. E. Jurica Professor of International Business, School of Business and Administration, St. Mary's University, San Antonio, Texas, USA.

David K. Tse, Professor of International Business and Director of Chinese Management Research Centre, Faculty of Business, City University of Hong Kong, Hong Kong.

INDEX

A

AACSB, 2, 7, 16, 18, 19, 20, 25, 32, 64, 71, 74, 102, 106, 122, 149, 150, 300, 301, 302, 303

abroad: education, 9, 16, 140, 145, 150, 179, 181, 221, 222, 230, 239; teaching and research, 5, 27, 46, 67, 89, 107, 116, 119, 120, 121, 136, 139, 140, 145, 214, 219, 234, 272, 278, 300, 303, 309

accounting, 4, 14, 19, 46, 47, 63, 72, 102, 139, 152, 183, 196, 299, 303

AIB, 2, 7, 16, 18, 19, 20, 22, 137, 150, 168, 204, 225, 238

awareness, 17, 21, 43, 62, 81, 88, 90, 164, 215, 217, 218, 220, 283

B

benchmarking, 9, 137

business administration. *See* internationalization

business education and research, 71, 74, 75, 78, 136, 146, 185, 308

business schools: Canadian schools, 1, 248, 298, 309; European schools, 17, 46, 51, 52; missions of, 7, 28, 119, 131, 169; strategies, 126, 239, 301; U.S. colleges and business schools, 4, 8, 14, 73, 108, 118, 140, 168, 177, 231, 274, 302

C

change: agents, 32, 123; need to, 21, 48, 90, 114, 152, 253; resistance to, 122, 128

CIBER, 1, 2, 103, 114, 135, 149, 150, 151, 152, 153, 154, 156, 157, 158, 193, 199, 202, 219, 223

cost-benefit consideration, 105, 107, 108, 110, 131, 246

culture: cross-cultural issues 4, 5, 89, 99, 113, 185, 216, 217, 218, 223, 230, 245, 248, 252, 258, 267, 293, 307, 309; cultural awareness, 278; culture-influenced learning, 81; differences in, 53, 170, 215, 267; faculty culture, 5, 98, 100, 165, 167; institutional culture, 5, 6, 115, 116, 118, 164, 175, 232, 306, 307, 309; program culture, 53

curriculum, 8, 25, 26, 27, 33, 37, 51, 55, 71, 98, 107, 116, 117, 118, 119, 122, 126, 139, 149, 164, 170, 176, 181, 183, 186, 191, 192, 193, 194, 196, 201, 204, 205, 209, 213,

315

215, 216, 217, 218, 219, 227, 228, 229, 231, 232, 233, 234, 268, 271, 273, 281, 282, 299, 302, 308

D

dean: activities of, 102, 124, 128; roles of, 5, 120, 121, 123, 124,128, 131
doctoral students, 27, 88, 109, 131, 150, 204, 230, 268, 290, 305

E

exchange programs, 87, 173, 174, 202, 213, 237

F

faculty: activities of, 56, 75, 125, 129, 165,173 177, 220; roles of, 4, 114, 120, 180, 192, 222, 263
foreign language: competency, 90, 141, 144, 272, 275, 281; of instruction, 54, 230, 234; requirement, 8, 16, 23, 91, 143, 184, 234, 274, 278; skills, 9, 145, 187, 277, 281; training, 22, 135, 138, 144, 147, 274, 282, 285
functional areas/specialization, 4, 72, 74, 89, 119, 125, 144, 209, 232, 262, 306
funding, 33, 153, 159, 183, 191, 222, 226, 297

G

German model, 4, 26, 49, 50
globalization, 2, 71, 87, 97, 98, 128, 136, 183, 191, 199, 213, 238, 251, 290, 294, 308
GMAC, 65, 69, 75, 97, 141

I

infusion, 97, 98, 124, 153, 156, 157, 158, 163, 168, 169, 227, 229, 309
INSEAD, 51, 55, 204, 221, 233, 293
institutional arrangement, 5, 115, 224
integration, 27, 28, 32, 37, 38, 52, 63, 64, 65, 77, 78, 79, 82, 115, 191, 225, 231, 238, 280
internalization, 193, 291
international: business, 1, 2, 7, 8, 10, 12, 15, 16, 17, 20, 45, 76, 80, 81, 103, 124, 135, 168, 179, 180, 184, 186, 201, 202, 203, 205, 206, 208, 213, 214, 217, 225, 227, 234, 235, 236, 238, 245, 257, 258, 272, 273, 274, 275, 283, 295; environment, 77, 126, 173; finance, 8, 14, 16, 187, 189; internships, 135, 145; marketing, 6, 12, 14, 16, 78, 152, 177, 182, 183, 235, 241, 245, 247, 253, 306; students,6, 16, 113, 172, 218, 224, 245, 296
internationalization: business Ph.D. programs, 5, 7, 9, 25, 31, 43, 76, 90, 97, 107, 149, 159, 173, 175, 177, 181, 213, 291, 300; business scholarship, 61, 133; doctoral education, 2, 49, 102, 105, 117, 120, 121, 125, 126, 127, 140, 144, 166, 172, 174, 225, 227; strategies, 5, 6, 122, 209, 230, 240, 293, 300, 306

J

journals: 45, 50, 55, 82, 101, 102, 124, 163, 168, 169, 171, 178, 180, 185, 208, 231, 251, 258, 259, 260, 289, 302, 303, 308

L

learning curve, 51, 183

M

management, 1, 6, 8, 12, 14, 58, 64,
71, 79, 83, 90, 131, 133, 137, 147,
148, 150, 157, 164, 173, 186, 187,
191, 202, 203, 206, 207, 212, 220,
224, 236, 238, 241, 242, 259, 269,
295, 306
marketing, 4, 19, 63, 92,
101,125,139,174, 183, 187, 196,
203, 212, 214, 234,248,249 296,
303

N

NAFTA, 70, 72, 77, 85, 135, 187

O

overseas experience, 16, 272, 274,
275, 295, 296, 306, 307

P

paradigms, 46, 70, 74, 75, 76, 77, 78,
80, 81, 85, 88, 89, 208
pyramidical approach, 138, 146
publications, 163, 165, 169, 202, 237,
279, 308

R

renaissance model, 4, 26, 44, 49
resources, 2, 7, 8, 48, 51, 52, 61, 62,
70, 88, 109, 116, 117, 118, 119,
120, 121, 122, 123, 124, 125, 128,
131, 132, 141, 154, 169, 171, 179,
180, 181, 183, 186, 193, 199, 203,
206, 214, 219, 222, 223, 229, 232,
233, 238, 239, 274, 290, 291, 294,
296, 300, 302, 303, 306, 307, 308,
309

S

silo enhancers, 4, 5, 65, 92
socialization, 65, 68, 73, 74, 75, 88,
139, 222
surveys: AIB, AACSB & USC, 7, 19,
171; Arpan, Folks and Kwok, 140;
Arpan, Folks and O'Donnell, 248;
EDAMBA, 59; journal project
team, 262; Kedia, 116; Kuhne, 8,
9, 14, 19; Myers and Omura, 4,
183; Nehrt, 26; Rose, 4, 7, 117,
163, 225

T

tenure and promotion, 105, 127,
129, 179, 187, 294, 297, 300, 308,
311
trade, 1, 108, 119, 128, 135, 136,
153, 158, 180, 195, 223, 234, 302

U

universal, 5, 7, 46, 47, 55, 57, 79, 85,
106, 109, 152, 153, 233, 248, 309

V

values, 1, 4, 5, 6, 26, 52, 53, 55, 62,
65, 71, 74, 136, 137, 163, 165,
166, 167, 184, 293, 308
visiting scholars, 172, 173, 219, 224,
229